Dublin Day by Day

Dublin Day by Day

Sean McMahon

LONDUBH BOOKS

For Marie D'Arcy

First published in 2014
by Londubh Books
18 Casimir Avenue, Harold's Cross, Dublin 6w, Ireland
www.londubh.ie
1 3 5 4 2
Origination by Londubh Books; cover by bluett
Cover image courtesy of the National Library of Ireland
Printed by ScandBook AB, Falun Sweden
ISBN: 978-1-907535-42-0

Acknowledgements

I would like very much to thank the staff of the Central Library, Derry, especially Jane Nicholas, for unfailing courtesy and helpfulness, and Philip Charlwood for a very special service.

WINTER

1 January 1801

'A Ship on Fire'

The rising of 1798 finally convinced prime minister William Pitt (1759-1806) that Ireland was, in his phrase, 'a ship on fire', and he used every means in his power to bring about its union with Britain. Fear of a French invasion that had almost happened was his chief spur but he felt that a parliamentary union was the best means of controlling the 'distressful country'. He soon found support in the Catholic Church, whose clerics, especially Archbishop Troy of Dublin (1786-1823), had denounced the United Irishmen. The trump card was the promise of full Catholic emancipation, which the 1795 relief acts had stopped short of granting. That proved an empty promise because George III (1738-1820) could not reconcile it with his coronation oath.

Orangemen opposed the union because they feared enfranchised papists and the ascendancy in Dublin was reluctant to lose the parliamentary independence won as recently as 1781. The main architect of the union was Viscount Castlereagh (1769-1822), the Chief Secretary, but the task of literally selling it was in the capable hands of Lords Cornwallis (1738-1805), the Viceroy, and Clare (1749-1802), the Lord Chancellor, who in their disdainful dealings with 'the most corrupt people under heaven' spent the equivalent of many millions of pounds by today's values in bribes.

The Act of Union became law on Wednesday 1 January 1801 and sent twenty-eight temporal and four spiritual lords to the upper house and a hundred MPs to the Commons. There would be a modicum of free trade between the two countries and Ireland would contribute two-seventeenths of the United Kingdom's expenditure. The terms seemed reasonable but there was an inevitable sense of departed glory and one wit, Edward Lysaght (1763-1811), painted a gloomy picture of a depressed Dublin:

> *Thro' Capel-street soon you'll rurally range,*
> *You'll scarce recognise it the same street;*
> *Choice turnips shall grow in your Royal Exchange*
> *And fine cabbages down along Dame-street.*

2 January 1905

The 'Indo'

The *Irish Independent* first appeared on the streets of Dublin on Monday 2 January 1905, after a complicated birth. It was a product of the serious Parnell split in the Irish Parliamentary Party when an apparently minor flaw widened into a crevasse. Its chief progenitor was the *Irish Daily Independent,* founded in 1891 by Charles Stewart Parnell (1846-91), while the opposition organ, *Daily Nation,* was owned by William Martin Murphy (1844-1919, an industrial magnate and nationalist MP, who became a hate figure during the 1913 Lockout. The older nationalist paper, the *Freeman's Journal,* founded in 1802, still supported the Parnell faction but Murphy, a man of strong convictions and an anti-Parnellite, acquired the *Irish Daily Independent* and marketed the new journal as a popular broadsheet in the style of the Harmsworth *Daily Mail* in Britain, with much use of photographs and lively presentation, and costing only a halfpenny. A companion weekly paper, the *Sunday Independent,* followed in 1906. Because of the new paper's success the *Freeman's Journal* lost readers and was eventually incorporated into the *Independent* in 1923.

The 'Indo', as it eventually was popularly called, became the organ of a conservative-tending Catholic middle class, especially the farming community. It strongly supported the employers during the Lockout, was fiercely opposed to the syndicalism and sympathetic strikes of James Larkin (1876-1947), deplored the Easter Rising and was strongly pro-Treaty, becoming the voice of Cumann na nGaedheal and later of Fine Gael. Its public denunciations of the IRA led to its being attacked and its plant destroyed on 21 December 1919.

The *Irish Independent*'s circulation rose from 20,000 to 40,000 in three years and it is still Ireland's leading daily. Its only Irish morning rival, *The Irish Times,* founded essentially as the voice of the Anglo-Irish ascendancy in 1859, managed to avoid any reference to its launch in the editions of the first week of January 1905.

3 January 1941

Bombs over Dublin

The first Luftwaffe bomb fell on Dublin on Thursday 2 January 1941, damaging two houses in the Rathdown Park area in Terenure and injuring seven people. It was the first raid on the city, although there had been damage, injury and loss of life in other parts of the country on five earlier occasions. Before the government could determine the cause of this inexplicable act with visits to Eduard Hempel, the representative of Nazi Germany in Ireland, the Luftwaffe struck, again inexplicably, but with greater force.

The centre of attention was the Donore area that includes Dolphin's Barn and the South Circular Road. The first bomb's point of impact was Donore Terrace, but damage was widespread. The second demolished Nos 91 and 93 South Circular Road and seriously damaged fifty other buildings. Thirteen people were buried under rubble but, although some of their injuries were serious, all survived. Among the non-domestic buildings hit or damaged by the blast were the Presbyterian Church in Donore Avenue and the Boyne Linen Company and the Hospice for the Dying, both in Harold's Cross. The main damage was to buildings on the South Circular Road itself: the White Swan Laundry, the Wills Cigarette factory, the National Boxing Stadium, St Catherine's Rectory and a synagogue.

This last target was considered highly significant by those very knowledge-able men who had a much better grasp of national and international affairs than anyone in the government, in spite of never seeming to budge from their dedicated seats in the corner of the snug. After all one of the houses hit the morning before had been owned by an Isaacson and another by Simon Lapeden (not quite certain about that one but the Simon was significant!). That and the synagogue were proof enough: the Nazis were targeting the Jews worldwide.

4 January 1961

A puckish Oirish character

William Joseph Shields was born in Walworth Road, Portobello, on 10 March 1888 and educated in Skerry's College before becoming a civil servant. Like his younger brother, Arthur, he was fascinated by acting and both joined the company of the Abbey Theatre, where, because of the day job, he used the stage name Barry Fitzgerald. He played Fluther Good in the first production of *The Plough and the Stars* by Seán O'Casey. A protester in the audience jumped on the stage during disturbances and struck Maureen Delany, who was playing Bessie Burgess, on the face. Fitzgerald, although only 5ft 4in in height, knocked him back into the pit with a single blow.

He was a reliable and versatile member of the Abbey company, as convincing as an intellectual in Shaw as a jackeen in O'Casey. One of his first film roles was in Hitchcock's version of *Juno and the Paycock,* made in 1931, but it was his replication of his stage role as Fluther in John Ford's *The Plough and the Stars* in 1936 that fixed him firmly in the lucrative job of a Hollywood character actor. He made more than forty films, being nominated as best actor and best supporting actor in the 1944 Academy Awards for his role as Father Fitzgibbon in *Going My Way.* The film won four Oscars, best film, best director, best actor and best support for Fitzgerald, the rules afterwards changed to prevent a double nomination in the future.

He died in Dublin after brain surgery on Wednesday 4 January 1961, remembered as a puckish Oirish character, especially after the ultimate stage-Irish movie, *The Quiet Man* (1952), in which he played Michaleen Oge Flynn, the garrulous jarvey. But he could chill when necessary, notably in *And Then They Were None* (1945).

5 January 1826

By canal from Dublin

The office of Grand Canal Passage Boats, the firm that carried passengers from Dublin to Shannon Harbour, eighty miles and forty-seven locks away, was situated in 49½ William Street. The company had been set up in 1802 and provided a service that was smoother and quieter, if rather slower, than journeys by coach over the rocky roads. By the end of the 1820s it rivalled most other means of transport and for legal as well as publicity reasons Edward Lawson (1767-1843), the company secretary, published a bill for display in each canal port along the route and as a leaflet available from the William Street offices on Thursday 5 January 1826.

The tightly printed document covered all aspects of the service, including details of sailings from Dublin, Tullamore and Athy. The canal at that time branched near Robertstown, one line going south to Athy, the other west past Tullamore to Shannon Harbour. The 'day' boats served Hazel-Hatch, Sallins, Robertstown, Rathangan, Monasterevan, Vicarstown, Athy, Ticknevin, Edenderry Branch, Ballybritain, Philipstown and Tullamore. The night sailings left Portobello at 2pm and Shannon Harbour at 4pm. The boat from Dublin was listed as reaching its terminus at 9.05am the next morning.

The bill covered every aspect of the system, advising that breakfast with eggs for first-class passengers cost 1s/3d, whereas in the second-class cabin dinner and breakfast with 'an egg' cost 10d. No servant in livery was allowed as a passenger in the first-class cabin. No smoking of tobacco was permitted in either cabin and no gaming was permitted on Sundays. No person was permitted to stand on deck, 'so as to interrupt the view of the steerer'. A private room was provided for ladies, to which no other person could be admitted. In spite of the company's confidence, implicit in this bill, the service, so seemingly buoyant, had virtually disappeared by 1850.

6 January 1818

The GPO

The first postal service that provided Ireland with a system we might recognise today was created in 1657 when the General Post Office of England, Scotland and Ireland was established as a monopoly. As demand increased, rates charged to the recipients became cheaper, with a Dublin local rate of one penny by 1765. The service had a significant effect on more than just personal communication; railway and road transport systems relied on Post Office contracts for a large part of their income and it was a pioneer in the use of the new steamships for more rapid transport.

After the Act of Union and the cessation of internal turmoil when the war with France had finally been settled in Waterloo in 1815 the resulting period of peace saw an increase in demand and provision. This received its greatest recognition with the building of the General Post Office in Sackville Street (as O'Connell Street was officially known until 1924). Earlier locations were in Dame Street and College Green. The foundation stone was laid by Earl Whitworth (1752-1825), the Lord Lieutenant, on 12 August 1812 in the company of the Post-Masters General Earl O'Neill (1779-1841) and Earl of Rosse (1758-1841) and the magnificent building was open for business on Tuesday 6 January 1818, at a cost of £50,000.

It was designed in Greek revival neoclassical style by Francis Johnston (1760-1829), the Armagh-born architect who had also been responsible for, among other city edifices, the House of Commons that became the Bank of Ireland after the Act of Union, St George's Church and the Chapel Royal in Dublin Castle. It was an obvious site for the 1916 Proclamation, although it was not the best headquarters for the Volunteers from a tactical point of view. It suffered greatly during Easter Week but with the façade intact it was lovingly restored by the Free State government in 1929.

7 January 1960

The Pillar

Nelson's Pillar in Sackville Street (now O'Connell Street) was Dublin's best-known monument. Erected in 1808-9 in memory of Horatio Nelson (1758-1805), the hero of Trafalgar, it was for more than one hundred and fifty years the 'centre' of the city and in spite of its British associations cherished by the nationalist majority as the 'ould Pillar'. By the start of the 1960s, with the city's traffic already reaching gridlock, it came to be regarded as a cause of congestion.

On Tuesday 7 January 1960 the press carried details of a meeting of the Corporation held the previous day. Noel Lemass TD, the son of the Taoiseach, proposed a motion asking the Streets Committee to examine the desirability of improving traffic conditions in O'Connell Street by removing the Pillar. To his mind it was a major obstruction in the city, ruined the view in the street and netted very little income. (It was a popular tourist attraction, mainly because of the views from its parapet, 120 ft above the ground.)

Many of the councillors agreed with Deputy Lemass, taking care to insist that the demand for its removal was based on contingency, not politics. One stated truthfully that many Dubliners would be opposed to its removal on sentimental and aesthetic grounds but they might well agree to the removal of Nelson at its top. Already a debate about traffic was spinning out of control and sinking into Treaty politics. The choice of candidate, after all, had no bearing upon the traffic problem. There would be many discussions about the Pillar's future for the next six years until an IRA bomb solved the problem for good.

8 January 1898

A new dawn

The 1897 annual report of the Gaelic League contained the following item: 'It has long been evident that a weekly newspaper was obviously necessary for the effective propaganda of the movement, and the committee are glad to announce that at last a publisher, Mr Bernard Doyle, has been found sufficiently enterprising to take the risk.'

The journal was called *Fáinne an Lae* (The Dawn) and first appeared on Saturday 8 January 1898. The opening edition had an editorial entitled 'Teanga na h-Éireann' (The Language of Ireland) and carried a profile of the co-founder Douglas Hyde (1860-1949). The editorial (in English) roundly stated: 'A great responsibility rests on the present generation of Irishmen. The battle for the retention, or the loss forever, of the Irish language has to be fought out within the next twenty years. That it is still possible to save the language we confidently believe. The continuing success of the Gaelic League abundantly proves his. But it is a race against time. Year by year the sands are running out.'

The paper had stories both in English and in Irish, cost one penny, and typical news items in Irish included: 'John Redmond MP landed in New York last Wednesday. He hopes to return within a fortnight' and 'Prince Bismarck is reported to be very ill.' It praised the Belfast newspaper, the *Irish News,* for printing in Irish an account of a mission given in west Donegal. A letter from Archbishop Walsh of Dublin to the editor stressed the need for a handy student dictionary.

Fáinne an Lae lasted until March 1899, when Doyle left the League after the committee felt that he had used the paper's columns to favour his own entrepreneurial ambitions. It successor, *An Claidheamh Soluis* (The Sword of Light), proved to be a much more vigorous organ.

9 January 1594

College of the Holy and Undivided Trinity

Although by the year 1592 English domination of Ireland was far from complete, Elizabeth I (1533-1603) realised that some institution of reputation and reliability need to be established to help with the de-Gaelicisation of the country. Already in 1570 she had caused the Dublin parliament to pass an act for the establishing of 'a free school in every diocese of Ireland…the schoolmaster shall be an Englishman of English birth of this realm…' A third-level institution was a logical development and work began in 1592 on land confiscated from the Augustinian Priory of All Hallows.

It was established as: 'the college of the Holy and Undivided Trinity near Dublin whereby knowledge and civility might be increased by the instruction of our people there, whereof many have heretofore to travail into ffrance, Italy and Spaine to gett learning in such foreign universities, whereby they have been influenced with poperie and other ill-qualities, and so become evil subjects.'

The implication in the phrase 'our people' was that Catholics and dissenters were not necessarily excluded and indeed they were accepted until 1637, when Catholics were excluded. It was not until 1793 that they were again permitted to attend.

The main supporters of the project in Dublin were the city corporation, chiefly representing the New English, and Adam Loftus (*c.* 1533-1605), the Protestant archbishop of the primatial see. As a result the ethos of the college remained firmly Calvinist. It was the main source of Church of Ireland clergy and it was the perceived need to proselytise the Gaelic western half of the country that enabled William Bedell (1571-1642), Provost of Trinity 1627-9 and Bishop of Kilmore and Ardagh from 1629, to establish Irish as a university subject.

Trinity College opened its doors on Sunday 9 January 1594 and enrolled Abel Walsh as its first student and the young James Ussher (1581-1656), later Archbishop of Armagh, as its second. The college's handsome modern library (2002) is named for him.

10 January 1980

A 'tiger' kidnapping

The Irish Farm Centre branch of the Allied Irish Bank in Bluebell in west Dublin was the target of a bank raid on Thursday 10 January 1979. It involved the nasty expedient of kidnap and hostages the previous evening, when a gang of at least six men, one with a northern accent, descended on the home of Thomas Scully, the manager of the branch, in Grangewood, Rathfarnham. Noreen Scully and her two daughters Anne (17) and Claire (15) were bundled into the back of a Ford Transit van and taken to a cottage in the country north-west of the city. Scully was ordered to stay in the house overnight and collect £100,000 from the bank. This was to be delivered to the West County Hotel in Lucan. He was warned that should he alert the Gardaí his family would instantly be killed.

The house had no telephone, strange as it may seem today; equally odd was the fact that no one was left to guard Thomas. He left the house by a rear window and immediately got in touch with the Rathfarnham Gardaí who called a midnight meeting involving senior officers and AIB officials. A suitcase containing £30,000 in marked notes and an electronic bug was prepared and Scully took it to Lucan. The taxi that was to take him from the hotel was driven by a plainclothes detective and it proceeded by a deliberately circuitous route to a telephone box in Ballymun. There the money was picked up by a motorcyclist, who was followed by detectives. At 9.00 o'clock that night six men, all members of the Irish Republican Socialist Party (IRSP), were taken into custody, some arrested at the party's headquarters.

Three hours earlier Noreen Scully and her daughters, shaken but physically unharmed, had walked into the Garda station in Dunshaughlin, County Meath, about twenty miles from where they were kidnapped.

11 January 1934

A pious myth

For more than two hundred years St Patrick was represented in pictures and prints as bearded and dressed in episcopal robes of verdant green, with matching mitre and ornamental crosier. Usually he was shown beside the sea driving one or several snakes or serpents into the tide, with a round tower and a Celtic cross somewhere in the background. Of these appurtenances only the round tower was authentic; the rest were the pious accretion of years. The correction of this was part of a salutary lecture given by Henry Morris (1874-1945) to the Academy of Christian Art in Wynn's Hotel, Abbey Street, on Thursday 11 January 1932.

The universal depiction of St Patrick is entirely wrong and unhistorical. The green chasuble belongs to a period at least four hundred years after his time, the mitre is a thousand years premature, the crosier should have no shepherd's crook but end in a Tau cross and, unless the snakes are taken to be metaphorical, they had no existence in Ireland. Morris's sources for the dispelling of these anachronisms were the extant ancient monuments, on only four of which St Patrick is represented. In all historic representations from the tenth to the 18th century he is beardless. Morris cited a Harvard professor's statement that shaving the beard 'was as much a part of the Irish tonsure as shaving the head'.

After a vote of thanks by the renowned bibliophile, Stephen Brown SJ (1881-1962), L.S. Gogan (1891-1979), Assistant Director, National Museum of Science and Art, concurred that the 19th-century model should be abandoned and suggested that a fair substitute might be found in the work of Seán Keating (1889-1977) whose recent large canvas had corrected the anomaly. (It was later issued as a postage stamp.) He hoped that similar corrective work might be done on Ireland's other iconic cult figures, St Brigid and St Columcille.

12 January 1965

The oral Irish

In November 1964 Patrick Hillery (1923-2008), Minister for Education, announced certain changes in the oral examination in Irish for the Leaving Certificate. Up until then the orals had been conducted by department inspectors who visited each school in the weeks before the written examinations began. They were assisted in the work by a nominated teacher in each school. The minister felt that to commit his inspectors to this work at that time of year was inefficient and even wasteful and proposed instead that the tests would be carried out by class teachers in a way that would be seen to be without any suggestion of bias. The same method of testing was already in operation for other languages.

On Tuesday 12 January 1965 Comhar na Meánmhúinteoirí, an organisation founded the previous April for teachers in secondary schools who taught Irish or other subjects through the medium, announced that it had not been consulted about the changes in the oral examination for 1965. This seemed to them a significant oversight and they felt that if the new system were forced through, harm would be done to the language. The oral was in their view 'as least as important educationally and nationally as the written examination'. The perceived downgrading of it would lower the status of Irish in secondary schools. Its direct imitation of the system regarded as adequate in Northern Ireland degraded Irish to the level of a mere school subject. It would make no contribution to the achieving of the national aim.

Comhar iterated that its aim was to foster cooperation between school and department and ended with an admonition to the minister that it was not 'too late to review the case by genuine consultation with the managers and teachers of secondary schools'.

13 January 1801

The Liberator

The Act of Union uniting the parliaments of Great Britain and Ireland became law on Thursday 1 January 1801 and almost immediately Daniel O'Connell (1775-1847), not yet known as 'The Liberator', began his fruitless agitation for its repeal. He noted that on that day 'the hatred which all classes (except the small government clique) bore to the measure had settled down into sulky despondency' and he was determined to rouse them from that slough. He was present at a public meeting (known in those years as an 'aggregate') of Dublin Catholics to support a motion of John Philpot Curran protesting against 'the extinction of Irish liberties and the reduction of Ireland to the subject condition of a province'. It was held in the grand Royal Exchange on Cork Hill (now City Hall) and it was there on Tuesday 13 January that the clever advocate became an orator, with his first political speech.

Hearing of the meeting in the Exchange, Major Henry Charles Sirr (1764-1841), the local 'peacekeeper' (town major) arrived with a party of yeomanry ready to quell any hint of 'unrest'. He read the wording of Curran's resolution, tossed it aside with a scornful shout and announcing, 'There's no harm in this. These talking shops!' withdrew his troops. O'Connell, with glowing face and ears tingling at the sound of his own voice, as he afterwards admitted, reminded his audience that a great calumny had been perpetrated on them, that they had supported the union on the promise of Catholic emancipation: 'I know that the Catholics of Ireland still remember that they have a country and that they will never accept any advantage as a sect, which would debase them and destroy them as a people.'

The applause was thunderous and O'Connell would have the same tumultuous response again and again over the next forty-five years.

14 January 1957

A catalogue of offences

Two cousins, James William Davis of Drimnagh Road and Anthony Meehan, Robinhood, Clondalkin, both eighteen years old, were each given multiple sentences in Dublin Circuit Criminal Court on Monday 14 January 1957. They had taken part in a series of escapades, including car theft, bank robbing, carrying an offensive weapon, stealing the same, burglary and larceny. The criminal rampage began on 2 October 1956 when with a .22 automatic pistol that they had stolen from John Carr, South King Street, on the previous 20 September, they entered the sub-branch of the Hibernian Bank in Clondalkin and demanded money from Herbert Croaghan. He was the only official present when the two marauders, wearing dusters as masks, made him hand over £460, the property of the bank. No doubt imitating some heist movie they had seen, the one carrying the gun fired a shot into the ceiling, from which the bullet was later recovered.

The master criminals also pleaded guilty to breaking into shops and stealing two overcoats and five wristlet watches, as well as admitting to the larceny of thirteen gallons of petrol. Davis said that he had stolen a suit valued at £14, the property of Denis Molloy, Cherryfield Avenue, Walkinstown. After the bank raid they drove off in a car later found abandoned. They had taken it from Garville Road that morning, driven to Kilmacanogue, broken open a petrol pump and gone to Bray, where they stole the watches. They took the scenic route via Brittas to Clondalkin, arriving at the bank at 1.28pm, two minutes before closing time.

Judge Conroy sentenced each to five years' penal servitude for possession of the gun, five years for the armed robbery, and six months' hard labour for the other offences, all to be served concurrently. He was unmoved by parental pleas as Davis had re-offended.

15 January 1970

The conservation caravan

The first year of the 1970s was declared Conservation Year and as part of the government's contribution a caravan bristling with ecological rectitude was fitted out to travel about the country, visiting schools to remind the young and their parents how casual the Irish were about their unrecoverable heritage. The caravan was twenty-four feet long and had illustrated panels round its exterior picturing important aspects of Irish outdoor life: landscapes and seascapes, wetlands where ducks and geese can flourish, native plants and trees. One that looked like a lunar landscape turned out to be an untouched deep brown shot of the Shannon estuary.

The caravan was not quite ready when it was rushed to the lawn in front of Leinster House to be officially launched, if that is the best word, by Taoiseach Jack Lynch (1917-99) and Seán Flanagan (1922-93), his Minister for Lands on Thursday 15 January 1970. Two important people who had significant roles in the project, Ray Kennedy from Flanagan's department and Éamonn Doherty, who taught architecture in Bolton Street, arrived early to make sure that all was in order for the official opening. When they reached Leinster Lawn they divested themselves of their shoes but not their socks.

One could imagine the ghost of Arthur Conan Doyle burning to write another Sherlock Holmes story for the Strand: *The Adventure of the Shoeless Visitors*. 'My dear Watson, why not socks as well, if respect for the institution was their aim?'

The answer was elementary, not at all a three-pipe problem: there should not and therefore could not be any marks of mud or grass on the virgin floor of the nature study caravan when the really important feet, wearing shoes, of course, would enter.

The ecological roadshow spent five weeks touring Dublin and its environs and then went nationwide.

16 January 1947

Mistreating the hired help

Mrs Patricia Caulfield, aged twenty-four, of 79 Gilford Road, Sandymount, was sentenced to four months' imprisonment on Thursday 16 January 1947 on four counts of assault and ill-treatment of a young domestic servant. The assaults had taken place in September, October and November 1946 when Caulfield had used fists, a hairbrush, a walking cane, two coat hangers, a saucepan, a potato pounder and a blackthorn stick. The girl, Josephine Carroll, from Kilkeeran Cross, County Kilkenny, was taken to Sir Patrick Dun's Hospital and it was there discovered that she had two bumps on the head, a half-inch cut on the right temple, two blackened eyes, swollen nose and lips, a severely swollen and cut ear and discolourations on her neck, shoulders and arms. Proceedings against her employer were immediately initiated by the National Society for the Prevention of Cruelty to Children and Caulfield was found guilty.

In extenuation it was stated that in the three years of her marriage to John Caulfield, a tax inspector, the defendant had had two miscarriages, two children (the second born in July 1946) and was expecting another baby in May 1947. Her gynaecologist had asserted that she was much more irritable and highly strung than normal. The maid's situation was grim too. Hired at eight shillings a week, with an unfulfilled promise of a rise to ten, she was told by her mother that if she took the bus home her father would be waiting for her with the stick. The pathologist was able to inform the court that a splintered blackthorn stick with human blood in the grooves had been found in the Carroll homestead.

At a continued hearing the following day Caulfield had her sentence suspended and she was granted personal bail of £50 and released on two sureties of £100 arranged by her husband.

17 January 1947

The Gorgeous Gael

Joseph Alphonsus Doyle appeared in Rathfarnham court on Friday 17 January 1947 on charges of assault and refusal to leave a public house in Knocklyon, Firhouse. Many similar cases were being heard all over the country but this had a special publicity angle in that the thirty-four-year-old Jack Doyle (1913-78), as he called himself, was a personality, known as the 'Gorgeous Gael' in films and variety theatre appearances. He was born in Cobh and, having joined the Gardaí in 1929, soon became an army boxing champion, a career aided by his height (6ft 5in) and a murderous right hook. A civilian career as a pugilist started well but his lifestyle with regard to women and liquor eventually proved his undoing.

He was still able to trade on remarkably good looks and a professionally trained voice and for a time a career in films beckoned. His addiction to drink led to unreliability and physical violence but for a while he remained employable. He married a Mexican actress, Movita Castenada, in St Andrew's Church in Westland Row and they toured these islands with a variety show in which they both sang. Drink and violence finished that relationship and by the time of his arrest his public life was essentially over.

On 18 October 1946 Doyle and a number of friends visited the pub in Knocklyon. They refused to leave at closing time, Doyle slamming the door violently. Kathleen Delaney, the licensee, sent for the Gardaí and when Detective Officer McGarry in turn asked Doyle to leave Doyle caught him by the throat, pushed him against the bar and threatened him with a bottle. He finally left at 12.40am. Mr Justice Reddin imposed a sentence of fourteen days and bound him over on a total surety of £50 with a further month's imprisonment on default.

18 January 1905

Post with wings

In the days before universal air travel the chief carrier of the all-important post was the express train. For transatlantic mail the need for urgency was greater after the rather stately progress of the ocean liners. In the early 20th century there was considerable competition between westerly ports such as Bristol and Liverpool for Post Office contracts and, much further west, Cobh, then still known as Queenstown. There the Great Southern and Western Railway Company set out on Wednesday 18 January 1905 to prove that it could have the US mail reach Dublin for distribution to all parts of the United Kingdom the following day, much earlier than from any other centre.

The White Star Liner *Teutonic* arrived in the Cove of Cork at 11.05, carrying the second largest load of mail ever recorded: 2889 sacks of post for Ireland, England, Scotland, 2500 of which had addresses in England. Three tenders were used by the railway company to convey the mailbags ashore; there they were loaded on to a special train by fifty porters under the management of the local postmaster, the Cobh stationmaster and the local representative of the White Star Company.

The 'special' consisting of nineteen carriages and two locomotives left the station at 12.49 and made only three stops on the way to Dublin: Mallow, Limerick Junction and Portarlington. It arrived in North Wall at 16.43, with the letters and packages already sorted by thirty Post Office experts sent down from Dublin the previous evening. At the terminus a number of drays had been drawn up, one to take mail to Amiens Street in time to put it on the 17.43 Belfast train for dispatch to Ulster and Scotland. It was a notable demonstration of what could be done but was it a little expensive?

19 January 1785

An aeronautic chariot

The first Irishman to make a flight was Richard Crosbie (1755-1824)from Crosbie Park, near Baltinglass, in County Wicklow. As a student in Trinity he was regarded as a mechanical genius, his room more like a workshop than a study. On 15 October 1783 Etienne Montgolfier had made the first fight over Paris in the hot-air balloon that he and his brother Joseph had invented. The news, when it finally reached Ireland, became a sensation and particularly excited Crosbie, who had been experimenting with balloon flight but using the safer hydrogen. The hot air generated by combustible material in the Montgolfier was likely to cause sparks that might ignite the balloon material.

For obvious reasons in a less sensitive age his first balloonauts were animals. He sent a tame cat aloft in a 'chariot' that was seen passing over the west coast of Scotland and then with a change of wind heading for the Isle of Man. (Both passenger and conveyance were safely picked up fortuitously by a passing ship.) With the feline success to encourage him Crosbie prepared himself for his own adventure. He exhibited his 'aeronautic chariot' for a fee to raise money for the project and then on Wednesday 19 January 1785, just fourteen months after the Montgolfier success, the thirty-year-old boarded his 'chariot', which was equipped with scientific instruments and the necessary ballast.

The launch pad was the pleasure gardens in Ranelagh, then virtually in the country. Such excitement was generated by the event that the city fathers had to impose travel restrictions: coaches were warned to keep well away from the garden and to park at the rear of Ranelagh House. Craft and passenger rose smoothly, headed north-west and 'landed in perfect safety on the strand, near the Island of Clontarf', as the *Freeman's Journal* reported it.

20 January 1957

'Inkblots' and 'crackpots'

One of the most successful entertainments ever devised occurs when 'personalities', those with well-known skills, are taken out of their professional comfort zones and 'star' in other spheres. The events are usually undertaken for charity and there is no limit to the crimes committed in that name. Typical was the annual revue/match featuring the 'Inkblots' (newspapermen) and 'Crackpots' (stage artists) in Dalymount Park, Phibsborough on Sunday 20 January 1957. In the circumstances any or all kinds of sporting events were possible. The arena, then the home ground of Bohemian Football Club, was properly a soccer pitch but that did not preclude rugby, hurling and hurdling, if they had the call.

The proceeds of the annual extravaganza usually amounted to £1000 and the money was used to ameliorate the plight of sick or underprivileged children. There was a contest between the two not necessarily internally cohesive teams and the Crackpots, as showbiz personalities, were more easily recognised that the Inkblots, who were used to hiding behind a byline. The Inkblots were also seasoned performers and soon adapted to playing 'in the round'. Since it was soon after the Suez Crisis it was no surprise that President Dwight D. Eisenhower (looking remarkably like the comedian Jack Cruise) should intervene between Anthony Eden and President Nasser.

UN forces had to separate rival warring parties and since the Grace Kelly-Prince Rainier wedding was still big news a newborn princess miraculously appeared. Noel Purcell, having recently recovered from a heart-attack, was present but was required to undergo a procedure there in the field, in which the chief surgeon was 'Mickser' Reid, the popular pantomime dwarf. When Dr Kevin O'Flanagan, the referee, announced that the result of the match was a draw 4-3, Brendan Behan led a movement to 'hang the ref'.

21 January 1980

Flooded with calls

The heavy rain that caused significant damage and disruption on Monday 21 January 1980 for once could only remotely be blamed on the seemingly endless Atlantic flow that has given the country its well-washed appearance since it originated in the Irish Sea. The deep depression centred there caused over thirty millimetres of rain to fall in Dublin between 6pm on the Sunday and the same time on the Monday. Such a deluge, coinciding with an unusually high tide in the early afternoon, caused widespread flooding.

The Fire Service announced, with unfortunate appropriateness, that they were 'flooded with calls', and with many roads under water there was travel chaos at the evening rush hour. Some children took things in their stride or rather made things go swimmingly, dragging out canoes and dinghies to float where no rivers previously ran free. Underground telephone cables were damaged in south County Dublin, cutting off many subscribers.

The winds also caused more damage to phone lines with poles brought down. Part of the roof of the Custom House was ripped off by the winds and the hoarding that had been placed round the demolished Ballast Office also fell victim to the gales. Transport by rail was disrupted when a waterlogged railway embankment between Inchicore and Hazelhatch collapsed on to the line. The effect was to cause severe delays on trains to and from Cork, Tralee, Limerick, Galway and Westport. The 9.20 from Cork took almost six hours to reach Heuston.

The Met Office reassured the public that the depression would move gradually away and colder weather with bright spells and wintry showers would occur over the next few days: 'We have got over the worst of the bad weather – at least for the moment' – a necessary qualification when dealing with the Irish climate.

22 January 1945

No further investigation

On the morning of 12 January 1945 a boy knocked on the door of a house in Harbour Cottages, Dún Laoghaire, to tell Thomas Graydon, the occupier, that he saw a man and a woman lying under the wall near the bandstand at the East Pier who did not appear to be alive. Graydon ran at once to the spot and found a man in army uniform lying on top of a woman wearing a fur coat and red shoes. The Gardaí were called, the usual forensic examinations held and ten days later on Monday 22 January, Dr J.P. Brennan, the County Dublin coroner, presided at an inquest held in St Michael's Hospital, Dún Laoghaire.

The verdict of the jury was that Commandant Peter Clerkin, a native of Tandragee, County Armagh, had killed Mrs Elizabeth McCormack, 75 Trimleston Park, Booterstown, and then shot himself. Dr Brennan said that from the beginning there was no evidence of any immoral relations between Commandant Clerkin and Mrs McCormack. The statement was, by today's more judicious usage, inappropriate but at the time it was taken as a kind of palliative for her family.

It seemed from the carefully chosen words of the non-technical witnesses that Clerkin was a model soldier, teetotal and a non-smoker. He was married with one daughter and went home to his house in Leinster Road as often as he was relieved from duty in Gormanstown. He had met Mrs McCormack in her home in Booterstown the previous November on military business. Her husband, Commandant James A. McCormack, had once been Clerkin's commanding officer and he remained on friendly terms with both. Just what deepening of the relationship occurred that winter remains unfathomed but no further investigation was deemed appropriate by the Gardaí, the army or the rather sober unsensational press of the time.

23 January 1803

The black liquidation

Ireland's national drink, once described as 'a black liquidation with froth on the top' and now generally known, at least to advertising copywriters, simply as 'the black stuff', was first produced in Dublin in 1759 by Arthur Guinness (1725-1803), known not always affectionately as 'Uncle Arthur'. He was born in Celbridge, County Kildare, the son of the land steward to Dr Arthur Price, Archbishop of Cashel. He and his brother Richard were each left £100 (£12, 600 today) in the will of the archbishop and with the money he leased a Leixlip brewery in 1756. Moving to Dublin in 1759, he obtained a 9000-year lease on a brewery in St James's Gate at £45 per annum, where in 1778 he began to brew the 'porter' that made his name world famous.

Until his time Dublin ale had a mediocre reputation as a blended liquor but he had learned that a stronger darker product made from roasted barley, known as 'entire' (as coming from a single barrel) was greatly favoured by London porters. It was known there as 'stout' because of its strength, so he labelled his brew as 'extra stout porter'. By the time of his death on 23 January 1803 it had an international reputation. (Thirty years later it would figure as an advertisement in an illustration to the first edition of *The Pickwick Papers*.) By May 1796 Guinness was exporting half the output of St James's Gate and by then, with the same steely determination that had led him to face down the Corporation when it tried to deprive him of water, he sold the stout as 'Guinness's Dark Protestant Porter'. This was to make clear his opposition to the rise of the United Irishmen, who nevertheless still drank it, an attempt at a local boycott having failed.

24 January 1934

Going to the zoo

Dublin Zoo, properly the Zoological Gardens, was opened on a twenty-eight-hectare site in Phoenix Park on 1 September 1831. It exhibited forty-six mammals and seventy-two birds donated by London Zoo. It soon became a popular, if somewhat expensive, attraction. Its condition formed the main business of a meeting of the Royal Zoological Society of Ireland in the Royal College of Surgeons, St Stephen's Green, on Wednesday 24 January 1934. Lord Holmpatrick, the society's president, was in the chair. The chief preoccupations were inevitably finance and livestock. The 'gate' of £3559 for 1933 was, disappointingly, £375 down on the 1932 total. The uncertain financial position and the reduction of the government's annual grant to £750 meant that no new purchases of stock could be made. This was a serious matter 'if the gardens are to be kept up to the level of former years'. On the positive side the educational value of the gardens had been recognised by school authorities and a supervised visit counted as school attendance.

The animal collection was doing well. The mortality was very low, partly as a result of improved housing and partly because of the warm summer. The lion house held nine lions and six lionesses, with three cubs born in 1933. This brought the total number born in the zoo since 1857 to three hundred and seventy-five. Food for the stock in 1933 cost £1567, including horse meat and dried flies. The sea-lion needed 20lb of fish every day while the rare Tuetara lizard from New Zealand ate nothing but worms that it foraged for itself.

The meeting concluded with a lecture on 'Animal Life in the Antarctic' by Dr Stanley W. Kemp FRS, in which he proposed, among many other interesting facts, that the blue whale was probably the largest animal that ever lived on the earth.

25 January 1988

Playing the stock exchange

It is not common although not entirely impossible for a student of Trinity College to appear before the High Court in Dublin but it is surely bizarre that one such, John Murray, was arraigned (on Monday 25 January 1988) for having run up debts of £114,000 (£259,000 today). He was regarded as being exceptionally knowledgeable about shares but this knowledge seemed eventually to have deserted him, for J. and E. Davy, the Dublin stockbrokers, were seeking an order against Allied Irish Finance (AIF) for the return of that amount lodged with them.

Peter Keane, Davy's investment manager, testified that because of certain instructions from Murray that were carried out, a total of £115, 546 was owed to the firm. He visited TCD in October 1987 to discuss the matter with Murray, who assured him that his brother Maurice would pay the money in full but Maurice, who lived in Boston, said that he too was a student and had no money. Gerard Butler, solicitor for Davys, said that AIF had paid the amount of £71,079 to two accounts under Murray's control but in the names of Breda and Veronica Smith. When asked about these transactions they disclaimed all knowledge of them.

Murray, who represented himself, admitted that he had opened accounts with AIF and had lodged money with them. He told Miss Justice Carroll that his brother had never at any time instructed J. and E. Davy and was not involved in the transactions. Asked if he had any objection to the money being paid out he said he had no control over it. The judge granted the order and gave costs against AIF but instructed that all the relevant documents should be examined by the DPP for forgery and if there were forgeries the DPP could decide whether or not to prosecute.

26 January 1946

'The pearls are so great.'

Robert Burns (1759-96), Scotland's national poet, was born on 25 January and the commemoration of that event, called Burns Night, is celebrated worldwide on that date or the nearest convenient one. In Dublin in 1946 it was held in the Royal Hibernian Hotel, Dawson Street, on Saturday 26 January. The host was the Dublin Scottish Benevolent Society of St Andrew. All the traditions were observed, including the piping in of the haggis, described by the poet as 'great chieftain o' the puddin' race' with the hope that its 'honest sonsie face' would 'fare fa'. The piping was done by Pipe-Major Andrews, who also played selections on his instrument.

The guest speaker was the Very Reverend D.F.R. Wilson, Dean of St Patrick's, who, faced with the problem of the bawdy nature of the poet's life and some of his work, reassured the squeamish among his listeners with an aplomb worthy of his illustrious predecessor: 'Some of Burns's censors have been unkind, some untrue. The accretions of falsehood around the grains of truth are as astonishing as the growth of pearls of great price in an oyster. So it was with Robbie Burns. I read the censors with impatience; the pearls are so great.'

J. Hubbard Clark, the society's honorary treasurer, in his toast to the guests, urged members to do even more to propagate the work of Burns, fearing that the newly formed Tom Moore Society would distract from the enthusiasm for the Scot. In reply he was reassured, with some polite exaggeration, by the most famous of all the editors of *The Irish Times*, R.M. Smyllie, that even if Burns was not the greatest poet that Scotland had produced he had become a national hero. 'Moore means nothing here but Burns is everything to the Scot.'

27 January 1936

Technicolour

Films first came to Dublin in April 1896 when Dan Lowrey Junior changed his music hall temporarily into a cinema, thereby unwittingly writing its death warrant. Forty years later the city was full of cinemas and citizens who read the papers on Monday 27 January 1936 were made aware of the wide choice available. Dublin's own magical theatre star, Jimmy O'Dea (1899-1965), who would twinkle for another thirty years, had made his first film, *Jimmy Boy*, and it was being shown in the Corinthian. It was as Oirish as only a British film could be, with shots of Bantry Bay and lots of blarney but it was felt that O'Dea, in spite of the company of Harry O'Donovan and Noel Purcell, 'was not given a chance to do the kind of thing which everyone knows he can do so well'.

Coincidentally another Irishman, a champion boxer, recorded singer and now cinema actor was on screen in the Grand Central that week. Jack Doyle, known as the 'Gorgeous Gael', was multi-talented; the film, *McGlusky, the Sea Rover*, he made when he was only twenty-one but alcohol and the rest destroyed all his possible careers. The film was damned with faint praise: 'Lively but no great strain on the intellect.'

The big cinema event of the week was *Becky Sharp*, playing in the Capitol, not because of its quality – a dumbed-down version of Thackeray's novel *Vanity Fair* – but because it was the first full-length film all in colour, 'the process Disney used for his cartoons'. Technicolour had definitely arrived, although thousands of movies would continue to be made in black and white. Just as the silent films had had their late sophistication replaced by trivial 'talkies', so now it seemed that colour might drive the industry again to childishness.

28 January 1802

Pelted with dead cats

The streets of inner south Dublin were crowded with people gathered to watch a funeral procession that led from the home of the deceased in 6 Ely Place, near St Stephen's Green, to St Peter's Churchyard in Aungier Street. It was appropriate that the funeral of John Fitzgibbon, 1st Earl of Clare (1749-1802), first native Irishman in modern times to hold the office of Lord Chancellor of Ireland, should have attracted a crowd but as it passed through the mean streets that coexisted with the very grand in Georgian Dublin the hearse was pelted with dead cats, or so the story goes. Clare was not only the most powerful man in Ireland but the most detested.

He had two non-personal ambitions: the preservation of the union with Britain and the prevention of Catholics from achieving the status of full citizens. He correctly linked the two, aware that the pesky unenfranchised majority would become uncontrollable if given any economic or political power. He was the principal native contriver of the Act of Union and is credited with convincing George III without much difficulty that concessions to Catholics either in Ireland or Britain would be a violation of his coronation oath and persuading George IV with even greater facility to follow his father.

His father John had been born a Catholic but joined the Church of Ireland so that he could become a lawyer. He became very rich and it was clear that his son's brilliance and ruthlessness marked him out for high office. Any slight measure of Catholic relief Clare attacked vehemently and made the United Irishmen his especial target as they intended to unite Protestant, Catholic and dissenter, working against his chosen methods of virulent sectarianism. The history of Ireland the next century was therefore vitiated by the persistence of such attitudes.

29 January 1907

The Playboy *riots*

The *Playboy of the Western World,* the crowning drama of the genius of J.M. Synge (1871-1909), opened in the Abbey Theatre on Saturday 26 January 1907, two and a half years before the playwright's death of Hodgkin's disease at the age of thirty-eight. In it he put the distillation of his sojourns in County Wicklow, County Kerry, Connemara and especially the Aran Islands, in representing the passion, resourcefulness, danger and, supremely, the use of language, 'as fully flavoured as a nut or an apple', as he described it, by the people who lived here.

The Abbey had been generally welcomed as a counterblast to the essentially British fare offered in the Queen's and other theatres but it was viewed with suspicion by the growing band of nationalists, members of Arthur Griffith's Sinn Féin, Conradh na Gaeilge and the GAA. These movements had generated an idealised vision of Irish peasant life and any supposed besmirching of this ideal was regarded as an attack by the unionist ascendancy, especially as personified by the Protestants, Yeats, Gregory and Synge.

The play was routinely attacked by the *Freeman's Journal* and the *Irish Independent* and after a troubled performance on the second night the scene was set for a serious confrontation. On Tuesday 29 January, a number of 'athletic' TCD students were admitted free into the best stalls while the pit at the back was filled with equally 'athletic' Gaelic Leaguers bent on mutual barracking. Yeats went on stage to announce that the play would nevertheless continue to be given. The melée that followed did little credit to either side, while rival versions of 'God Save the King' and 'A Nation Once Again' drowned out the actors. The play continued and after the final curtain there were scuffles and arrests by the police who were present in expectation of trouble.

30 January 1988

'No property in a dead body'

A meeting of the ethics committee of the Irish Medical Organisation (IMO) scheduled for Wednesday 3 February 1988 to discuss the issue of multiple organ donation, would also consider the related and grisly question of ownership of dead bodies. The announcement was made on Saturday 30 January, by Professor Patrick Bofin, the Dublin City coroner, who drew attention to the fact that under current archaic legislation 'when a person dies the body does not belong to the family or, indeed, to anyone else, and that surgeons could legally remove organs for transplant operations, contrary to the bereaved family's wishes.'

He underlined the absurdity by using the example that if a motorist killed a farmer's chicken, the chicken remained the farmer's property but if a motorist killed a farmer's daughter her body did not belong to anybody. He explained that Ireland was the only country in Europe without the protective legislation that would prevent a person from taking a heart from a dead body. He had been campaigning for such legislation for seventeen years, from the time that Ireland had signed up in Strasbourg to a general agreement concerning organ transplants while the other matter remained unresolved. He had devised then a 'fairly loose code of practice' but the state of the law at the moment was that there 'is no property in a dead body'.

As to whether there should be a single dedicated team of surgeons to remove all the donated organs from a single donor or whether there should be specified teams for liver, heart and kidney. Professor O'Higgins of St Vincent's Hospital, who had performed the first liver transplant four years earlier, recommended the single team option with a central agency for dissemination. It was a matter that the IMO needed to determine.

31 January 1957

'The quick and the dead'

'Pa' O'Donnell (d. 1970), the Minister for Local Government in the Fine Gael-led interparty government, introduced in one of his last acts a number of regulations associated with new traffic signs. These required amendments to existing by-laws, the details of which were announced by Daniel Costigan, the Commissioner of the Garda Síochána, on Thursday 31 January 1957.

The primary change was to improve the lot of pedestrians, giving them right of way at crossings and at 'traffic refuges'. Motorists were required to stop at a marked 'stop-line' when yielding right of way at pedestrian crossings. If the crossing had a central 'island' the portion on either side would be deemed as separate crossings. At an uncontrolled or unpatrolled crossing every person on the roadway within the limits of such a crossing should have right of way over any vehicle, which must yield if the pedestrian has reached the roadway first. The only trouble was that not all the crossings had been 'brought into conformity' with the regulations. Any improvement, however, was welcome for until the new rules were formally stated there were in the words of one cynic only two kinds of pedestrians, 'the quick and the dead'.

Other rules applied to the now obsolete hand signals required from a driver, specific to slowing down and turning left: 'moving the fully extended arm with palm turned down slowly upwards and downwards' and 'rotating the extended right arm in an anti-clockwise direction'. With riders of motorcycles and pedal bicycles, 'the left arm and hand should be extended to the left.' Those leading a horse not attached to a vehicle might use either side of the carriageway (instead of only the left as hitherto). Approved by the Safety First Association of Ireland, the measures were to come into force on 8 February.

SPRING

1 February 1968

Tonehenge and other monuments

The sculptor Edward Delaney (1930-2009) is known to Dubliners for two prodigious public statues of Irish patriots, Thomas Davis in College Green (1966) and Wolfe Tone (1967) in St Stephen's Green. The same witty Dubliners named these installations respectively as 'Urination Once Again' from the fountains at the figure's feet and a tribute to his authorship of 'A Nation Once Again, and 'Tonehenge' from the stark pillars surrounding the statue.

Delaney was the defendant in the Dublin Circuit Civil Court on Thursday 1 February 1968 on a charge of breach of covenant of the lease of premises in Stoneview Place, Dún Laoghaire, the site of the artist's home and workshop. The case was brought by Cyril, Robert and Herbert Allen Sharpe, who sought damages of £300 and an injunction that Delaney should demolish his workshop and desist from further building on the site. They suggested that his occupation, which required a furnace for the preparing of molten metals that he used as an artist, was an 'offensive trade' and as such in breach of the covenant.

Delaney countered with the argument that he was neither ironmonger nor businessman but a sculptor who needed to pour the metal himself. The furnace was very small, rather like a central-heating unit in a house. Anyway he thought he might give up sculpting, being now more concerned with painting. In his decision Judge Wellwood found that although the defendant had been in technical breach of the contract it would be unreasonable to grant a mandatory injunction to demolish the new workshop. He admitted not to understand art but could not in any way regard the work as 'offensive'. He dismissed the plaintiffs' case but said that they were entitled to damages, which he assessed at £10.

2 February 1882

John Stanislaus Joyce

James Joyce (1882-1941), the logodaedalic author of *Ulysses* and *Finnegans Wake,* was born on Thursday 2 February 1882. It was Candlemas Day and the day after the feast of St Brigid, feasts full of significance for a man with a lifelong, almost sacerdotal, absorption in religious rites. His father, John Stanislaus, was thirty-three, his mother, May, ten years younger and the family, in a never-to-be-repeated period of affluence, had a very good address, 41 Brighton Square West, Rathgar. He was baptised James Augustine Joyce, the names of his grandfather. In fact he was incorrectly listed as James Augusta, perhaps unwittingly prophetic of the feminine empathy he would show in his work.

Over the next twenty years the father's spendthrift ways reduced a prosperous middle-class family to abject poverty with sixteen changes of address, many of these flits proving necessary. Joyce never completely lost his patience with his flamboyant father but summarised him tersely in Stephen Dedalus's description of his father Simon in *A Portrait of the Artist as a Young Man:* 'A medical student, an oarsman, a tenor, an amateur actor, a shouting politician, a small landlord, a small investor, a drinker, a good fellow, a storyteller, somebody's secretary, a tax gatherer, a bankrupt and at present a praiser of his own past.'

It is interesting to note that many of these boxes could have been ticked for Stephen as well.

In 1884 the family moved the short distance to 23 Castlewood Avenue, on the other side of Lower Rathmines Road. They stayed there for three years before moving again, this time to 1 Martello Terrace, Bray, from which young Jim, just 'half-past six', as he put it, was dispatched as a boarder to Clongowes and to which he returned for the poignant Christmas dinner, one of the high points of his writing.

3 February 1905

Irish lights

The first known form of coastal warning light in Ireland was a fire beacon set up by monks in Hook Head, County Wexford, in the fifth century. It wasn't until 1867 that the responsibility for coastal safety was assigned to the Commissioners of Irish Lights. This all-Ireland body still maintains the lighthouses that are, with one exception, now automatic. At the start of the 20th century most were manned and the 'six weeks on – six weeks off' system usually worked well, although access was often difficult and at times the periods of duty lasted longer than the six weeks.

The sense of romantic isolation made the keepers' lives a topic of great interest to landlubbers and lectures about the service were usually popular. On Friday 3 February 1905 a lecture by Sir Robert Ball LLD FRS (1840-1913) entitled 'A Cruise with the Irish Light Commissioners' in the theatre of the Royal Dublin Society premises attracted a packed audience. The talk was illustrated with 'limelight views' (an improved form of lantern slides) and it described a journey of 1200 miles beginning and ending in Kingstown (Dún Laoghaire). The itinerary took three weeks because of delays at some of the ninety points of call.

Hall divided his journey into four sections: Kingstown to Tory island, Tory to the Shannon, Shannon to Bantry Bay and back to Kingstown. He opined that the most interesting part of the cruise was the stretch from Tory to Fastnet, south-west of Cork – the 'steep Atlantic stream'. Among the pictures screened were those of the ship, the *Alexandra*, and the various lighthouses, with fascinating stories from the lecturer about the perils faced by those who built them in the first place. Ball finished his talk with an account of the latest illumination techniques that gave a warning flash every five seconds.

4 February 1971

Student in contempt

Martin Dolphin, a twenty-year-old former UCD student, had had a troubled career ever since he was arrested on the Belfield campus during a demonstration when, on Tuesday 29 September 1970, President de Valera was officially opening the new Arts Block. He had assaulted a Garda and security men at the scene. Arraigned in the District Court, he was sentenced to seven days' imprisonment for contempt of court. Because of his condition he was transferred to the Central Mental Hospital in Dundrum, where he stayed until the last week in January. At this point he was discharged.

On Thursday 4 February 1971 he was taken before District Justice Ó hUadaigh but he stated that he did not recognise the authority of the court. There were a certain number of interruptions and in the end the judge sentenced him to a further seven days for contempt but required medical evidence of Dolphin's fitness to plead. When Dr Eveleen O'Brien, Governor of Dundrum, was being sworn in, Dolphin shouted, 'It is only a court of injustice and a tool of oppression against the people.' When the judge warned him of the danger of contempt he replied, 'You are a lackey, Ó hUadaigh. It is not me who is on trial. You are on trial and the whole imperialistic system.'

As he was being forcibly taken from the court the judge said, 'Be careful of him.' The prisoner shouted back, 'Long live the Irish Communist Party, the Marxist-Leninists and long live Chairman Mao.' He was back in the afternoon when in an all but empty courtroom Justice Ó hUadaigh again advised that in the face of the court he was guilty of contempt because of his abusive language and faced another seven days in Mountjoy. 'I have nothing but contempt for your court,' was his only response.

5 February 1934

A halfpenny on the pound of sugar

The chief preoccupations of the first Fianna Fáil government that succeeded Cumann na nGaedheal in 1932 were the necessity of keeping the Free State in existence, waging the Economic War with Britain consequent on refusing to pay land annuities, dealing with residual extremism – the quasi-fascism of the Army Comrades Association, known for obvious reasons as the Blueshirts and the still active IRA republicanism – and maintaining the country's economic reputation in the eyes of the world. This balancing act led in the government to a kind of paternalism with regard to the population and the arrogating of emergency executive powers to the cabinet outside the Dáil.

On Monday 5 February 1934 it was announced that from the following day the price of a pound of sugar would be increased by one halfpenny, the equivalent of 50-60 cent today. The increase was part of a series of new duties imposed by the Executive Council of the Free State Government under the Emergency Imposition of Duties Act. Additional duties were also imposed on molasses, glucose and saccharin. The main purpose of the 4s/8d per hundredweight increase that brought the total imposition to 16s/4d was to boost the sale of existing home-grown sugar beet and encourage sugar factories, located in Carlow (the longest-established centre of the sugar industry, from 1926), Thurles and Tuam. These could produce 55,000 tons of the state's total sugar requirement of 105,000 tons. When all the factories had reached full output, as they were expected to do before the end of the year, there would no longer be any need to import at all. No mention was made of the difference in texture and quality between the coarse home product and the finer cane that came largely from the West Indies. A decade later, when Second World War exigencies largely cut off imported sugar, the beet factories became virtually the only source.

6 February 1966

McGahern and the Censorship Board

The Dark, the second novel of John McGahern (1934-2006), published in 1965, was banned by the Irish Censorship Board, which seemed to direct its trivialising and Puritanical venom with greatest energy against native Irish writers. Its harrowing account of adolescent life in rural Ireland was declared pornographic because of its bleak account of the protagonist's episodes of masturbation and that suggestion that a priest might be homosexual. McGahern was awarded the MacAuley Fellowship that enabled him to take a year's leave from his post as a teacher in St John the Baptist Boys' National School, Clontarf. Just before the new academic year began in 1965 he had had a minor motorcycle accident that prevented his resuming work on 20 September, the day his leave ended. Four weeks later he notified his headmaster that he was ready to return on 11 October.

He was told by him that Fr Patrick J. Carton, the school manager, had said he was not to resume work and that they would meet when the priest returned from holiday. At their meeting four weeks later it was clear that he had been dismissed on the orders of Carton's own superior, Archbishop McQuaid, partly because of the book ('What entered your head to write that book!' were the priest's opening words) and because he had married his Finnish wife in a civil ceremony.

These details were given by the writer on Sunday 6 February 1966 at the height of the controversy about his dismissal from his teaching post. Though he was refused reinstatement, the case virtually finished the censorship system, already reeling from its moral and aesthetic dysfunction. McGahern was reclaimed for Ireland and Irish writing and by the time of his death on 30 March 2006 was treasured as one of the finest of its authors.

7 February 1947

Mr Holiday

'Billy' Butlin – actually Sir William Heygate Edmund Colborne Butlin (1899-1980) – did not actually invent the holiday camp but made it one of the most significant aspects of 20th-century British popular holiday-making. He described his camps as 'luxury hotels for the middle-classes' but they were essentially bargain holidays for ordinary working-class families. From 1936, with the opening of his first venture in Skegness in Lincolnshire until the development of cheap continental holidays, he was Mr Holiday.

On Friday 7 February 1947 he called a press conference in the Shelbourne Hotel to reveal his plans for Ireland's first Butlin paradise. The site was in Mosney, near Layton in County Meath, and would have accommodation at first for 1500 guests but that number would increase as necessary. The chalets would have two to four beds with heating, lighting and hot and cold water. Extensive public rooms would include dining-rooms, ballrooms, bars, shopping centres, children's playrooms and a first-class theatre. Conscious of the Ireland of the time Butlin announced that a Catholic Church would be built on site and representation would be made to the diocesan authorities to appoint a resident chaplain. Other denominations would be similarly catered for. He would also establish a railway station for the site as he had done for one of his Yorkshire camps.

He emphasised the employment that would be created in building the camp and said that four hundred people would be needed to run it. Every possible post from managing director to chalet maid would be filled by Irish people and the clients' only expenses for a week's stay after paying the all-in fee of between five and a half and six and a half guineas would be for drink and cigarettes. All was in train for the opening of Butlin's in Mosney in April 1948.

8 February 1964

'Trinity needs more Irish Catholics for its own good.'

In 1874 religious tests for undergraduates were no longer imposed in Trinity College and the automatic prohibition of Catholics from membership was finally rescinded. The reaction of the Catholic hierarchy was to accuse the college of secularism and ban Catholics from attendance under pain of mortal sin, unless with an individual dispensation, not exactly easy to obtain. The effect was for Trinity to be regarded as an unpatriotic outpost of Britain, elitist and formally unIrish. The consequences were serious for the college, deprived of 75 per cent of the academic population, and for the country, virtually cut off from its oldest university.

With most social, national and moral objections associated with the college removed by the 1960s and in the surge of liberal thinking influencing even rooted Ireland, agitation to have the ban removed grew in intensity, both within the college and outside it. Yet as the clamour grew the Church's adamant opposition kept pace with it, finding a prime place in the Lenten pastorals of Archbishop McQuaid. The ban was not removed until 28 October 1970 but by that time many interested parties had chosen to disregard it.

Typical of the recurrent theme was a debate in the Literary and Historical Society on Saturday 8 February 1964 when a motion calling for the ban to be lifted was carried by a large majority. The chief speaker was Professor W.B. Stanford, who said that Trinity needed more Irish Catholics for its own good. 40 per cent of the students were from overseas, he said, and it would be preferable if 75 per cent were Catholic and Irish. From the highest level down Catholics were represented; the new chancellor was Catholic, the college had been the first in these islands to remove restrictions on Catholics and the authorities actively welcomed them.

9 February 1964

The broad Church of John Charles McQuaid

It was customary that on the Sunday before Ash Wednesday each year the bishops of Ireland should utter a 'Lenten Pastoral' that would be read at all Masses. Its message was partly catechetical, restating the complicatedly precise rules for the Lenten fast; partly devotional, urging the faithful to use the season as a time for spiritual renewal; and mainly admonitory, to underline the permeation of clerical authority in the premier Catholic country in Europe, as the laity were constantly reminded. Easter was unusually early in 1964 so the episcopal letters were published on 9 February that year.

The pastoral for the Dublin diocese was written by Archbishop John Charles McQuaid (1895-1973) then in the twenty-fourth year of his thirty-two-year term of office. It was also the third year of the Second Vatican Council, with whose changes he was singularly ill at ease. The document showed not a hint of ecumenism nor of a greater role for the laity and could have been issued at almost any time since his appointment in 1940. It showed his capacity for detail, his excellence as an administrator, his assumption of automatic and total obedience – even approval – by his audience and his adamantine demonstration of his authority. What did not emerge was his unpublicised work for charity and attempts at amelioration of social ills.

The absolute defence of the need for Catholic education of children and third-level adults, refusing permission under pain of mortal sin to attend Trinity College, was the most controversial of the Irish Church's edicts, only less strong than the stringent conditions imposed on those couples who would enter into in a 'mixed marriage'. The archbishop's admonitions did not stop there but penetrated into many aspects of social life: joining societies, driving, suitable reading. It was indeed a broad church.

10 February 1936

Fatal accident on Merrion Road

R.T. Callan, a solicitor with a practice in Suffolk Street, lived with his wife Elizabeth in 48 Sandymount Avenue. On Saturday 8 February 1936, at about 8.30pm, they went for a stroll along the avenue in the direction of Merrion Road. They were hit by a car as they attempted to cross and both received fatal injuries. These were described at the inquest held on Monday 10 February 1936 by Dr J.P. Brennan, South Dublin coroner, in the Royal Dublin Hospital, Baggot Street. Dr P. Walsh, house surgeon in Baggot Street, reported that Callan had a fractured skull and wrist, and compound fractures in both legs. He had died of a cranial haemorrhage after a few hours. Mrs Callan was dead on arrival in St Patrick Dun's and the pathologist Dr Ellerker, who carried out the autopsy, gave the same cause of death – brain haemorrhage – and noted that she had sustained a fractured skull and rupture of kidney and liver.

Patrick Smith told how he had been aware of a car coming from Ballsbridge at about 30-35 mph and had seen the couple on the pavement opposite. A few seconds later they were lying in the middle of the road as the car reversed back to the point of impact. He ran to help but there was little he could do. The Garda report on the condition of the car showed that the front had been extensively damaged. The radiator had been bent back, the bonnet smashed and the right panel of the windscreen deeply dinged. The jury had difficulty at first in arriving at a verdict but after a second session a majority returned a verdict in accordance with the medical evidence, exonerating the driver, who was not named in any press report, from all blame.

11 February 1926

'There are no women like that in Ireland.'

The Abbey Theatre, in its one hundred and ten years of existence, has staged at least three plays that caused riot in the legal definition of that term. Each was caused by a sense of affront in people, generally not regular theatre goers, who felt that the fair name of Ireland and/or that of Irish Catholics had been traduced. In 1907 the objection to Synge's *The Playboy of the Western World* lay in its portrayal of Mayo peasants. In 1955 Seán O'Casey's *The Bishop's Bonfire* was riotously deemed anti-clerical but it was the first week of the same author's most famous play, *The Plough and the Stars,* that saw the most characteristic of Abbey rumpuses.

It opened on Monday 8 February 1926 and by the Thursday night the word was out that once again Ireland's peerless morality and sanctified heroes were being traduced. O'Casey, as a member of the Citizen Army, had been about Dublin during Easter Week 1916 and had witnessed for himself the opportunistic looting from big and small shops by a working class as deprived as any in the western world. He was wary of Pearse's adulation of blood sacrifice, having the off-stage character, 'The Voice of the Speaker' utter phrases like: 'Bloodshed is a cleansing and satisfying thing…' This attack on the tenth anniversary of the Rising was too much for some patriots.

It was, however, the character of Rosie Redmond, the prostitute, that caused the greatest rage, as missile-throwers hissed, 'There are no women like that in Ireland.' It was a singularly empty claim, uttered within a quarter of a mile of the notorious 'Monto'. Barry Fitzgerald, who played Fluther Good, knocked a would-be assailant off the stage and Yeats's voice thundered above the din, 'You have disgraced yourselves again!'

12 February 1988

'Engaged in homosexual activity'

On Friday 12 February 1988 the Circuit Criminal Court in Dublin was the scene of the imposition on a thirty-four-year-old man from New Cabra Road of a five-year suspended sentence for blackmail. He had pleaded guilty to demanding money from a thirty-eight-year-old man from Finglas who had 'engaged in homosexual activity' with his twenty-two-year-old flatmate. They had met in the Erin's Isle GAA club and after that first meeting had come together again on 8 February 1987. They moved on to the New Cabra Road flat, the Finglas man inviting himself. The thirty-four-year-old left, saying he was 'going home' and when he returned his flatmate informed him that further intimacy had taken place.

Here the story took a bizarre twist. When he returned, he claimed that he was a detective assigned to 'protect' the younger man and that the bedroom conversation had been taped. He suggested that the visitor should pay £3000 compensation to avoid a fifteen-year jail sentence. The man was distraught but agreed to these terms, promising to pay £1000 of it on the following Wednesday. In fact he went to the Gardaí, who provided him with a concealed recording-machine. When the blackmailer arrived in a red Escort car he repeated his demand for the money and was subsequently arrested.

Fr Michael Cleary (1934-93) then a well-known media priest, appeared as a character witness, testifying that he had known the thirty-four-year-old for many years as an honest hard-working man, whom he had trusted with the keys of the church in Ballyfermot when he lived there. His doctor had written to say that he was epileptic, had had two car crashes and could never drive again. The judge agreed that prison was not the best place for an epileptic and bound him over for three years. A similar charge against the younger flatmate was dropped.

13 February 1820

Lawyer, librettist and government spy

On Sunday 13 February 1820 a Dublin lawyer, Leonard McNally (1752-1820), died in his home in 22 Harcourt Street. He was buried in Donnybrook four days later. The public prints, especially *Saunder's Newsletter,* carried full details of a remarkable career in law and the theatre. Leonard McNally had been a United Irishman and in the trials of such revolutionary leaders as Wolfe Tone, Napper Tandy, Lord Edward Fitzgerald and Robert Emmet his eloquence as defence counsel was notable if never quite successful. His public stance as the United Irishmen's legal adviser never seemed to get him into trouble with the authorities, especially the relentless Major Sirr.

He was born in 1752, the son of a Catholic grocer of St Mary's Lane, off Capel Street, a career he followed at the beginning. His talent was such that, although totally unschooled, he was called to the Irish bar in 1776 at the age of twenty-four and the English bar seven years later. The young Dubliner revealed a rich dramatic ability, having twelve plays staged between 1779 and 1796. He also wrote libretti for Covent Garden and one of his songs, written in tribute to his first wife, with whom he eloped in 1787, is still in the repertoire as 'Sweet Lass of Richmond Hill' and contains the first mention of the phrase 'a rose without a thorn'. In 1892 his book *The Rules of Evidence* formulated the concept 'beyond reasonable doubt'.

Dubliners were startled when, a few days after his supposed death, he wrote a letter to the newspapers protesting that he was very much alive and intended to sue; the Leonard McNally who had died was his son. He survived for another four months and it was only after his death that it was revealed that he had been the government's chief spy all during the revolutionary period.

14 February 1981

St Valentine's Night in the Stardust

The Stardust nightclub was situated near the Artane Castle Shopping Centre in north Dublin and for St Valentine's Day 1981 the management advertised a disco. On possibly the most commercialised and spuriously romanticised date in the year after Christmas and Hallowe'en it was not likely that they would fail their niche audience, young people with a modal age of eighteen. They came in their hundreds – 841 in all – and all went merry as a marriage bell. A fire may have started from an electrical fault in the roof space next to a storage room that held flammable material. The staff failed to contain it but sounded no alarm.

Soon flames and thick black smoke soon began to burst from the ceiling, causing the fiercely hot material to melt and drip on the patrons. A growing hysteria became naked terror when all the power failed and the stricken customers tried in the darkness to reach safety outside. The surge of people mistook the doors to the men's toilets for the exits but as they crowded in they found that the windows were barred with iron grilles. Some of the real exits were found to be padlocked. Rage, fear and hysteria reigned outside as those who had escaped harangued the emergency services to do more to rescue their friends, still trapped.

In all forty-eight people died and two hundred and fourteen were injured, some seriously. Most were 'local', coming from Artane, Coolock and Kilmore, and the sense of loss devastated the community. A tribunal chaired by Mr Justice Ronan Keane in November 1981 concluded that the cause was probably arson, a judgement that enabled the Stardust owners to claim compensation from the city amounting to £580,000. They were, however, reprimanded for a serious breach of fire and safety regulations. New legislation followed.

15 February 1971

Decimal Day

Once upon a time and a very good time it was, money in Ireland was known as £/s/d – pounds, shillings and pence. The '£' stood for *libra*, the 's' for *solidi* and the 'd' for *denarii*, obscure Latin words that all took in their stride, for nothing sharpens the mind like finance. So it was until the exigencies of the modern computer-driven world required that Britain and Ireland should follow most of the western world and introduce decimalisation. The old elegant coinage with such exotic names and decorations as farthing (woodchuck), halfpenny (sow with piglets), penny (hen with chicks), threepenny piece (hare), sixpence (Irish wolfhound), shilling (bull), florin (salmon), half-crown (horse) had to yield to the modern world.

For Ireland, Monday 15 February 1971 was designated Decimal Day and there was considerable concern that the change to the new coinage (and the simpler arithmetic) might be painless. Dubliners, on the whole, took the change in their urban stride. They had generally obeyed the national injunction: 'Pay more and get change!' Shop assistants had been given training but they needed calculators from that date. With the old system bill totals in the banished duodecimal coinage could be worked out mentally in £/s/d. Now adding 35p to 50p, a sum that used come to 17 shillings, became a tricky 85p.

One elderly person refused to accept new money in change; another, having tendered a ten-shilling note for an item costing 41p, got only three new pence in change. An old Kerrywoman assured an RTÉ reporter: 'It'll never catch on here, son!' The banks said that all £/s/d transactions had been cleared by Friday evening. CIÉ found that travellers made no demur and the busmen, although reluctant at first, eventually agreed to have their float in the new money. Decimalisation had arrived.

16 February 1966

The case of the nylon stocking

The body of Peggy Flynn, a forty-seven-year-old waitress, was found in Sandycove on Tuesday 15 February 1966 with a nylon stocking tied tightly round her neck and the following day Chief Superintendent Bernard McShane, who was in charge of the investigation, said there was a possibility that she could have committed suicide. Tests on the nylon stocking suggested that it was possible that the first loop was tied sufficiently tight to cause strangulation. The body was lying face downwards with the arms tucked under the chest and facing towards the neck. There were no signs of any other marks on the body apart from an abrasion on the nose that could have been caused by her fall.

If she had been murdered the perpetrator had gone to an awful lot of trouble to place her body neatly on very slippery rocks. 'He would have had to negotiate a slipway and rocks which were treacherous with rain and seawater. The natural thing would have been for him to either throw the body over the small wall fronting the rocks or from the slipway but there was no evidence to show that he did this.' It was difficult to see how one stocking was removed from her without some evidence of a struggle. No trace of her shoes and handbag was found.

Anticipating the expected inquest finding the Gardaí nevertheless carried out their enquiries as if in a murder investigation. The shore in Sandycove was thoroughly searched and all the shops and cafes in the Dalkey area frequented by the deceased were visited. There were several false leads: a taxi passenger to Sandycove at the critical time was located safely at home and a pair of shoes found in an abandoned car in Dún Laoghaire were found not to be hers.

17 February 1946

Eleanor Roosevelt in Ireland

Anna Eleanor Roosevelt (1884-1962), fifth cousin and wife of Franklin Delano Roosevelt (FDR), was of all first ladies until Hilary Rodham Clinton the only one with real political influence. She worked vigorously for her husband in his gubernatorial and presidential campaigns in 1928, 1930 and 1932 and was a strongly liberal effect on his policies throughout his periods of office, 1932-45. She wrote a syndicated newspaper column, 'My Day', and had a personal schedule of speaking engagements and press conferences. Two years younger than FDR, she continued her public career after his death. She was US delegate to the United Nations under Truman and Kennedy and a lifelong campaigner for the improved status of women.

She landed in Baldonnel Aerodrome in a US Naval aircraft on Sunday 17 February 1946, after a journey from Bevington that took 105 minutes. She wore black and was smiling when she walked down the gangway to be greeted by her aunt, the wife of the generally uncooperative American minister, David Gray, who was also in the welcoming party. The chief Irish person in the group was Helena Early, from the Women's Social League. Eleanor Roosevelt's chief concerns were the UN – the United Nations Organisation (UNO) it was known then – and the advance of feminism in Ireland.

Both were of immediate concern to her, especially the good start the UNO had made, and neatly to link with her other preoccupation she urged a greater involvement of women in the organisation's affairs. She urged Irish women to vote, probably sensing that their formal power in the Ireland of the time was slight but insisting that 'they can nearly always get what they want'. Later she entertained the Taoiseach and other distinguished guests to tea in the American Legation.

18 February 1936

Abandoned car dripping blood

At 9 o'clock on the morning of Tuesday 18 February 1936 an abandoned car was discovered near a cliff in County Dublin. It had been parked at the foot of Corbawn Lane, Shankill Cross. What alarmed passers-by and brought the Gardai hurrying to the scene was the seepage of blood on to the rear wheels. It had dripped from the back seat, which was completely saturated, and a blood-stained towel lay on the floor. The lane where the car was found was lined on both sides with trees and at the end was a kind of palisade of earth and wooden posts to prevent any traffic from falling over the steep drop.

The car, an Austin Seven, was found to be the property of Mrs Vera Ball (53), the wife of Dr Charles Preston Ball of 81 Pembroke Road, although she lived with her son, nineteen-year-old Edward, in 23 St Helen's Road, Booterstown. She had left her home at 8.30 on the Monday evening and had not been heard from since. When the car was found in such a bloody state the Gardai instituted an immediate search of the area. The blood and the pieces of broken glass that littered the floor made them suspect the worst and their search was intensified.

Among the possibilities considered by the Gardaí were that Mrs Ball's body might have been buried or that she might have been thrown over the cliff into the sea. All costal stations were alerted and the search was extended to include Shankill and the coast north and south of the area. The forensic team led by Dr John McGrath examined the car and the house in Booterstown, while statements were taken from the husband and the son. On 22 February Edward Ball was charged with the murder of his mother.

19 February 1957

A coming man

After the 1957 general election Jack Lynch became, at thirty-nine, the youngest cabinet minister in Ireland, with the portfolios of the Gaeltacht and Education. Unlike some contemporary politicians he exuded a kind of transparent honesty and a face in which there seemed no guile. He had had a stellar career as a sportsman for his native Cork – a kind of political reincarnation of the Bould Thady Quill. Later in his career as Taoiseach he was thought to be the most popular Irish statesman since Daniel O'Connell. Even as a young man his serious mien, wreathed in pipe smoke, and his sober vocal register gave him the avuncular air of someone much older and wiser.

He was, then, the ideal man to give a party political broadcast on behalf of Fianna Fáil in the lead-up to the election that ousted Costello's second coalition. On Tuesday 19 February 1957 fourteen days before the polls, he made an effective attack on the previous government's record in office. In those days before television had begun to be transmitted the radio was only medium for universal communication and although the recipients could not actually see the slightly prominent but oh so sincere eyes the voice, with its mixture of righteous indignation and pathos, more than compensated.

He excoriated the interparty government for its dereliction of duty towards the Gaeltacht in both its terms of office. A Gaeltacht committee set up by Fianna Fáil in 1951 met over forty times in the two and a half years up to the election in 1954 but had met only eight times since. Under Fianna Fáil a Gaeltacht Housing Bill was passed enabling water schemes, housing grants and tourist roads, to be financed by expenditure of £40,000 a year for eight years. It was clearly the talk of a coming man.

20 February 1910

Miss Horniman of the Abbey

Annie Horniman (1860-1937) once described herself as 'a middle-aged, middle-class, suburban, dissenting spinster'. She was also a remarkably independent feminist and the rich heiress of a prosperous tea company. She had two loves, theatre and, for a period, the poet W.B. Yeats. He was five years her junior when they met in the 1890s at a gathering of the Order of the Golden Dawn in London. She helped subsidise the performance of Yeats's play *Land of Heart's Desire* and after what she considered a favourable reading of the Tarot decided to subsidise the Irish National Theatre in 1903 with the active encouragement of Yeats but with less enthusiasm by Lady Gregory and Edward Martyn, the other founders.

Over the next seven years she provided money for the company's salaries, bought and refurbished the Mechanics Institute as the Abbey Theatre and quarrelled with most Irish people she met, having no interest in nationalism nor cheap theatre seats. She tired of competing with Lady Gregory for Yeats's emotional attention, lost confidence in W.G. Fay as a director and after seven years was ready to leave again for her Gaiety Theatre in Manchester. On Thursday 20 February 1910 she agreed to pay the subsidy until 1 December and then to sell the Abbey outright to the company.

On 7 May 1910 Edward VII was buried and all theatres and other places of public entertainment were closed as a mark of respect, except the Abbey, which was kept open by the manager, Lennox Robinson (1886-1958). It was the excuse that Miss Horniman needed. She refused to pay the legally due remainder subsidy of £400 (£360,000 today) and left Ireland for good. It is estimated that her contribution to the setting up of Ireland's national theatre was the equivalent of a million Euro today.

21 February 1966

'The importance of the language'

Micheál MacLiammóir, although treasured at home in Ireland as actor, writer, dramatist and personality, achieved international recognition only after the success of his one-man entertainment *An Oscar of No Importance*, based on the life and work of Oscar Wilde and first presented in 1963. On Monday 21 February 1966 he announced from the stage of the Gaiety Theatre that he proposed to perform *Talking about Yeats*, another one-man show that he had devised. The performance scheduled for Monday 14 March would be in the theatre and the proceeds would help pay for new building work in Coláiste Mhuire, the Christian brothers all-Irish school in Parnell Square. MacLiammóir admitted that devising a programme about Yeats was much more difficult that one about Wilde, who offered so much humour and tragedy – and O'Casey had shown that in Ireland this mixture was necessary.

The event was conducted in Irish, in which he was fluent, using it for his diary each evening, and he reminded his listeners that more than once the poet had expressed his sorrow that he did not/could not write in Irish. 'He knew the importance of the language, its strength and how essential it was if the country was to survive.' Speaking of the school, he said that the country was indebted to Ernest Blythe, one of its founders, not only for his work for the language but for all he had done for the theatre. Blythe happily returned the compliment, saying that Dr MacLiammóir had done far more for the Irish language than many of the people who shouted about the movement without any effect on the public. When he saw his play *Diarmuid and Gráinne* in Galway he knew the language had been brought a step forward.

22 February 1926

Hobblers in Dublin Bay

'Hobbling' in the early years of the 20th century had an alternative connotation to limping progress on foot; it described an informal kind of piloting and mooring of larger boats intending to anchor in Kingstown or Liffeyside. The occupation was centuries old and essentially confined to a smallish number of seacoast families known as hobblers, who used to sail out into Dublin Bay to secure the right to moor any vessel of large draught at an appropriate berth. There was a dangerous element of competition involved, as the hobbler's boat had to be positioned in front of the vessel and hope to be thrown the line that established the contract. It was not unusual for several hobblers to approach the same vessel. The resulting fee was a good one and worth the effort.

Early in the morning of Monday 22 February 1926 a Belgian steamer, the *Hesbaye*, was sighted entering the bay and three hobblers from Kingstown set out to secure the mooring. They were Thomas Miller, a man of sixty, and two younger partners, James Pluck and Richard Brennan. It was thought that their boat was driven by a big wave right under the *Hesbaye*'s prow and crushed. Its master, Captain Celis, hearing cries, ordered his ship to stop and launched a longboat to try to rescue the hobblers but found no one. Another hobbler boat owned by Patrick Shortall joined in the search with no success. He had sent up a flare in the hope of getting help from shore but there was no response.

Later in the day Shortall, searching the shore, found the broken seat of a boat and an oar he recognised as the property of Millar. Reports that a body had been washed ashore in Howth and the wreckage of the boat seen floating out the bay were later proved true.

23 February 1988

Low-cost airfare

The battle for cheap airfares from Dublin was intensified on Tuesday 23 February 1988 when the beset national airline Aer Lingus announced a new low fare of £35 one-way to London. The airport was Stansted and the route had been granted to the carrier during the previous week. On the same day, Eugene O'Neill, then chief executive of the rival Ryanair, announced that they would announce a 'stunning and dramatic' fares package on the same route within a week. Aer Lingus said that their offer would operate 1-31 March, while the return tariff from Stansted to Dublin would be £29 sterling. Thereafter, from 1 April throughout the summer, the single fare would be £45 with a midweek special of £39 over the some period. The fares would be bookable up to the day of departure but could not be changed without penalty.

O'Neill's response was characteristically brisk, querying how Aer Lingus could justify their fare of £104 to Heathrow if their Stansted rate was so much cheaper. He was reticent about the details of Ryanair's tariff, saying merely, 'We are putting together a very good package but Stansted will be difficult, as access to London at the moment is very poor.' Later that night a Ryanair spokesman announced a new set of 'fun fares' targeting families, youth and senior citizens: £75 return from Dublin to London, Manchester and Cardiff and £87 return from Knock, Galway, Cork and Shannon to all destinations served by the airline in Britain. The groups favoured were husband and wives travelling together, people from twelve to sixteen, senior citizens and family groups consisting of at least one parent accompanied by a child under twenty-six. The spokesman added that the fares would become available once the several government departments gave clearance.

24 February 1797

Handy Andy

It is not generally known that Victor Herbert (1859-1924), the composer whose many operettas including *Naughty Marietta* were such a hit on Broadway, was born in Dublin in 1859, the grandson of Samuel Lover (1797-1868), the artist and writer. Herbert's song 'Sweet Mystery of Life' from *Naughty Marietta,* which opened in 1910, has become a standard concert piece but it will never outdo in popular success, at least in Ireland, his grandfather's songs, 'Molly Bawn', The Angel's Whisper' and 'The Low-back Car'.

Lover was born in 60 Grafton Street on 24 February 1797 and received his education in Samuel Whyte's school, No 79 in the same street. His father was a stockbroker and for a time he followed that profession but ceased to practise after a family row. He had already shown himself to be talented in music, writing and art. It was in the last of these that he decided to make his mark, painting mainly marine subjects and acquiring a sound reputation as a miniaturist. He was elected RHA in 1828 and published books of mythology, ballads and stories with his own illustrations. Like his younger contemporary Charles Lever – and, in a different field, Dion Boucicault – he was unjustly accused of perpetuating the extremes of stage Irishness. True his bestseller, *Handy Andy,* apart from giving the English language a useful near-proverbial phrase, erred in perhaps over-boisterousness but the characterisation was genial and sympathetic.

Lover's failing eyesight eventually precluded his work in miniatures. He wrote for periodicals, including the *Dublin University Magazine* that he had helped found, and *Bentley's Journal* with Charles Dickens. He devised a theatrical entertainment, featuring his own songs and stories, called *An Irish Evening* and toured it in Britain and America with great success. He died in St Helier, Jersey.

25 February 1946

Found guilty in Dublin courts

The Dublin courts on Monday 25 February 1946 were busy as usual with the hearing of a manslaughter charge in the Central Criminal Court and a 'false pretences' in the Circuit Criminal Court. The more serious case concerned thirty-four-year-old Thomas Ball, a native of Dublin, but with a current address in Tullinadaly Road, Tuam, County Galway. The charge had originally been one of murder, that of Patrick Flaherty (30), Tubberjarlath, Tuam, on the night of 14-15 December 1945, but a plea of guilty to manslaughter was accepted by the state.

R.J. McLoughlin SC said that Flaherty had died as a result of wounds inflicted by Ball, who worked as a joiner as well as playing with a dance band. Flaherty had been drinking on the night of 14 December and left Tuam some time before 11pm. After midnight he was seen by Ball on top of a wall at the back of his property. When challenged by Ball, Flaherty disappeared but returned and assaulted him on the green patch outside the house. Ball, defending himself, stabbed him with the chisel he had been using. He fell and Ball sent for the Gardaí but shortly after they arrived Flaherty died. In spite of his plea of self-defence Mr Justice Gavan Duffy sentenced Ball to two years with hard labour.

On the same day, Desmond D'Arcy (22) of no fixed abode was sentenced by Judge Shannon in the Circuit Criminal Court to six months' imprisonment with hard labour for a scam involving turf. He went to a number of Dublin houses and managed to persuade the occupants that they had won a load of turf in a raffle and he had been asked to collect money from them for the transport. In all he managed to bilk them out of £8/3/4d (£286.80 today).

26 February 1988

Eccles Street

Eccles Street is to be found in Dublin postal district 7 and runs from Berkeley Road to Dorset Street. The street acquired its name in 1772, after Sir John Eccles, the Belfast property developer who had been rewarded for sheltering William III and was Lord Mayor of Dublin, 1710-11. The Mater Hospital occupied most of the ground between it and North Circular Road and had steadily acquired most of the street because of expansion needs. The left-hand side, as one looks south, once held the Dominican College, while on the right was a terrace of stately Georgian mansions. More than two hundred years later they were in a state of virtual dereliction.

The street's most famous denizen, known for eating with relish the inner organs of beasts and fowls, was the fictitious Leopold Bloom, who lived in No 7 (really the home of his creator's friend, John Francis Byrne, the 'Cranly' of the novels). One assumes that his attitude to what some described as the destruction of the other side of the street would have been a weary shrug of his Hebraic shoulders.

The Mater's authorities had been required to demolish three Georgian houses. An Taisce and other interested parties had hoped to obtain an injunction preventing the demolition but on Friday 26 February 1988 the Dublin High Court refused it. The corporation's sanitary department had issued notices to the hospital to demolish two of the houses to second-floor and the third to first-floor level. The corporation's demand was based on the dangerous state of the buildings. This would have been enough to persuade Mr Justice Murphy but he also found an error in the basis of the plea, which had used planning permission law that was not relevant to the case.

27 February 1947

A thaw in an endless winter

The winter of 1946-7 was one of the coldest of the century with, it seemed, endless arctic conditions, serious blizzards with mountainous drifts and a punishing lack of the then staple fuel, coal, which could not be delivered because of a catastrophic breakdown in road and rail transport. The unnatural wintry conditions made any kind of travel hazardous and cuts in power, not so debilitating in an Ireland only minimally electrified, still made city life wearying. The 'big freeze' as the press universally called it, was so persistent that by the end of March there were fears for vegetation and even bird life. In fact by Easter Sunday (6 April) the weather was warm and in unusual meteorological compensation the late spring and summer were almost continuously sunny.

Although the air temperature stayed well below freezing, now and then the usual Atlantic stream would cause a sudden thaw which in turn would mean slippery slush, serious flooding and then more hazardous reglaciation. One such thaw was warily welcomed on Thursday 27 February 1947. It meant a slight relief for those trying to keep warm but bus drivers, plumbers, railway workers, linesmen, and delivery men had to work under appalling conditions as they tried to get Dublin working again.

Goods trains that had left the capital on the Monday for Sligo, Athlone, Tuam and Westport had still not arrived, five milk lorries were still missing since the Tuesday and when buses managed with difficulty to reach Enniskerry there was general relief. Roundwood in Wicklow, one of Ireland's most elevated villages, was still completely cut off and food was dropped by an army plane. That evening, the temperature in Dublin airport, which had reached 35.8°F at noon, had dropped to 14° and was still falling.

28 February 1957

The Comets rock to Dublin

On the evening of Thursday 28 February 1957 there were a lot of Gardaí on duty in Poolbeg Street. Their purpose was to control the crowds of youths had gathered to catch a glimpse of the first great pop group of the rock-and-roll era. The Gardaí were startled by the numbers of people who had gathered around the Theatre Royal on the date of the final performance given by Bill Haley and the Comets. They had come to pay strident homage to the band, who had been rocking round many clocks since they assumed the quasi-astronomical title in 1952.

The rise of 'youf' culture during the 1950s had not passed Ireland by, as testified by the presence of the lads who sang 'Shake, Rattle and Roll' with their tubby leader, William John Clinton Haley (1925-81), who always sported an obvious kiss-curl in the center of his perspiring forehead. Unlike later stars of the genre he was folksy, even hillbilly, and generally wholesome in his songs and demeanour. That was not the mien of his fans, who claimed to be driven to violence by the relentless 'beat' of the twenty-four-hour rock music. The band's arrival in the London station generated such crowds and obligatory violence that the event came to be known as the 'Second Battle of Waterloo'.

It was almost inevitable that the second of the two concerts given in the Royal would cause a minor riot. The films 'Knock around the Clock' and 'Don't Knock the Rock' had caused such damage to cinema seats that they were banned in Belfast. The trouble in Dublin was slight compared with what the city would suffer later but stones and bottles were thrown, batons were drawn and the crowd moved to Burgh Quay and Lower O'Connell Street, where windows were broken. The Comets wisely left the theatre by a side entrance.

29 February 1968

'A menace to the community'

John Patrick Ward, a 23-year-old native of Trim, County Meath, was sentenced to two years' imprisonment for a long list of offences in the Dublin Circuit Criminal Court on Thursday 29 February 1968. Judge McGivern, who imposed the sentence, seemed quite startled at the level of criminal activity, noting that Ward was not content to commit single crimes but went for several each night. He paid him the unintended compliment of being 'an experienced and determined type of criminal and a menace to the community'. Ward, in his defence, said that it was lack of permanent employment that caused his downfall. He had planned, he said, to go to England to obtain work.

The brake to Ward's wide-ranging career had occurred on the previous Tuesday when his targets were Drages premises in Grafton Street; the burglary netted £111 worth of goods, of which £76 worth was recovered; Newell's in the same street had been relieved of goods amounting to £83 (£50 worth recovered). Other premises broken into that night were Richard Allen, Grafton Street, and buildings in South King Street, including the Gaiety Theatre, where the cost of deliberate and pointless damage to the safety curtain exceeded £200.

Arrested, Ward was charged with the burglaries but also with the felonious acquisition of gelignite and ten detonators from the Meath Lime Company near Trim, where he was once employed. He had use this material twice to blow open a safe in the Metropolitan Laundry, Inchicore (the first time unsuccessfully) in August 1967. The mere mention of 'jelly' had made the case more serious and profoundly affected the judge. At the hearing he asked that many other offences be taken into consideration. These included breaking and entering and malicious damage, mostly in Dublin but also in Gorey, Clane and Kildalkey, County Meath.

1 March 1955

O'Casey's Bishop's Bonfire

The love-hate relationship of Seán O'Casey (1880-1964) with the Irish public began early in his career. Hailed as the great Abbey playwright of the 1920s, only heir to Synge, his accurate portrayal of Easter Week in *The Plough and the Stars* and the creation of Rosie Redmond, an unashamed portrait of a Dublin prostitute, led to general execration. His exile after Yeats rejected *The Silver Tassie* and the writing of such anti-clerical, 'communist' plays as *The Star Turns Red* (1940) damned him in the eyes of non-theatre goers, although *Juno and the Paycock* and *The Plough and the Stars* continued to be staged.

In February 1955 Cyril Cusack presented *The Bishop's Bonfire* in the Gaiety Theatre, a risky venture considering the current orthodoxy; the very title was clearly anti-clerical! The opening night was a sell-out but there were the inevitable protesters. The following night, Tuesday, 1 March 1955, saw an even greater crowd. The ghost of Yeats could fancifully be heard intoning, 'You have disgraced yourselves again, again.' The fact that British critics from the *Daily Telegraph*, *Daily Mail*, *Daily Express* and the London *Times* received it warmly only convinced the protesters that they were right; clearly it was anti-Irish as well.

Gerard Fay, son of W.G. Fay, who had directed the original *Playboy*, in reviewing the play for the *Manchester Guardian* had the advantage of lack of prejudice, national and religious. He wrote, 'It succeeds beyond the hope of it enemies. It fails a little more than O'Casey's friends would have wished. But it remains one of the best of his works for several years.' It was a fair critique of play, author and protestors. When in 1953 *The Drums of Father Ned* was the spur for what O'Casey felt was clerical interference in the Dublin Theatre Festival he withdrew permission. Disgrace abounding!

2 March 1926

Collision in Ballsbridge

Pembroke, Northumberland and Lansdowne Roads meet at a junction with an obvious capacity for accidents, even in 1925, a time of comparatively light automotive traffic. On 1 September 1925 a collision occurred between two cars, one owned by William McMahon, a commission agent, of 81 Iona Road, Drumcondra, and Dr William J. Dargan, 47 St Stephen's Green. McMahon alleged that he had been seriously injured, was suffering from shock and that his car had been wrecked. His action against Dargan was for personal injuries and damage to his car. Dargan denied negligence and pleaded contributory negligence on the part of the defendant. The hearing was concluded on Tuesday 2 March 1926 before Mr Justice Hanna and a common jury.

Dargan, giving evidence, stated that he had fourteen years' experience of driving and that on the day he had been driving along Pembroke Road with his daughter and four children. At the junction he carefully looked for traffic coming from Ballsbridge. Seeing none, he was turning right, still on Pembroke Road, when a car coming fast down Northumberland Road struck his left front wheel and crashed into a tree. Cross-questioned, Dargan said he had been going slowly and had stopped dead after the collision. His daughter Ena testified that their speed along Pembroke Road was moderate and at the junction not more than ten miles an hour. She thought that McMahon's car had been travelling 'at a terrific speed'.

Dargan's speed was estimated as 'a walking pace' by witness Martin Egan, a tram conductor, but Dr Francis Cronin, who had been walking on Northumberland Road, thought that his speed as he approached the junction was about 30 mph. In spite of some inevitable confusion about the facts, the jury found for McMahon and awarded £220 damages.

3 March 1947

Tragedy in Sundrive Road

The winter and spring of 1947 was one of coldest of the century and the icy grip persisted until Easter. All lakes, dams and quarry holes were frozen hard and the Arctic conditions gave the young unimaginable scope for hair-raising adventure. Even in the city the ponds seemed frozen solid and the more daring took advantage of these new playgrounds supplied free. The icebound quarry in Sundrive Road, Kimmage, proved tragically irresistible to three local lads.

On Sunday 2 March, three boys, Christopher Byrne (13½) of Slane Road, Anthony Burke (16), Saul Road, and Edward O'Toole (8), Leighlin Road – all local addresses – were part of a larger party playing a form of hockey on the ice, using piles of rags as goalposts. Christopher saved two of his friends before he disappeared under the ice. He had refused his father's invitation to come with him to an international football match, preferring to play with his friends. The father heard the grim news on his way home and spent the rest of the day by the quarry's edge as the Gardaí dragged it.

His body was recovered on the Monday morning at 11.15, as was Anthony Burke's but the third, youngest, victim had not been found. Christopher's father had been on watch late on the Sunday night and again from 7 o'clock that morning. The Gardaí had continued to chase children from the pond but they returned by other routes. They had urged many times that such potentially dangerous locations should be filled in or fenced off but no firm moves had been made and it was of little comfort to the grief-stricken parents. The local papers noted that Anthony was the fifth of a family of five boys and three girls and his father, a widower, was unemployed.

4 March 1964

Airbrushing history

The Department of External Affairs caused to be published on 4 March 1964 a book called *Facts about Ireland*. To say it was slanted by the government in power may be a bit harsh but it may truthfully be said that it contained nothing to make Fianna Fáil uncomfortable. This comfort was not shared by everyone. Little exception was taken to the aesthetic aspects of Irish life, although it was felt that not enough Irish writers were included. The only pictures were of Joyce, O'Casey, Shaw, Wilde and Yeats.

Inevitably there was a brisk and well-written account of the history of the country from 'Recorded Irish history begins with the coming of Christianity about the beginning of the 5th century...' right up to 'the repeal of the External Relations Act (1936) and provided that the description of the State shall be the Republic of Ireland.' Its 1500 words handled the minefield of Stephen Dedalus's nightmare rather neatly but history is always written by the victors – or at least the survivors. A closer look shows a terseness about the Civil War that is tantamount to obfuscation. The account of the Ulster plantations and the persistent problems that this adventure created is barely mentioned but then the north-east as a whole was virtually ignored.

These lacunae might have been forgiven, even ignored, except that two unignorable Irishmen were not included, largely because the moral fission caused by the 1921 Treaty still seared the political fibre of the twenty-six counties, essentially the territory covered by the historical sketch. The names of Michael Collins and Arthur Griffiths, whose deaths within ten August days of each other in 1922 had an incalculable effect on Irish history, did not merit inclusion. The term 'airbrushing' may not have been in use then but the practice clearly was.

5 March 1939

Lighting Dublin

One of the most notable things about Dublin during what was called in Ireland the 'Emergency' but others called the Second World War, was how brightly the lights shone in comparison with those of Belfast or Derry or, indeed, London or Birmingham. A whole mythology was generated about them as a sign of reassurance in the darkness and as a handy beacon for the Luftwaffe or the RAF. The system had been installed only a year when war broke out and it was the subject of a paper read by F.X. Algar BE BSc, the Public Lighting Engineer of the Electricity Supply Board, to the Institute of Civil Engineers of Ireland on Monday 5 March 1939. The paper was entitled 'Two New Public Installations' and described the setting up of the system in central Dublin and the Dublin-Dalkey road.

The two sites were completely different in conception and execution. The first difficulty arose because of the famous width of O'Connell Street, which seemed to require no less than three lines of lanterns, one along each kerb and one down the centre of the roadway. This was undesirable and several options were tried before the final system was arrived at. The six-foot bores revealed all kinds of obstructions: electricity mains, telephone cables, water pipes. In thirty-six cases they were over existing cellars where new brick foundations had to be built. The standards which would throw sufficient light from each side without the need for a central line were finally sourced in France.

On the Dalkey Road it proved possible to attach lanterns to existing tramway poles. These extended for six feet over the roadway and provided the 'best diversity of brightness' while eliminating glare. Algar described the laboratory examinations that tested the fittings far beyond what they would ever be called upon to bear.

6 March 1966

A call to Irish Protestants

The fiftieth anniversary of the Easter Rising saw an Ireland confident enough to celebrate the first overt move to establish its independence. The years 1916-23 had mixed violence and glory and it was fitting to celebrate the courage and sacrifice of many who had contributed to the period's partial success. Not all the inhabitants of the country known as Éire or the Republic of Ireland felt there was much to celebrate. Some mourned the incomplete nature of the independence while the 5 per cent of the population that was Protestant felt that there was indeed little to celebrate.

It was, therefore, courageous and salutary that on Sunday 6 March 1966 as speaker in the first of a series of Sunday-night Lenten talks given in the Dublin Central Mission in Abbey Street under the general title 'Protestants in the New Ireland', the Reverend Gerald Myles, Principal of Wesley College, should urge Protestants in the Republic to make a whole-hearted and unreserved entry into the public life of the nation, chambers of commerce, city and county councils, political parties, trade unions and a host of other community activities – not least the Dáil.

In the early 1920s many men and women who belonged to denominations other than Catholic left the country because they felt that they had no place in the new Free State. Ireland had lost a deal of necessary talent then and those who either could not or would not leave retreated into cells of self-sufficiency. Myles suggested that the fault was largely their own but that there were factors outside their control. He urged them not to look back in anger, realising that they had instinctively shied away from social engagement with Catholicism because of the penalties imposed by the Ne Temere decree that had impoverished both sides.

7 March 1988

Ice cream in the Phoenix Park

The 'Phoenix' part of Dublin's great park, although it looks Greek, is actually Irish, coming from its Gaelic title *Páirc an Fhionnuisce* (clear water park). Covering seven hundred and seven hectares (1752 acres), it was given to the people of Dublin in 1745 by the Earl of Chesterfield and remains one of the largest and finest urban parks in Europe. It houses Áras an Uachtaráin, the home of the President of Ireland, once the Vice-regal Lodge, the residence of the United States Ambassador and the Zoological Gardens.

Once a place of fashionable parade, the amenity had begun to show the marks of time and attrition by the 1980s. Maintenance is the responsibility of the Office of Public Works (OPW) and they instituted a series of improvements that, it was hoped, might help it regain some of its former grandeur. The grand avenue that runs north-west from the main entrance in Parkgate Street to the Castleknock gate was furnished with new ornamental gas lamps and many new walks and picnic areas were laid out. New gates were hung at the main entrance and most side roads were made free of traffic.

On Tuesday 7 March 1988 the OPW, in a sudden fit of nostalgia, discouraged the modern ice-cream vans with their sirens and unsteady whipped-cream cones and asked that an older vending system be restored that 'would be more in keeping with what we are trying to achieve'. They had in mind handcarts or carts with a pedal cycle. These could still be found on the streets of many European cities and were obviously more attractive to tourists than the raucous, siren-equipped vans. The OPW further announced plans to introduce traditional horse-drawn transport. By the end of the summer, interested parties, having stopped and bought an ice cream, could take a turn about the park in a barouche or its modern equivalent.

8 March 1966

Up went Nelson

Nelson's Pillar stood in Sackville/O'Connell Street for more than a hundred and fifty years, execrated by extreme nationalists, respected by the Anglo-Irish ascendancy and loved by the Plain People of Dublin as the city's omfalos, a trysting place before the time of Clery's clock. Its spiral staircase interior was first opened to the public in October 1809, four years after the subject's victory and death in Trafalgar. From the top of its nautical head to the street was a distance of 134ft 3in and as it became the Dublin landmark it was noticed that fewer citizens made the laborious ascent, leaving such delights to tourists, bogmen or both.

The voices agitating for the pillar's removal, as an 'eyesore' and traffic hazard, were drowned by the shrieks advocating the destruction of the effigy of the man Joyce called the 'one-handled adulterer'. After several suicides a wire mesh added nothing to its appearance but as the years went by the cost of demolition always seemed too dear to the city fathers. Then at 1.32 on the morning of Tuesday 8 March 1966 there was a tremendous explosion and the statue and tons of rubble crashed down into the roadway. There may have been some glee on the part of the splinter group of the IRA who did the deed as their contribution to the fiftieth anniversary of the Easter Rising but a majority mourned the loss of the tallest Dublin landmark.

Colonel Patrick McCourt, the chief explosives expert of Eastern Command, reluctantly admitted that the demolition had been an 'expert job' and the collateral damage was comparatively slight. On Monday 14 March, the remainder of the column except the plinth was blown up by army engineers, the blast causing more damage to buildings in O'Connell Street that the original explosion.

9 March 1932

'Slightly constitutional'

Fianna Fáil, the political party Seán Lemass, its economics expert, called 'slightly constitutional', came into being in 1926 when its leader, Éamon de Valera, sloughed off the original name Sinn Féin (Ourselves Alone). Forty-four members took their seats in the Dáil after the general election of 16 May 1926, having found themselves able to disregard the once worrisome Oath of Allegiance as 'an empty political formula'.

Already in its own estimation the 'party of government', it geared itself for office and with seventy-two members elected in the general election of 16 February 1932 was able, with the support of the seven Labour members, to form a minority government on Thursday 9 March 1932. Cumann na nGaedheal, the previous administration, although it had worked the near-miracle of setting up a viable Free State, had only fifty-seven members.

With characteristic ruthlessness de Valera assigned no cabinet seat to the Labour Party. It was as if he was already confident that he would soon be leading a majority government. This was the case after the snap election held on 24 January 1933 when his party secured seventy-seven seats that gave it an overall majority of one. He continued to lead the government party without interruption for the next fifteen years. The 'gunmen', as their adversaries dubbed them, proved as resourceful in government as in guerrilla war. De Valera continued throughout as President of the Executive Council (later Taoiseach of the Dáil) and Minister for External Affairs. Lemass, his Minister for Industry and Commerce (and Supplies during the Emergency) in credited with the modernisation of the country but had perhaps to wait too long to succeed his master as Taoiseach. Two Ulstermen, Frank Aiken and Seán MacEntee, served with distinction in Defence and Finance.

10 March 1962

Horses to courses

With today's universality and almost total reliability of air travel it is hard to entertain conjecture of a time when standards were not so high. On Saturday 10 March 1962 flights out of Dublin airport had to be cancelled. That weekend had been characterised by continuous drizzle, affecting the whole country. The miserable meteorological conditions kept vehicular traffic to a minimum; even pedestrians were noticeably absent from the streets. At the airport, visibility of less than 100 yards led to the cancellation of twelve flights and the delay of as many others. The catering staff worked overtime to provide snacks and drinks for those whose travelling arrangements had been affected.

Among them were the professional golfers Christy O'Connor, Joe Carr and Noel Fogarty who were to play in a competition in Wentworth in south Yorkshire. They left as soon as they realised the situation and found themselves berths on the evening steamer. In fact the afternoon flights to Glasgow, Manchester and London got away, although rather delayed. Three Irish army officers, Commandant S. Lynch, Captain J. Sweeney and Captain P. Broe, were given permission to book midweek flights.

The most troublesome aspect of the disruption was the problem of getting horses to courses. Twenty-three were due to be flown to Cheltenham – the most Irish meeting in Britain – and had to return to their stables. They were back on the Sunday, as was the fog; it looked as if they would not be able to run in Tuesday's card. Four BKS planes were chartered – BKS was a UK-based airline of the period – and one had to circle for half an hour before finding a gap in the clouds that enabled it to land. With weather conditions steadily worsening, the animals were hustled on board but all the carriers got away safely and were in time for the races.

11 March 1596

A spark in the gunpowder

In 1596 Ireland was in the grip of the Nine Years' War. The 'modern' tactics of warfare of Hugh O'Neill, Earl of Tyrone, were working and might well have succeeded had he continued to use them. He controlled most of the three provinces outside the Pale but had no support among the Old Catholics in Dublin. The city, with a population of about 10,000, was the main port of supply and depot for the English forces and high priority was given to arms and ammunition for their use. On Monday 11 March, word came that a squadron of English ships with a cargo of gunpowder, stored in barrels, had arrived in the bay and had begun to be transported to Wood Quay by river lighters from the deeper waters. The wharf, on the Liffey in Winetavern Street, was in the heart of the old Viking city and surrounded by the mansions of the leading merchants of the day.

The Crown official in charge of the docks was John Allen and relations between him and the port workers were poor. Most of them had been refusing to work and previous consignments of explosive, amounting to a hundred and forty barrels, were still stacked on the quay. At about 1 o'clock, while a wooden crane was landing four barrels of gunpowder, a spark ignited them and caused all the casks on the dock to explode. No one could say whence the spark originated. In *Annála Ríoghachta Éireann*, written forty years later, the Four Masters could only speculate:

> ..a spark of fire got into the powder; but from whence that spark proceeded, whether from the heavens or from the earth beneath, is not known...

A hundred and twenty-six people were killed and many more injured; forty houses were completely destroyed and crane and crane houses obliterated. The event is considered to have been Ireland's worst disaster.

12 March 1905

Almost totally deanglicised

The Gaelic League, founded in 1893, had by the first decade of the 20th century become a significant part of the cultural, social and, increasingly, political life of Ireland. The League's approach from its inception was what we nowadays should describe as multi-media. On Sunday 12 March 1905 it held for the third time an outdoor event consisting of a procession, a display of tableaux illustrating its work and an address by the president, Douglas Hyde, also known by his pen-name, An Craoibhín Aoibhinn.

The League's success as an organisation for the revitalising of Irish as a spoken medium and its development as a modern language through literature and technical vocabularies was patent. It was helped by the perception of it as a non-sectarian movement and, until the tensions associated with the Home Rule agitation in Ulster, had support from all sides of the political spectrum. Then it was to play a significant role in the rise of the Irish Volunteers and the seismic struggles of the decade 1913-23.

That Sunday in March involved nearly 100,000 participants, including marching bands, football, hurley and the recently formalised camogie teams, floats showing Irish industries, academics, writers, painters, members of trades councils, the Catholic Church – a broad panorama of Irish life, almost totally deanglicised, to use Hyde's famous phrase. They assembled in St Stephen's Green and moved towards Smithfield by York Street, Aungier Street, Dame Street, Sackville Street (as O'Connell Street was then known), Great Britain Street (Parnell Street) and North King Street. In Smithfield Hyde described the League's victory over the Post Office, which had refused to handle mail addressed in Irish. Also on the platform was William J. Walsh, Archbishop of Dublin, a potent reinforcement of approval by the Church of what the League stood for.

13 March 1939

Dr Faustus *in the Gate*

The Gate Theatre was founded by Micheál MacLiammóir and Hilton Edwards in 1928 and found a permanent home in the converted supper rooms of the old Assembly Buildings (1785) in Parnell Square in 1930. Chronically short of finance, they accepted Edward Pakenham, 6th Earl of Longford, long a supporter, as a member of the board in 1934. After disagreement about policy in 1936 he formed his own Longford Productions that occupied the theatre for six months, while the Gate company toured.

Both companies continued to offer drama complementary to the output of the Abbey, which tended more towards Irish, especially contemporary Irish plays. It was typical of the Longford ethos and courage to offer, on Monday 13 March 1939, *The Tragical History of Dr Faustus* by Christopher Marlowe, who was stabbed in a Deptford tavern probably on the orders of the Privy Council but ostensibly in a row over a bill. The play was staged in 1604, the same year as *Othello*, and is as full of passion. Apart from its protagonist's deal with the devil it is usually known for its line about Helen of Troy: 'Is this the face that launched a thousand ships?' and his Latin plea for time to slow: '*Lente, lente, currite noctis equi!*' (Run gently, night's horses) to delay his final damnation.

The critics were greatly impressed by the production: 'Wonder Wrought on Small Stage' was a typical headline. Apart from the turbulent hero, played by John Stevenson, the other great part was that of Mephistopheles (the Mephisto of Gounod's opera), Satan's emissary, whose company both elates and terrifies Faustus. It was played with great brio by Noel Iliff. Other significant parts were played by Ronald Ibbs as Satan, Dermot Kelly as Beelzebub and Michael Ripper as one of the clowns who provided the necessary comic relief.

14 March 1966

An Conradh in Harcourt Street

Number 6 Harcourt Street, built in 1798, has been home to various enterprises. John Henry Newman lived here in the 1850s while serving as rector of Archbishop Paul Cullen's Catholic University, his riposte to the Queen's Colleges in Belfast, Galway and Cork. In 1910 it was the Sinn Féin Cooperative Bank and later it was used as the headquarters of the movement. The work of the First Dáil was organised from there and it was there that Michael Collins ran the Department of Finance. It was bought in 1924 by the Commissioner for Public Works and was in turn Coláiste Mhuire and the headquarters of the engineering branch of the Department of Posts and Telegraphs.

On Saturday 14 March 1966 nearly seventy-three years after the organisation was founded, it became the headquarters of Conradh na Gaeilge, the opening ceremony conducted by President de Valera. The hall was dedicated to Thomas Ashe, who had died while on hunger strike in 1917, and contained a table once owned by Patrick Pearse. Cathal Ó Feinneadha, the League's president, told how their old premises in Parnell Square had been condemned by the Corporation and that they had faced the prospect of 'retreat into a back room'. Thanks, however, to the generosity of the Irish government they now had fine new premises that would greatly increase the efficiency of the League's work; he found it necessary to add that there was still work to be done to save the language.

Among those who attended the event were the Tánaiste, Frank Aiken, and his wife, Pádraig Ó Fachtna, the Parliamentary Secretary to the Minister for the Gaeltacht, Earnán de Blaghd, who Gaelicised the Abbey Theatre, and Dónal Ó Móráin, the chief executive of Gael Linn, the cultural organisation dedicated to the furtherance of Irish.

15 March 1979

The Irish Oral (again)

On Thursday 15 March 1979 the Department of Education announced measures to have the Leaving Certificate oral examination in Irish carried out. The members of the Association of Secondary Teachers in Ireland (ASTI) would normally have carried out the tests but they were in dispute with the Department over payment for the examination work, which was not a normal part of the teachers' duties but undertaken by them on a voluntary basis for payment. The crisis arose just before the annual conference season and the Teachers Union of Ireland (TUI), the union to which most staff members of vocational schools belonged, intended to hold the examinations as usual on 2 April, pending the decision of their conference, to be held later in the month. They made it clear that they would not do the work in any school in which ASTI members were in dispute.

The Department had to find examiners to avoid the whole system of school-leaving and third-level education ending in stasis. The number of candidates for examination was 31,000 and the attempt to have the tests done by a hundred and twenty inspectors was thwarted by the directive of the Institute of Professional Civil Servants that forbade the inspectors to do the work. In that day's papers the department had placed an advertisement explaining the alternative arrangements. Dominic O'Laughlin, the secretary of the department, insisted that the examination would go ahead: 'We do not want a fight with the ASTI but we have an obligation to the schools to see that the exams take place.'

He iterated that all offers to the ASTI were still open. They had asked for a 100 per cent increase in payment but the Department had offered an immediate 20 per cent and a review with ASTI members to revise the whole system of payments. This was also refused.

16 March 1927

The cost of petrol

In the days before OPEC, inflation and the universality of the car, petrol for those who could afford it or needed it was relatively cheap. On Wednesday 16 March 1927 the price of a gallon was reduced by twopence to 1s/6d (£4 with today's purchasing power) following the cost in London, the source of supply. It brought the price to its lowest since 1904 and was caused by a great overproduction of crude in the United States, 'the country that dominates the market'. It is noticeable that at the time there was a difference of one penny in price between petrol at the pump and that bought by the can (the dearer).

The Dublin papers gave comparative tables of cost by time and location. In 1904 the cost per gallon was 1s/4d. The Great War caused a hike because of scarcity aggravated by the U-boat campaign in the North Atlantic. By 1916 the cost was 2s/2d. The War of Independence caused a sharp rise, to 3s/6d, and the price of 4s/7d recorded in August 1923 was a direct result of the Civil War. With the establishment of the Free State prices returned to the pre-war levels. The regional variations concerned London (1s/3d), the rest of England and Wales (1s/4d), Scotland (1s/5d) and Northern Ireland (1s/6d), the variation probably caused by transport costs.

That same day Dublin motor agents called a meeting to protest against the Garda commissioner's order to remove all petrol pumps in the city. They agreed to approach Richard Mulcahy, Minister for Local Government, to overrule the order on the grounds of safety, convenience and slowness. The alternative was the use of cans, seven or eight of which were required to fill the average petrol tank.

17 March 1968

Demo on St Patrick's Day

'St Patrick's Day will be jolly and gay/And we'll waken them up in the morning', as the old song has it. A well-known Broadway song claimed it as 'a great day for the Irish' and indeed it has been an important holiday for many years in New York. In Ireland its falling in early spring meant that any festivity was at the mercy of the rain and wind that often blighted the occasion. Most years the meteorological situation made mock of the old folk belief that on the feast of the national apostle 'the warm side of the stone turns up'.

St Patrick's Day in 1968 may have been jolly and gay but it was also wet and windy. The children representing Irish dance schools wore light costumes that were totally inadequate as protection against the bitterly cold showers that seemed at their worst when the parade was passing the GPO. An indication of the parade's size is that it took forty minutes to pass the platform where Charles Haughey, then Minister for Finance, took the salute dressed formally in tails and top hat. Some of the floats were very colourful; others showed little imagination. There were trucks carrying loads of sand and gravel and others empty except for the names of the sponsoring firms.

Just after the Fianna Éireann float had passed the GPO there was a protest by the Dublin Housing Action Committee. It was not clear how they had managed to be part of main procession but at the crucial moment a number of people jumped out and displayed banners, while several youths showered the street with leaflets that read: 'You may have a home; there are 10,000 families in this city who have none.' It was an eerie anticipation of the demo culture that was to characterise the next forty years.

18 March 1899

The sword of light

An *Claidheamh Soluis*, the bilingual journal of the Gaelic League, first appeared on Saturday 18 March 1899. Its editor, Eoin MacNeill (1867-1945), himself a Gaelic scholar, approved the title, which came from the legend in Celtic mythology of Nuada of the Silver Hand, who possessed an invincible sword. The writer Desmond Ryan suggests that its potency and persistence as a symbol sprang from 'a memory transmitted from some poetic observer who first saw the glint of steel in the Bronze Age'. It appeared weekly, its position central to the intellectual and public growth of the League. The forum for much discussion and the chief medium for propaganda, it served the purpose as a practical text for learners. It received the doubtful accolade of mention in George Moore's novel *The Lake* (1905), in which a character called Scanlan makes the large claim: 'I was travelling in Mexico for a firm of dry-goods-men and one day I came across a copy of the League's newspaper, *An Claideam* [sic] *Soluis* and it was out of that copy I learned to read Irish.'

Patrick Pearse (1879-1916) became editor in 1913 and with a combination of modernisation (enlarging the format, introducing illustrations) and increasing militancy made it profitable. The edition of 1 November 1913 carried an article by MacNeill called 'The North Began' about the foundation of the Ulster Volunteer Force (UVF) and the need for an equivalent nationalist armed force. Twelve days later the Irish Volunteers were founded by MacNeill and Bulmer Hobson and the seeds were laid for the Easter Rising, although neither of the two founders was permitted to take part. The journal was suppressed in 1916 and two years later took the title of its predecessor, *Fáinne an Lae*, continuing in existence until 1930.

19 March 2003

Tunnelling under Dublin

The Dublin Port Tunnel, an extension of the M50, was begun in June 2001, after being included in the *Dublin City Development Plan* 1999-2005. The volume of HGV traffic had grown so intense that some means of diverting the southbound trucks away from the gridlocked city centre had to be devised. Hard-rock boring in the spring of 2003 and the resultant vibration caused some damage in the Marino area.

On Wednesday 19 March, one householder reported a notable fracture in a 10in reinforced concrete column in his kitchen. His name was Stephen McQuillan (81) and he lived in Annadale Estate in Marino. Just before midnight one night in the first week of March, hearing a loud bang, he rushed downstairs to find that the pillar was cracked right through just inches above the floor.

In the days before the fracture, mirrors and pictures on the walls had been shifted by a vibration that shook the whole house. The noise of the tunnelling mechanism at work under the house was audible from early morning and cracks had appeared in the main walls, along the junctions of walls and ceiling, and the kitchen was badly damaged. Outside in the porch there was debris from falling cement, and doors and gates became hard to open and close.

Neighbours of the McQuillans had similar stories to tell of noise, structural damage and lack of prior consultation. They were considering a series of sit-ins at the tunnel work sites and other types of civil disobedience. Finian McGrath, the local TD, was vigorous on their behalf and managed to secure from Michael Phillips, the City Engineer, the promise of funding for any repairs. There were altogether two hundred and forty-one claims and these were settled from a fund of €1.5m set aside for the purpose.

20 March 1964

The biggest funeral since Michael Collins

On Friday 20 March 1964 Dublin saw the biggest funeral since that of Michael Collins, 'the man who won the war' in the words of Arthur Griffith. The city was paying its last tribute to a native son who was generally loved, even if some were embarrassed by what they took to regarding as his posturings. Brendan Behan (1923-1964) was born in Dublin on 6 February 1923 and educated by the Christian Brothers and his own well-read and heritage-saturated family, who would have been notably ambivalent about the Cork hero. They were strongly anti-Treaty and maintained a 'diehard' attitude to Irish politics.

Behan left school at fourteen to join Fianna Éireann, the cadet branch of the IRA, and learn the family trade of house painting. He was arrested in 1939 for IRA activity in England and spent three educative and formative years in borstal in Suffolk. He returned to Ireland and in 1942 was sentenced to fourteen years' imprisonment for attempting to kill a detective. He was released five years later and resumed his trade, while determined to become a writer. An early piece, 'I Become a Borstal Boy' appeared in *The Bell* in June 1942 and his other prison experiences generated his best book, *Borstal Boy* (1958) and his finest play *The Quare Fellow* (1954).

Because of the success of that play in the Joan Littlewood production and some notorious television appearances, Behan, who had become a regular columnist in the *Irish Press* and gathered a nighttown reputation for drink and bilingual wit, became public property. *The Hostage* (1958), which was so modified by Littlewood that the original play was almost lost in revue, increased his international reputation. The years of success were marked by alcoholism, attempts at drying out and undiagnosed diabetes. The Dublin meteor burnt himself out at forty-one.

21 March 1988

Criminal arrogance

An editorial in the *Garda Review* on Monday 21 March 1988 drew attention to 'a new breed of malefactors' that showed 'a ruthlessness and disturbing criminal arrogance'. A recent incident involved the digging up of greens and the slashing of car tyres in Stackstown Garda Golf Course and seemed to indicate that the 'new breed' had made the Garda Síochána its particular target. The gangs were prepared to go to extreme lengths, the writer opined, 'to show their contempt for the law and for those whose job it is to enforce the law'.

That attitude was essentially one that could lead, if maintained, to mere anarchy. The real target of the perpetrators was the very fabric of society. 'It is not so much the Gardai but the State and its right to maintain the rule of law and the State will not be intimidated.' Two attitudes could be discerned in the editorial: a warning of potential civic unrest and an equal determination not to exaggerate it. The media, as usual, did not escape some censure, perhaps making the attacks 'a titillating sideshow of no great personal concern except to those directly concerned'.

The reminder again that 'the fight against crime is not a fight which Gardai carried on on their own behalf but on behalf of the citizenry' somehow diminished the effectiveness of the chaos that the earlier paragraphs foretold. A hint of special pleading with an appeal for the cooperation of the public turned the piece into at once a lay sermon and an exculpation. Perhaps after all the attacks were just yobbo-ism – 'Boys will be boys' – and the Gardai were smarting a little because there was a prima facie case that, as the most obvious representatives of the oppressive state, they were deliberately chosen.

22 March 1848

Sarah Purser: artist and patron

One day in 1938 a lady in her ninetieth year anxious to inspect the condition of the roof of her house arranged for an aviator to fly with her over the property the better to see any deterioration. The pilot was Oliver St John Gogarty (Joyce's 'Buck Mulligan') and the fabric-inspecting passenger was an artist, a portrait painter and a patron of stained-glass design in Ireland. Sarah Purser (1848-1943) was born in what was then called Kingstown on Wednesday 22 March 1848. Her father, a prosperous miller, emigrated to America when his business failed and Sarah and her mother moved into the city, where she began a career in art.

Having become an accomplished portraitist in Paris, Purser persuaded Countess Markievicz and her sister Eva Gore-Booth to sit for her and so popular did her work become that commissions came pouring in. As she pungently put it she 'went through the British aristocracy like the measles'. Her charge for a portrait, completed from a photograph, was thirty guineas. This work and judicious investment in Guinness shares made her a rich woman and she used her wealth to encourage Irish artists and hold a groundbreaking exhibition of the work of Jack B. Yeats and the neglected Nathaniel Hone in 1900.

In 1903 with the help and advice of Edward Martyn, the founder with Yeats and Lady Gregory of the Abbey Theatre, she established a workshop for stained glass in Upper Pembroke Street, appropriately called *An Túr Gloine* (The Glass Tower). When the Free State was established she persuaded her friend, the president, W.T. Cosgrave, to adapt Charlemont House in Parnell Square as the Municipal Gallery. This was an important element in the final resolution of the controversy about the housing of the Lane pictures. Sarah Purser became the first female member of the Royal Hibernian Academy in 1923 when she was seventy-five.

23 March 1966

In a dangerous condition

Even as late as the 1960s many Dublin inner city dwellings were more than two hundred years old years old and clearly showing signs of that great age. This was true of some streets in Dublin 8. Miss Annie Armstrong of 48 Pleasant Street, off Camden Street, was advised by the Corporation on 28 July 1965 that two houses belonging to her, 2 and 3 Great Longford Street, off Aungier Street, were in a dangerous condition. The order required that she 'take down, repair or rebuild them in order to remove the danger'. She ignored the notice and received a further order on 19 November, giving her forty-two days to carry out the work. In the event of failure the Corporation would do the work and further prohibit any use of the houses.

Armstrong appealed to the Circuit Court but Judge Conor Maguire dismissed her appeal at a hearing on Wednesday 23 March 1966. He was extremely sympathetic when the full facts of the case were made known. Four houses in Great Longford Street, the two in question and Nos 6 and 7 as well, had been left to Armstrong in her father's will when he was killed in 1916. Numbers 6 and 7 had been demolished because of their unsafe state and her inability to afford the necessary repairs. The demolition bill came to £800.

Judge Maguire commented that now she faced actual hardship since the only compensation the Corporation offered was £425 and with the cost of the demolition, she still owed about £300. With the same conditions obtaining for these latest houses she would have no site, no houses, no income and still owe about £650. Since the space would be utilised for a necessary carpark the judge suggested that a more generous compensation could be financed by a charge on users.

24 March 1979

Pride in our national games

As the national broadcasting service RTÉ is regularly criticised for what the Irish public sees as its failings. One regular charge arises out of its perceived attitude to the national language and culture. During the late 20th-century Northern Troubles the Irish language became a factor in the propaganda of all sides, meshed, it seemed irretrievably, with politics and another cause of complaint about RTÉ's broadcast provision. On Saturday 24 March 1979 Con Murphy, the outgoing president of the GAA, used his valedictory address at the annual conference to opine that the whole attitude of RTÉ to things Irish was in question.

His chief concern was, unsurprisingly, the need 'to give due recognition to our national games and the other cultural characteristics of Ireland'. He did not blame the members of the sports department, the personnel of which 'did their best in difficult circumstances,' but the policy-makers and controllers, He implied that the GAA was regarded as a political entity in parts of Ulster. He drew attention to the plight of its members in Crossmaglen, where they had to face 'the harassment and intimidation by the British forces', who had taken over part of the grounds and seemed determined to make it a 'military fortress'. This led to a discussion about the plight of the H-Block prisoners in Long Kesh and Murphy emphasised that the association 'deplored the indecent and inhumane treatment being meted out to the H-block prisoners'.

Murphy ended on a more positive note, praising the work of the now retiring stalwarts Seán Ó Síocháin, Pádraig Ó Caoimh and Bríd Ní Mhuircheartaigh. His peroration called upon the delegates at the conference to have faith in the GAA, 'pride in our national games, respect for our country and a loyalty to what is Irish and our own.'

25 March 1795

The Royal Botanic Gardens

One of the most beautiful amenities of Dublin is the National Botanic Gardens in Glasnevin, five kilometres north-west of the city centre. On Wednesday 25 March 1795 Sir Walter Wade (1750-1825) of the Dublin Society purchased a sixteen-acre site with the enthusiastic aid of the Irish Parliament. The place had a kind of literary aura: its original owner was a poet, Thomas Tickell, and already there was a double line of yew trees, called 'Addison's Walk' after the co-founder (with the Irish writer Sir Richard Steele) of the *Spectator*. John Underwood was appointed head gardener in 1798 and over the next twenty-five years he collaborated with Wade in establishing the beds and conservatories.

After Wade's death for some years the gardens declined but under Ninian Nevin, director, 1834-8, they were extended. They continued to expand under the Dr David Moore, the next director, who was in charge 1838-79. During his tenure the elegant curvilinear range conservatory designed by Richard Turner was completed (1848) and the palm house added in 1862. This wooden structure was destroyed by gales on 1883 and was replaced by an iron model by Moore's son Sir Frederick (1879-1922). The gardens are famous as well for their cycads, orchids, herbaceous borders and conifers. In 1878 the government took over ownership of the gardens and named them the Royal Botanic Gardens. The name was changed again by the Free State government in 1922 and they have since been known as the National Botanic Gardens.

Although they are a public amenity the gardens' original purpose was scientific, studying plants for medicinal as well as agronomic reasons. It was in Glasnevin that *Phytophthera infestans,* the cause of the devastating famine of the 1840s, was identified. Such research continues. In 2002 a new complex with café and lecture theatre was completed.

26 March 1947

German sympathiser in court

The Dublin morning papers of Wednesday 26 March 1947 carried an account of an unusual case heard in Dublin District Court when the thirty-year-old John Francis O'Reilly of Leinster Road, Rathmines, was fined £3 (or in default two months' imprisonment) for having in his possession a revolver and fifty rounds of ammunition.

The accused had been in Germany during the war and had been dropped by parachute into County Clare, his home county. As Seamus Heavey, his solicitor, informed the court, he had been working on a farm in St Helier in Jersey when in 1940 the Germans invaded the Channel Islands. He and a number of other neutral Irishmen volunteered to work in Germany. In the last months of the war he returned to Ireland and was interned until May 1945, when he was released unconditionally, and in November bought a share in a hotel on the Esplanade, Kingsbridge, County Kildare. While there he was subject to harassment by Irishmen who had served in the British Army during the conflict. He moved to a flat in Montpelier Hill to leave room for guests and was aware of people lurking nearby. He was advised by senior members of the Gardaí and the Irish army that he might be extradited to England to stand trial for 'war crimes'. It was then that he decided to equip himself with a revolver that he kept in a locked box under the bed.

Questioned by William Synott, O'Reilly admitted that his experiences were not dangerous enough to merit arming himself. He had compared himself to William Joyce who, known as Lord Haw-Haw because of his posh accent, had broadcast Nazi propaganda during the war and had been hanged. Synott suggested that he was grossly exaggerating his own importance. The fine was paid immediately and O'Reilly left the court.

27 March 1979

Byrne's sausages

Dublin was for years justly famous for its sausages; one thinks of Olhausen's, Hafner's and Leopold Bloom's favourite, Dlugacz's. The individual brand name was important as evidence of quality so, as late as Tuesday 27 March 1979 a successful High Court application was made to protect the brand name of sausages made by Byrnes of Chatham Street, at the top of Grafton Street. The firm was older than the century and had been making Byrne's Sausages since 1930.

The order with costs was made against John Walsh, from Peacockstown, Mulhuddart, trading as 'Fay', with the business address of 49 Thomas Street. His family had had a meat business for nearly as long as the Byrnes; his grandmother, Bridget Fay, had founded 'Fay's Pork and Bacon Distributors' in Meath Street, off the Coombe, in 1900. Kevin Byrne, a director of the plaintiff firm, testified that his father had founded the company in 1879 and they had been making 'Byrne's Pork Sausages' since 1930. With more than five hundred retail outlets they had sold 1,243,000 lbs of sausages the previous year. The Thomas Street product sold as identical to those from the Chatham Street firm were cheaper, inferior in quality and intended to confuse the shoppers.

Walsh, in rebuttal, claimed that when his mother and father were running the business in the 1940s they employed a sausage-make called Joseph Byrne, who had a personal recipe for the product that he gave to the Walshes to use. Their sausages were then literally 'Byrne's'. Mr Justice Murnaghan, who was hearing the action, said he could bring his own Dublin knowledge to bear in the matter. He adverted to the fact that although in former times the product was sold loose in known shops, packaging and supermarkets had changed that but Byrnes still made Byrne's Sausages, so he found for the plaintiff.

28 March 1966

The Late Late Show *and the bishops*

The *Late, Late Show*, RTÉ's flagship television programme, began broadcasting in 1962 and had what many regard as its golden years with presenter Gay Byrne. Although generally light-hearted, in its treatment of controversial subjects its approach was serious and often therapeutic, and as a free entity it often clashed with the government and the Church. On Saturday 12 February 1966, during a game of *Mr and Mrs* in which couples were asked questions about their spouses out of earshot, a wife, asked about the colour of her nightie on her wedding night, suggested that she had not worn any. The result was outrage from the Bishop of Clonfert, Thomas Ryan, who had his secretary protest to RTÉ and the *Sunday Press*. Loughrea Town Commissioners, Mayo GAA County Board and other bodies joined in denouncing 'such lewdness'. All the objectors were soon silenced in the wave of mockery that followed.

Six weeks later, on 26 March, the show received another slap from the crosier, this time from Michael Brown, Bishop of Galway, who objected to the description of his new cathedral as a 'ghastly monstrosity' by Brian Trevaskis, a TCD student. Trevaskis also suggested that the million pounds spent on building it had been raised largely by coercion and would have been better used to address social problems. The bishop uttered a strongly worded statement the following Monday, rebutting the charges. In this he had a stronger case about the coercion than about the cathedral's design, since many more than Trevaskis found it unpleasing. Galway County Council joined in the criticism of the programme and demands were loud for its suppression. The following week Byrne invited Trevaskis to apologise but he merely compounded the offence by enquiring whether the bishop knew the meaning of the word 'Christianity'. The show continued on its perceived iconoclastic way.

29 March 1844

The Atmospheric Railway

Railways came to Ireland in the 1830s with the first iron-horse journey from Dublin to Kingstown (as Dún Laoghaire was known from 1821) on 17 December 1834. The engineer was the energetic William Dargan and over the next dozen years the Dublin and Kingstown Railway carried more than 2.3 million passengers on what was essentially a suburban line. In the way of these things it did much to open the coast south of the city to residential development, turning both Kingstown and Dalkey into urban dormitories and tourist resorts.

A kind of tramway already existed from the Dalkey quarry that was used in the construction of Kingstown Harbour and this became the basis of the first atmospheric railway in the world when the line was extended to Dalkey. The new extension was officially opened on Friday 29 March 1844, although trials and unofficial journeys took place from 19 August 1843. The line from Kingstown to Atmospheric Road was 2800 metres in length with an average uphill gradient of 1 in 110 but for the last 512 metres the vacuum tube that provided the propulsion ceased to work and the train's momentum had to carry it powerless into Dalkey station.

The power was provided by a stationary steam engine that drove the train by means of a tube 38cm in diameter. This enabled the engine to reach speeds of 64 km/h on the outward journey, about as much as the human frame could bear, according to the physiologists of the time. That journey required that the train be pushed by hand until the piston engaged with the tube but the run back to Kingstown needed only gravity as propulsion. Many engineers, including I.K. Brunel, were intensely interested in the process but it proved neither popular nor economical to run and in 1854 the atmospheric trains reverted to locomotion.

30 March 1880

Laureate of the Dublin poor

Seán O'Casey (1880-1964) was born to Michael and Susan Archer Casey in 85 Upper Dorset Street on Tuesday 30 March 1880. His family was Protestant, working-class but with genteel aspirations crushed by the early death of the father in 1886 when Seán was six years old. With thirteen children to look after, Mrs Casey had many shifts to make, including occasional changes of address. Trouble with his eyes made O'Casey's attendance at school sporadic but he was a relentless autodidact, an omnivorous reader and apprentice scribbler by the age of fourteen, when he left school.

A relative who worked in the Queen's Theatre in Brunswick Street provided him with free passes to the 'Gods'. As with Shaw, that Victorian colossus with its fare of sentimental and 'sensation' plays laid the basis for O'Casey's grasp of dramaturgy. He was also conscious of the plight of the Dublin working class and the need for amelioration made him a lifelong socialist. (He lost his job in Easons, a firm that employed only Protestants at the time, for keeping his cap on when collecting his pay.) His own colourful version of his life is told in a series of garrulously impressionistic and not entirely reliable autobiographies (1939-54).

Seán O'Casey was a member of the Gaelic League (as Seán Ó Cathasaigh), the IRB and Larkin's Citizen Army (he wrote its first history). His thorough grounding in Irish nationalism made him the ideal clear-eyed laureate of the Dublin of the decade of the Troubles. His trilogy, *The Shadow of a Gunman* (1923), *Juno and the Paycock* (1924) and *The Plough and the Stars* (1926) did for the slum-dwellers of Dublin what Synge had done for the peasants of Connacht and Wicklow, earning the same gratitude. After the rejection of *The Silver Tassie* by the Abbey in 1928 he went into permanent exile in Devon. He died there in 1964.

31 March 1951

'A valley between peaks'

On Saturday 31 March 1951 the weekly meeting of the St James's Gate Literary and Debating Society heard a paper read by Michael Hogan, the society's auditor, entitled, 'Will the Irish Theatre Stage a Comeback?' The title suggested that that protean entity, Irish theatre, had somehow gone away or fallen behind, but equally it called for a rebuttal. There was more to Dublin theatre than the Gate and the Abbey. The Gaiety, the Olympia, the Theatre Royal, the Capitol and others carried on in their commercial way but it was clear that the contributors were concerned with the theatre as the temple of dramatic art.

The Gate, under the suzerainty of Hilton Edwards and Micheál MacLiammóir, had made the slightly buttoned-up Dublin aware of the work of international dramatists, while the Abbey, although claiming to be the national theatre and in receipt of a small government grant, was essentially inert, conservative and apparently unconcerned with young writers.

Lennox Robinson, whose name was that most closely associated with the Abbey after the death of Lady Gregory and Yeats, gave a short metallic summary of the theatre's history: a golden age until the death of Synge, an iron age to which he and T.C. Murray had contributed and a silver age that included the early works of Seán O'Casey. He did not attempt to classify the 1950s but advised the society that the theatre was losing money.

It did not answer the auditor's question but the general feeling of the meeting was expressed by Dorothy Macardle (1889-1958; author of an account of the national struggle, *The Irish Republic*): 'The Irish theatre was in a valley between peaks.' The coming peak would include John B. Keane, Samuel Beckett, Brian Friel and Tom Murphy but that summer the Abbey was destroyed by fire.

1 April 1966

Myles na Gopaleen

A famous photograph from the early 1950s shows a smallish man, hatted as was still the custom, with the face of a stern cherub, beside an arrowed sign reading: 'Dublin Diversion'. The man was Brian O'Nolan (1911-66), aka Flann O'Brien, aka Myles na Gopaleen aka Brother Barnabas – and no unwitting caption was more apt. He was born on 5 October 1911 in Strabane, County Tyrone, where he is not inappropriately remembered in the name of a pub. His father was a customs officer whose final posting was to Dublin in 1923. The family was Irish-speaking and his sprightly English was well learned from books.

O'Nolan began writing when an undergraduate in UCD, finding an outlet as Brother Barnabas for his polyglottal paronomastic humour in *Comhthrom na Féinne* (fair play), edited by Niall Sheridan. He joined the civil service in 1935 and published his first uncategorisable novel-complex *At Swim-Two-Birds* in 1939 – now an internationally appreciated text about texts. Wartime restrictions prevented the publication of *The Third Policeman*, ready in 1940 but not published until after his death.

From 1941 he began to write a column in *The Irish Times* called 'Cruiskeen Lawn' (Full Jug) which he signed as Myles na Gopaleen, the true hero of Boucicault's *The Colleen Bawn*. This was the name he also used in 1941 for *An Béal Bocht* (*The Poor Mouth*), a hilarious satire on a kind of writing fostered by some elements of the language revival movement. The tri-weekly (health and hangover permitting) Cruiskeen Lawn ration of jokes, puns and increasingly savage satire that continued for more that twenty-five years made him a countrywide celebrity and overshadowed his later novels and plays. Called 'our Gaelic satirist' by Austin Clark, O'Nolan's verbal pyrotechnics both revealed and concealed his serious fascination with language. He died of cancer on Friday 1 April 1966, a date that somehow suits.

2 April 1914

Cumann na mBan

The Irish Volunteers were founded in November 1913 as a direct response to the establishment of the Ulster Volunteer Force the previous January and soon the idea of a women's organisation that would work in conjunction with the men's group was considered. A number of largely middle-class women met in Wynn's Hotel, Lower Abbey Street, at 4pm on Thursday 2 April 1914. The time and day essentially precluded any working-class attendance and indeed the whole occasion was marked by a great deal of informality.

Many in the company were wives of men who would figure in the Easter Rising and later in the War of Independence. They included the spouses of Thomas Clarke, Éamonn Ceannt, the O'Rahilly, and Eoin MacNeill, with a mixture of doctors, teachers and civil servants. Mary (Sheehy), the wife of Tom Kettle, the nationalist MP, was also present, as was Countess Markievicz, who later joined the Irish Citizen Army. Kathleen Lane-O'Kelly was persuaded to take the chair and that afternoon Cumann na mBan (Association of Women) came into existence.

When John Redmond formed the National Volunteers on the outbreak of the First World War more that two thousand volunteers led by MacNeill broke away and a majority of Cumann na mBan sided with them. By now there was a substantial number of working-class women in the cumann. They were active at Easter 1916 (one of the members, Margaretta Keogh, was shot in St Stephens' Green and it was a midwife member, Elizabeth O'Farrell, who carried Pearse's terms for surrender to General Lowe) and in the War of Independence, and they split along Treaty lines during the Civil War, the majority opposing it. The rump who supported the agreement changed its name to Cumann na Saoirse (The Association of Freedom).

3 April 1846

Zozimus

Until the opening of Prospect Cemetery, Glasnevin, in 1832 no Catholic funeral ceremonies were permitted in Dublin city graveyards. Daniel O'Connell (1775-1847), as part of his lifelong agitation for Catholic rights, succeeded in having opened a consecrated burial ground, in which Catholic and Protestants could bury their dead with appropriate rites. O'Connell himself was buried in Glasnevin and close to his tomb was a patch known as 'poor ground' where the destitute found a final resting place.

On Holy Saturday 3 April 1846 Dublin's 'last gleeman', Michael Moran, was buried there, a year before O'Connell. The proximity was appropriate since the Liberator was one of the subjects of the many topical ballads that Moran rapped – he had no ear for music – for a living at various 'stands' in the inner city. He was universally known as 'Zozimus' from a mishearing of 'Zosimas', a priest who saved St Mary of Egypt from vice, as told in a poem that was part of his repertoire. Many of his most popular pieces were of his own composition, including a parody of 'An tSeanbhean Bhocht', when O'Connell was released from Richmond jail in 1844: '"You put me in the cage/The people to enrage/But I'm once more on the stage, "/ said the Dan van Vocht.'

Moran was born 'in Faddle Alley, off Blackpitts, near the Coombe' in around 1794 and was blind from the age of two weeks. He had a prodigious memory and a gift for topical balladry. Some of his ballads, set to music, are still singable, including, 'St Patrick was a gentleman, he came of decent people./In Dublin town he built a church and on it put a steeple.' His own version of the finding of Moses is still recited: 'On Egypt's banks contagious to the Nile/The Ould Pharaoh's daughter, she went to bathe in style.'

4 April 1984

Tenant in Grattan Street

On 4 August 1914 eight-year-old Robert Quinn first went to live in 20 Grattan Street, off Mount Street. He was later made aware that it was the date of the beginning of the First World War. He continued to live there after his mother died in 1960 and was evicted from the house by the city sheriff on 28 March 1984, at the second attempt. The story of the tenancy and the drama surrounding it were revealed in the Dublin Circuit Court on Wednesday 4 April 1984, when he was restored by Mr Justice Martin to possession of his rented property, thereby rescinding the previous week's order by the District Court.

The eviction order had been obtained by Margaret Pierce, the landlord, for non-payment of rent, in arrears to the amount of £1750, and a writ for recovery of the debt and possession of the property had been issued in December 1983. District Justice Maura Roche had on that occasion ruled that Quinn be given time to appeal her decision.

The property had come into Pierce's possession on the death of her husband in 1974 and in May 1983 the controlled rent of 60p a week had been increased to £34, which Quinn said he was unable to pay. His situation was aggravated by his refusal or reluctance to attend either the valuation tribunal or engage with the appeal mechanism. When Pierce arrived with the eviction notice he attacked her verbally and tore up the order, throwing the pieces of paper in her face.

Martin allowed the appeal, while stating that his colleague had had no alternative but let the process be served. Since Quinn's pension of £41 a week was totally inadequate, arrangements had been made for social services to contribute £31 of rental subsidy retrospective to the date of the increase.

5 April 1984

Detectives move from Dublin Castle

The plainclothes division of the Garda Síochána for the city of Dublin had its headquarters for many years in Dublin Castle. This accommodation dated from the time of the Dublin Metropolitan Police, which was founded in 1786 and assimilated into the Gardai in 1925. By the spring of 1984 it was found necessary to move the detective force to Harcourt Street, to a three-block building erected on the site of the High School, which had relocated to the leafy suburb of Rathgar. The Central Detective Unit, with responsibility for drug-associated crime and fraud, was already in situ but they were very displeased with the arrangement and complaints about the new venue soon reached the ears of the Garda Representative Association (GRA) and the Association of Garda Sergeants and Inspectors (AGSI).

At a joint meeting of the GRA and the AGSI on Thursday 5 April 1984, it was decided unanimously that the detectives 'would not move to the new headquarters in Harcourt Street because of the inadequacies of that building.' The wording of the statement was agreed by both bodies and as a result most of the five hundred officers involved refused to leave the Castle. The main complaints concerned security and inadequate parking but there was an element of rootedness about the detective branch. It seemed to those involved that a new purpose-built block within the Castle estate would be much more desirable. Failing that, they would settle for a suggestion, made by planners several decades earlier, to remodel part of the existing Castle buildings.

Members of both groups were keen to discuss the affair with the Minister for Justice at the time, Michael Noonan, and asked as a precondition for a delay in the move. Whatever the final outcome of the struggle, the question of 'disturbance money' would figure largely in the discussion.

6 April 1978

Sin ceist eile

Thursday 6 April 1978 was a not untypical day in Dáil Éireann. Charles Haughey, then Minister for Health, gave a not untypical response to a question about abortion. It came from Dr John O'Connell, then a Labour TD, and referred to the fact that there had been a 21 per cent increase in the number of Irish girls going to England to have terminations. The minister replied that he had no responsibility for the law in Britain – and did not wish to comment on it. He was, however, aware of the figures, and also knew that a number of Irish bodies that were receiving assistance from his department were encouraging pregnant women to let the baby go full term. When O'Connell criticised the quality of the back-up services Haughey assured him that improvements were in hand.

O'Connell's next question also dealt with a percentage increase: 8.4 per cent in the number of elderly people, 30,000 in the next ten years: what were the minister's proposals for expanding the health services to deal with them? The answer was not only enigmatically Irish but typically stonewalling: *Sin ceist eile.* They were politic responses to questions about two of the persisting issues of Irish life and did not mean lack of concern on the part of the minister but rather that he was inadequately briefed.

He more expertly fielded a suggestion from a Fine Gael TD that he had interfered to prevent a prosecution of a hotelier who had been arraigned for failing to observe adequate standards of hygiene in his premises. He denied the imputation, indicating that his only input was to iterate that the campaign, 'Clean up the Kitchens' that he had sponsored was intended to persuade and encourage people to improve standards. If they could indicate good faith prosecutions would not follow.

7 April 1973

'No change need worry the tranquillity of your Christian lives.'

When in 1965 the Primate of Ireland, Archbishop John Charles McQuaid (1895-1973), then in his seventieth year, returned from the last session of the Second Vatican Council he was at pains to reassure his flock: 'No change need worry the tranquillity of your Christian lives.' The deconstruction of that sentence is problematic. Was it a deliberate attempt to turn the ecclesiastical clock back? Was it wishful thinking, a form of whistling in the dark? Or had the man who ruled the Dublin diocese with such authoritarian and remote austerity for twenty-five years finally lost touch with the reality of the modern Church? He had taken a strong conservative line during the early sessions and had accepted the changes only with obedient reluctance.

McQuaid was an able and energetic administrator, building thirty-four churches and sixty-seven secondary schools during his thirty-four year term. He had also set up agencies to alleviate the harsh poverty of his people and provide care for emigrants. He was one of the architects of de Valera's 1937 Constitution that seemed to many to have created a confessional and repressive state that banned divorce and contraception. Famous for the terseness of his correspondence, he was adamantine in his refusal to allow Catholics to attend TCD (a ban not lifted until 1970) and achieved a kind of notoriety as the orchestrator of the clerical, to complement the medical, opposition to Noël Browne's Mother and Child scheme in the early 1950s.

When McQuaid resigned in 1972 his country and Church had changed; many of the certainties that had made his stance so confident had been modified and his own clergy had become restive under his authoritarian leadership. His conviction that all Irish social agencies should essentially be clerically controlled was no longer acceptable, as the media regularly pointed out. He died on Saturday 7 April 1973.

8 April 1927

Scotts jam

The government in the first ten years of Saorstát Éireann was preoccupied by the need for industry to supplement the country's agriculture, the basis of its economy. It was something of a relief when a British firm of preserve manufacturers announced on Friday 8 April 1927 that it intended to open a jam factory in Dublin. R & W Scott had been in business since the 1850s with factories in London and in Carluke, a town in Lanarkshire overlooking the Clyde, It had secured extensive premises near Annesley Bridge in Fairview and hoped to have the plant up and running for June, when the fruit season would start. The two existing firms employed a total of 1500 people and it was expected that the Dublin factory would have work for a further two hundred staff. Some outside workers would be used to train the Irish hands but ultimately only Irish workers would be employed.

The site for the Sotts factory had been deliberately chosen because the region was rich in fruit farms and it was company policy to use local products where possible. They had already been in touch with the Carlow beet factory (the first sugar factory opened in the Free State) to obtain as much sugar as it could provide. At the time Ireland was not rich in fruit, although it was known that Irish soil is particularly good for growing raspberries, strawberries and blackcurrants. The last of these did not do well in England and Scotland, although a popular source of jam. The company intended to scour the country for local produce and implicitly suggested that with such demand fruit-growing would become a profitable industry. The firm reminded the public that homemade jam would not be subject to the import tax of threepence on a pound jar and assured them that theirs would have 'the same high quality at a considerably lower price'.

9 April 1962

Contrasting entertainments

The Dublin playgoer in the week beginning Monday 9 April 1962 had quite a choice – from Irish plays in the Damer Hall to dance drama in the Gate Theatre. There was a forgivable air of second-city condescension as Joan Denise Moriarty (1912-92) brought her Cork-born Irish Theatre Ballet to town. The company offered a series of items incorporating the work of both modern Irish composers and classical standards, mixing such local themes as 'West Cork Ballad' with the *Don Quixote Pas de Deux*. The composer-conductor of the former had initially been named Seán Reidy before, as Seán Ó Riada, achieving much greater fame with *Mise Éire* (1960).

The Damer had *Na Mairnéalaigh* (The Seamen) by Eoghan Ó Tuairisc, in which the action takes place on board the ship bringing home the body of Daniel O'Connell for burial in Glasnevin in 1847. The second piece was Mairéad Ní Ghráda's *Stailc Ocrais* (Hunger Strike) about the unrelieved misery of this situation. The contrast with the other entertainments available was striking. The top of the bill in the Theatre Royal was the brilliant Dave Allen – labelled incredibly as one of 'the modern school of American comedians' as if he had not been a Dubliner – the Olympia had a jazz concert led by Ian Henry and the Gaiety had three farces played by the cast of the ATV series *Doctor in the House*. The Abbey, still in exile in the old Queen's in Pearse Street, seemed scarcely able to shake itself out of its torpor. It preferred past successes rather than risk the untried. Louis D'Alton, like George Shiels, had kept the money rolling in during the lean years and *They Got What They Wanted,* his play on offer, was a good old-fashioned comedy with an unlikely plot.

10 April 1962

'Early 20th century Paintings'

Brown Thomas, the department store, has since 1848 been regarded as the Harrods of Dublin and its Little Theatre was a unique cultural extra used for performance and as a gallery of fine art. On Tuesday 10 April 1962 an exhibition began of oils, watercolours and bronzes from the first quarter of the 20th century. The chief contributor was Matthew Smith, an English painter who had studied under Matisse and was known for his studies of the female nude. He had died aged eighty in 1959 and this was his first retrospective.

Irish masters represented were Roderick O'Connor (1860-1940), the Irish benefactor of Gaugin in Pont-Aven, who refused to accompany 'that madman' to Tahiti and whose work, like that of his mentor Van Gogh, brought little return while he lived but was now soaring in price, and William Orpen. Two oils by the former were on show and a large landscape of fishermen in Howth by Orpen, the most fashionable society painter of his day, who became a stark recorder of the First World War.

Other exhibits included work by Dame Ethel Walker (1861-1951), famous for delicate landscapes and many studies of women, Charles Ginner (1878-1952) a British artist born in France who founded with Sickert the Camden Town Group dedicated to artistic realism, and whose paintings, looking as though made of fabric, made poetry out of unglamorous street scenes. A Jacob Epstein bronze showed the Roman god of wine and ecstasy as a child entering puberty and already geared for bacchanalian revelry.

The show was probably too diffuse and eclectic to make a strong impact outside of the city's inner artistic circles; 'Early 20th century Paintings' was not sufficiently thematic to have a wider impact. Nowadays it would seem quite remarkably rich and unmissable.

11 April 1900

Housing the poor of Dublin

By the end of the 19th century, Dublin had some of the worst slums in Europe. The contrast between the opulence of the worshippers in St Patrick's Cathedral at Sunday evening service and the condition of the poor children in Patrick Street as seen by the young John M. Synge put him off religion for life. So appalling was the situation that Edward Guinness, Baron Iveagh, the chief executive of the St James's Gate brewery, determined to use his money and influence to do what he could to ameliorate the situation.

As the richest man in Ireland he was able to put his ideals into practice. The Iveagh Trust, which he founded in 1890, was responsible for considerable urban renewal and now on Wednesday 11 April 1900, at a meeting in the Sackville Hall, Sackville (later O'Connell) Street, R. O'Brien-Smyth, a local government inspector, announced the details of Lord Iveagh's proposals. He began by stating what everyone already knew: that the area round the cathedral had been condemned as unsanitary and that the scheme required demolition before new dwellings could be built.

This had caused some concern – voiced by the local parish priest – as to where the displaced should be housed. They were reassured that any tenants left homeless could find shelter in rooms in Derby Square (now vanished) and as far as possible rehoused in new houses in the place they lived before. The arrangement had been made by Lord Iveagh in consultation with the Association for the Housing of the Very Poor. The crowded meeting was very pleased with the proposals and applauded his intention to see the scheme carried out with the least possible inconvenience. It was noted that sixty-two houses in the area were homes to nine hundred and forty-nine persons, including one hundred and sixty-four 'nightly lodgers'.

12 April 1984

Honoured by degrees

Thursday 12 April 1984 was conferring day for honorary degrees by the senate of the National University of Ireland. The ceremony took place in Iveagh House in St Stephen's Green. There were eleven people so honoured, including an Irish-speaking cardinal who was also a historian of the early Irish Church, a leading Irish poet, a virtuoso flautist, the president of the European Commission, three professors, a prime minister, a leading Irish business magnate, the president of the GAA and a Sister of Mercy.

The most widely known internationally was James Galway, the 'Man with the Golden Flute', a publicity title that was an accurate description, both literally and metaphorically. The president of University College, Cork, when presenting his degree to Tomás Ó Fiaich, noted that his appointment as Archbishop of Armagh was the first in history of a man not already a bishop. Among other praises he heaped upon his head was that 'he can sing a ballad with the best' and hoped that before the night was over he would sing his favourite, 'The Old Orange Flute' to an accompaniment by Mr Galway.

Thomas Kinsella was honoured not only for his poetry but for 'his work in scholarship, translation and creative redaction' that 'had drawn the attention of the world to the epic and lyrical riches of our literary inheritance'. This was especially true of his rendering of the *Táin* and his great bilingual anthology, *An Duanaire: Poems of the Dispossessed*, created in collaboration with Professor Seán Ó Tuama.

Other recipients were Gaston Thorn from Luxembourg, Professor Erickson of Minnesota, Professor Bernard Crossland of Queen's University, Belfast, Professor Eoin O'Malley of the Royal College of Surgeons, Pádraig Ó Bogaigh (the GAA president), William G. Davis (Premier of Ontario), Patrick McGrath, the businessman founder of the Irish Heritage Trust, and Sr Canisius O'Keefe.

13 April 1742

The Messiah *in Fishamble Street*

George Frederic Handel was born in Germany in 1685, the same year and in the same country as Johann Sebastian Bach, although they never met. He travelled widely and enjoyed considerable artistic and commercial success with his operas and oratorios. When he was fifty-six, at a fallow period in his life, he gratefully accepted the invitation of the Duke of Devonshire, Viceroy of Ireland, to visit the country, arriving on 18 November 1741. The governors of Mercer's Hospital had asked him for a special composition and he brought with him the score of a new oratorio that he had completed in three weeks the previous September, the libretto, based upon scripture, having been written by his friend, Charles Jennens.

The venue chosen for this charity event for the benefit of 'poor and distressed debtors' was Neale's New Musick Hall in Fishamble Street, within comfortable walking distance of Handel's lodgings in Abbey Street. A public rehearsal set cultural and fashionable Dublin aflame. 'The finest Composition of Musick that ever was heard' was a typical critical response. Those who intended to attend the first performance were instructed: 'Ladies, come, please, without hoops; gentlemen without swords.'

At 12 noon on Tuesday 13 April 1742 Neale's Music Hall was densely packed with a swordless hoopless audience that heard for the first time one of the finest and certainly the best-known of all oratorios. It was repeated by public demand on 3 June, with the composer at the organ and men and boys from both Christ Church and St Patrick's cathedrals, the latter group by special permission of Jonathan Swift, the Dean, 'upon account of their being chiefly intended for the benefit of Mercer's Hospital'. The bills announced: 'This will be the last Performance of Mr Handel's during his Stay in this Kingdom.'

14 April 1920

'Going to Kells tomorrow'

In July 1919, during the War of Independence, Michael Collins asked his lieutenant Mick McDonald to set up an assassination unit specifically to target the Royal Irish Constabulary, especially members of the reserve force known as the Black and Tans on their arrival in March 1920 and the Auxiliary Police Force that joined them in June of that year. There were originally five members but the number was eventually increased to a dozen, forming the 'Twelve Apostles'. Their leader was Paddy Daly and the initial list of other 'apostles' included Patrick Buckley, Mick McDonnell, Ben Barrett, James Conroy, Seán Doyle, Joe Leonard, Pat McCrea, Jim Slattery and Bill Stapleton. They were on full-time duty and had headquarters in Abbey Street, where they had the cover of being carpenters in a legitimate cabinet-making business.

During exercise in Mountjoy jail one April morning in 1920, when about a hundred IRA prisoners were present, an army officer read out a list of twenty names. The prisoners were then marched to an open area opposite some steps where a group of men stood with their backs to them. These men quickly turned round and back again as if in some kind of identity parade. A prisoner called Clancy recognised one of them as Henry Kells, a detective-constable of the Dublin Metropolitan Police. A few days later Clancy was given a smuggled note reading: 'I am going to Kells tomorrow. M.C.'

The next day, Wednesday 14 April 1920, Kells was on plainclothes duty and as he neared the corner of Upper Camden Street and Pleasants Street he was shot three times by Daly, with one bullet passing through his windpipe. He was forty-two, married but childless, and had been with the DMP for twenty-two years. He was buried three days later in Mount Jerome cemetery.

15 April 1929

'A serious cause of complaint'

Mary Lamont Lee, known professionally as Mary Lee, lived in 16 Rathdown Road, which joined Grangegorman Road to the North Circular Road, and had a dance hall in her garden. It was really a large hut and she had been careful to win the consent of the neighbours before she had built it as a dance academy. Sessions were held strictly in accordance with the terms of the licence granted. The details of the origin of the amenity were revealed at a court hearing before Mr Justice Johnston on Monday 15 April 1929.

The case was brought by Adelaide Patterson who lived in No 17, on the opposite side of Rathdown Road. She asked for an interlocutory injunction restraining Lee from using the hut, pending the hearing. Patterson's objections concerned mainly the noise of the clients arriving and leaving, the music of the three-piece band and the nuisance associated with groups of people loitering in the laneway beside the house. She also suggested that there were often arguments and actual fights after the dances.

Lee denied most of these charges, saying that there was nothing undesirable about the patrons of her dance hall and she was unaware of any serious disorder or the use of offensive language, as complained of in Patterson's affidavit. She agreed that people did congregate in the laneway and had regularly complained to the Gardai about them. The judge took time to explain the nature of the injunction; there was a prima facie case for the temporary cessation of the hut's use. He revealed just a hint of bias in his language: 'The carrying-on of a dance hall…accompanied by so-called music of a jazz band consisting of three persons would give rise to a very serious cause of complaint…' Granting the injunction, he guaranteed that the hearing would not long be delayed.

16 April 1864

The Colleen Bawn *in the Theatre Royal*

The social and intellectual life of Dublin in the spring of 1864 was quite rich for those who could afford to partake of the entertainments on offer. The Royal Agricultural Society had held for the first time what later became famous as the Dublin Horse Show, on Friday 15 April 1864. But the skimpy local press paid little attention to the event, anxious instead to advise the interested public that the Saturday night had a remarkable variety of urban entertainments. Pride of place was given to the offering in the Theatre Royal, when Dion Boucicault (1820-90) and his second wife, Agnes Robertson, would appear in Boucicault's most famous play, *The Colleen Bawn,* only four years after its New York opening. Based upon *The Collegians,* the novel by Gerald Griffin about a real-life murder (Boucicault was an efficient and ruthless adaptor) it was a typical 'sensation' drama with full use of theatrical machinery, revolving stage and flying scenery.

Boucicault had moved the locale from the Shannon to the more beautiful Killarney lakes (but still sang 'Limerick Is Beautiful'). He kept the part of Myles na Gopaleen (Coppaleen), the comic hero who charms equally with his blarney and his courage, and whose dive into the lake to rescue Eily O'Connor, the Colleen Bawn, when the villainous Danny Mann tries to drown her, stopped the show each evening. The water effects were breathtaking – more exciting then than those of computer-generated effects in the movies of today. When the action slowed down there was always Eily (Agnes) to sing 'Cruiskeen Lawn' (Full Jug) or 'Cailín Deas Crúite na mBó' (Pretty Girl who Milks Cows) that became 'A pretty girl milking her cow' in later Broadway shows. No wonder the play had another incarnation as the opera *The Lily of Killarney* by Julius Benedict.

17 April 1962

Updating the study of chemistry

The 1960s was a decade of general educational reform, especially in the field of the teaching of science and mathematics. A typical tocsin was issued by Professor T.S. Wheeler DSc FRIC in his presidential address at the first annual meeting of the Irish Science Teachers' Association in University College, Dublin. In his capacity as Dean of the Faculty of Science in UCD he was in a position to give a diagnostic assessment of what he termed 'the stagnation in school courses of chemistry'. His address, called 'Billiard Balls and Hard Water', referred to the superficial way atomic science was dealt with in secondary-school classrooms: a student trained in 1880 or even earlier would have a good chance of passing the science papers in the present-day matriculation.

The 'Dalton billiard-ball atom' had been presented to students without any reference to modern knowledge of atomic structure. Furthermore, themes related to the hardness of water had figured in examination for elementary chemistry for more than a century. The stimulus for chemistry teaching in Britain had been the needs of industry for bleaching and metallurgy. Recent examinations were set by people who believed that chemistry stopped with simple molecular theory and August Kekule's representation of structural formulae. Change, however, was coming; the Department of Education had decided to modernise the chemistry courses in the curriculum and the examinations.

Wheeler praised the work of the association, saying that its inauguration in 1961 corresponded with a new epoch in school chemistry and that it had a vital part to play in that work. It was not mentioned in the address but there was a clear implication that as ever university staffs were not anxious to have to cram knowledge properly learned in secondary school into first-year undergraduates.

18 April 1927

Easter 1927

Good weather at Easter is as variable as the date of the feast but when the longed-for break coincides with sunny weather spring has undoubtedly arrived. Easter Monday 18 April 1927 was as sunny as ever a pessimist could wish. The date of the feast was on the late side – a week short of 24 April, the latest date it could be – which may have helped, and in clement Dublin, according to all the papers, 'a warm wind gave a summer-like atmosphere' and by the Monday the stringencies of Lent were easily forgotten. There was a lot of movement of population; the Howth trams had long queues of holidaymakers, as did the cars for places on the south of the bay. If the city seemed at least partially emptied of its citizens, visitors from the country and across the channel poured in by train and steamer to fill the vacuum.

There were plenty of holiday events for citizens and tourists alike: the Irish Grand National in Fairyhouse, a rugby semi-final in Donnybrook, soccer in Shelbourne Park, lawn tennis in Fitzwilliam and hockey in Foxrock. At night the theatres and cinemas did holiday business. For those without the urge or means to roam, the city parks gave sun and air. The seven hundred and seven hectares of the bountiful Phoenix Park attracted hundreds, especially parents with young families, who had literally wide-open spaces to roam, while in the city's festive centre a younger and trendier train was on parade.

Possibly the most popular amenity site in the park was the Zoological Gardens (a grand title that no one used). Crowded from early morning, the zoo's prime attraction was the plodding elephant, although the monkey house ran it close. For older folk the outdoor aviary with two recently arrived cranes almost upstaged the peacocks and the ostriches.

19 April 2000

'Go! Go! Go!'

On Wednesday 19 April 2000 an unnamed man was arrested as a suspected member of the IRA and known member of Sinn Féin in a house in Walkinstown. He was in his twenties and was held that night in Crumlin Garda station. The complicated story began at about 1.45am the previous morning at the Walkinstown roundabout. Two plainclothes Garda officers pulled up beside a motorcycle on Cromswellfort Road and at once the pillion passenger shouted to the rider, 'Go! Go! Go!' – a phrase learned from films. The rider obliged but took off at such a rate that his passenger fell off. He was taken into custody, with slight injuries to his face. A short while later, during an examination of the scene, the Gardaí found a snub-nosed Taurus revolver loaded with six bullets.

The next step in the investigation was to search the thirty-five-year-old's house, in Buckingham Street, off Summerhill, in what had come to be called 'the north inner city'. Here Gardai found documents with details of the location and movements of a man known to have been an associate of Martin Cahill, a notorious Dublin criminal, known popularly as the 'General', who had been killed by the Provisional IRA – or so it claimed – six years earlier. He had 'form', having served sentences for robbery, and his house was not far from where the pillion passenger had fallen off. The search led Gardaí to another address in Walkinstown where they arrested the second man. It was now clear that the case had its basis in the murky interface between the IRA and the Dublin criminal underworld. The pillion passenger had escaped death before this; in August 1998 he had been shot in the back outside a Walkinstown pub and it looked as if they had foiled another attempt on his life.

20 April 1896

Cinema in Dan Lowrey's Palace of Varieties

The Dublin theatre now known as the Olympia began life on 22 December 1879 as the Star of Erin Music Hall and became Dan Lowrey's Music Hall two years later. The Dan Lowrey in command was the son of the original owner. (Father and son had been the joint managers of the Empire Theatre in Belfast and the senior died in 1890.) In 1889 he changed the name to Dan Lowrey's Palace of Varieties, keeping that name until 1897. It was the heyday of the music hall and the stars from Britain, American vaudeville and Ireland sang, danced, did stand-up (although they did not use the phrase), juggled, walked on tightropes, did bird imitations and insisted that the girl/boy that they loved was up in the gallery.

But already as the raucous century was drawing to a close another all-conquering popular entertainment was slouching towards Bedlam to be born. Moving pictures had been invented by the Lumière brothers, Auguste Marie Louis Nicolas and Louis Jean, from Besançon. Their first film, *Sortie des Usines Lumière à Lyon* (1895), showing workers leaving their Lyon factory, was seventeen metres long, hand-cranked through a projector and ran for fifty seconds. It caused a sensation and with Léon Bouly's cinématographe, patented in 1894, they had begun, in however a flickering fashion, a new and exciting medium. Films ('flicks' as they called them) came to Ireland on Monday 20 April 1896, under the auspices of Dan Lowrey Junior. That day with the Palace of Varieties converted temporarily into a cinema, he screened such Lumière work as *The Sprinkler Sprinkled* and *Fishing for Goldfish*. As the art developed and the popularity grew local films were made with such titles as *A View from the Train on the Blackrock Line* and *The Fire Brigade Going out on a Call*.

21 April 1954

Killed by a fall from a horse

Captain Michael Tubridy called at Joseph McGrath's stud farm in Trimblestown, Trim, County Meath, on Wednesday 14 April 1954, saddled his five-year-old chestnut gelding and went for a gallop through the fields. Later word came that he was lying on his back some fields away and that the horse had run away. When Christopher McDonnell, one of the McGrath grooms, arrived, he found Tubridy unconscious. He was taken by ambulance to the Richmond Hospital, where he died two days later. The inquest was held by Dr D.A. MacErlean, the Dublin city coroner, on Wednesday 21 April, in the city morgue. McDonnell offered his opinion that since bridle and stirrups seemed perfectly in order Tubridy had not been thrown at a jump but had been walking the horse about the field.

The cause of death was stated to be shock and respiratory failure, secondary to cerebral haemorrhage, laceration and other injuries of the brain. This the coroner found unhelpful towards determining what exactly had happened. Edward Casey, another of McGrath's men, had testified that Tubridy had passed him while he was working with another man at a hayrick and had stopped to talk. He said he was going to exercise the gelding in the field but five minutes later he saw the horse run away from where Tubridy lay in the ground. The ground was hard at the time and there was nothing unusual about the scene.

MacErlean decided that there was no doubt that Tubridy fell or was thrown from the horse. The medical evidence also indicated that he had been a perfectly healthy young man and that there was nothing to suggest that he might have had a weakness or anything of that sort. He wished too to scotch any rumour that the deceased had suffered spinal injuries or had a brain tumour.

22 April 1955

'Rhode Island' holiday camp

Red Island Holiday Camp was built in the early 1950s in Skerries, north County Dublin. It was typical of the post-war phenomenon: the inclusive total holiday with accommodation, food and entertainment available without further charge. To maintain the cheapness of the cost a certain amount of organisation – not to say regimentation – of the campers was essential in all these amenities throughout the UK as well as Ireland and they became obvious targets for satire. One British film had a Grenadier Guard complaining that he could not stand the discipline and on 21 November 1954 the Radio Éireann comedy show *Living with Lynch* featured a sketch about 'The Rhode Island Holiday Camp', which Irish Holidays Inc., the owners of Red Island, claimed was defamatory.

The star of the show, Cork-born Joe Lynch, was a skilful actor and comedian and his programme in the pre-television era was extremely popular. The action was taken against Maurice Gorham, Director of Radio Éireann, and the scriptwriters Dermot K. Doolan and Michael McGarry. The plaintiffs complained that the script suggested that patrons 'were subjected to severe and unremitting regimentation and were treated like prisoners; that they were accommodated in small uncomfortable chalets and that the standard of morals was lax.' (This last slur had been anticipated: when the Butlin camp had opened in Mosney in 1948 it was declared inappropriate in Catholic Ireland.)

On Friday 22 April 1955, in a side issue to the defamation action, Irish Holidays Ltd applied to have a section removed from their statement of claim. This was Paragraph Five, except for the first sentence that claimed that the sketch was 'false and malicious and calculated to damage'. Mr Justice Murnaghan said the language used was extravagant and he deplored extravagance. He allowed the motion, adding that costs would abide the result of the trial.

23 April 1014

The Battle of Clontarf

The battle of Clontarf, fought between the armies of Brian Boru and the Leinstermen, led by Máel Mórda, who did not accept the Munsterman's claim to suzerainty, took place on Good Friday 23 April 1014. It was portrayed by romantic 19th-century historians as a simple struggle of Christianity against the pagan Danes in which the good eventually triumphed but the saintly seventy-three-year-old Imperator Scotorum (Emperor of the Gael) – a title suggested by his confessor, Máel Suthain – was treacherously slain by the fleeing Brodir.

Life even in the eleventh century, was a deal more complicated: the Ostmen, as the Irish Vikings preferred to call themselves, were nearly all Norse, most were already Christian through intermarriage; they and their Orkney, Hebridean, Manx and Icelandic allies were part of Máel Mórda's native Irish army. The Munster Ostmen in Brian's army were led by Sitric, his son-in-law, whose mother Gormflaith had been married to both Brian and Máel Sechnaill II, King of Meath, who played no part in the battle. It was that bewitching lady who persuaded Sigurd, Lord of Orkney, to side with Máel Mórda, offering her body as an inducement.

The battle was fought north and east of the Tolka and cost at least 10,000 lives. It destroyed the power of Leinster and the Ostmen in general and effectively ruined Brian's ambition to rule a united Ireland, an ideal yet to be achieved. Both his son Murchad and his son Tordhbelbach died in a battle so strikingly bloody that it is mentioned in the thirteenth-century Icelandic saga *Burnt Njal*, with Gormflaith rendered as Kormlada. Only Sitric benefitted, having been a mere observer of the carnage with his mother from the safety of Dublin, and ruled there for another twenty-eight years. Brian's body was taken to Armagh for burial.

24 April 2000

The Double for Ted Walsh

The Irish Grand National is a National Hunt chase for horses aged five years or older. It is run in Fairyhouse each Easter Monday over a distance of about 5834 metres, with twenty-four fences to be jumped. On Monday 24 April 2000 it was won by Comanche Court, which pleased his owner Dermot Desmond greatly but was an extra-special celebration for Ted Walsh, the trainer who had won the most famous of all steeplechases, the British Grand National in Aintree, with Papillon a fortnight before. It was a remarkable triumph to be the first trainer to achieve the double in the same year.

Bertie Ahern, the then Taoiseach, presented the trophies and the £78,000 prize money and some wags commented that it was something of a relief to find the juxtaposition of a senior politician, a wealthy businessman and a large sum of money changing hands in a way that was entirely above board. Everything contributed to the pleasure of the occasion. The day was sunny and the crowd of race goers was calculated to be about 23,000. The euphoric Ted Walsh paid tribute to 'the man above'. Ruby Walsh, his jockey son was more analytical: 'I didn't think he'd make the trip but coming into the straight and seeing how well the horse was travelling, I thought, "Jesus, not again!"'

The punters were pleased with the result although there was a lot less wagered than had been on Papillon, Ahern admitted to the press that he'd had a tenner on Tony O'Reilly's horse, Foxchapel King, that had shown well until the second-last jump. His tip for the sixth race was Farbeitfromme, a disclaimer title with a neat political ring, which actually did not finish.

25 April 1916

Francis Sheehy-Skeffington

Francis Sheehy-Skeffington (1878-1916), who was born in Balieborough in County Cavan, was simply Skeffington until his marriage in 1903 to the feminist Hanna Sheehy when, true to his egalitarian principles, he incorporated her name with his. In University College, Dublin, he was a notable eccentric, unfashionably bearded, wearing Norfolk jacket and knickerbockers and agitating for women's suffrage. He edited several nationalist and suffragist journals and became known for his socialism and pacifism, endeavouring without success to reconcile workers and employers during the Lockout of 1913. When the First World War broke out he campaigned as a pacifist against recruitment and was sentenced to six month's imprisonment but released after being on hunger strike for six days.

Sheehy-Skeffington did not support the Easter Rising but tried to organise a civilian militia to prevent looting. On Tuesday 25 April 1916 he was arrested by a captain of the Royal Irish Rifles called Bowen-Colthurst as an 'enemy sympathiser' and marched as a hostage on a raiding party with his hands tied behind his back. On this patrol he saw Bowen-Colthurst deliberately shoot a boy called Coade. The next morning Bowen-Colthurst had him executed, along with two journalists, Patrick McIntyre and Thomas Dickson, who had been held with him in Portobello Barracks. The operation, which had been ordered without authority, was bungled, requiring two firing squads.

A court-martial on 6 June, insisted upon by Major Sir Francis Vane, the Portobello commander, found Bowen-Colthurst of unsound mind, although Sir John Maxwell, Commander-in-Chief of British forces in Ireland, refused to arrest him. He was transferred from Broadmoor to a Canadian hospital and, deemed cured, released on full pension on 26 April 1921. Hanna's unrelenting agitation eventually led to a royal commission, an apology and an offer of monetary compensation which she refused. British army incompetence and official intransigence had hammered another nail into the coffin of constitutional nationalism.

26 April 1984

The Liberties Festival

The Liberties of Dublin, a term originating from the legislative organisation of the Norman invaders, forms part of the postal district Dublin 8. The name echoes the district's earlier independence of the central government and even today, when the term has no legal significance, its denizens celebrate its distinctive difference from other parts of the city. The idea of a cultural festival celebrating the district was suggested in the early 1960s and the first Liberties Festival was launched in 1972.

The 1984 festival, in its twelfth year, was launched on Thursday 26 April, and Larry Dillon, the creator and director, declared in his opening speech that two of the usual concert venues, the Tailors' Hall and St Catherine's Church, would not be available that year and that the festival would be dependent on local churches. The first of these, located in Back Lane and the last surviving relic of the Dublin guild system, had been transferred to An Taisce, while St Catherine's in Thomas Street, in front of which Robert Emmet was executed in 1803, was then in poor condition because of vandals. It had been taken over by the Belltower Trust, which had in hands a £48,000 refurbishment scheme. A possible alternative, the old school hall in Carman's Hall, off Francis Street in the Coombe, was closed for redevelopment.

The festival would be held, nonetheless, and it began with a 'Run for Life', a sponsored road race for the Leukaemia Trust Bone Marrow Fund. This was followed by a ballad session with the Fair Isle Folk. The entertainment would last for a week, its highlights being a concert by the Chieftains in St Audeon's in High Street on the Friday, followed by a late session in one of the city's oldest pubs, the Brazen Head in Bridge Street.

27 April 1752

Around Ireland by stagecoach

Travellers in Ireland in the 18th century were pleasantly surprised at the quality of Irish roads, especially those radiating from Dublin, Belfast and Cork. As the century progressed the demands of trade and the post office and the perceived need to move detachments of troops rapidly about the country caused these lines of communications to continue to improve. In fact until the rising of 1798 the country was remarkably peaceful and even some members of the disaffected Catholic majority became wealthy through trade, as the discrimination of the Penal Laws was not as severe in this area as in others.

A lot of travel was done on foot or on horseback, if the owners had sufficient means, but those for whom neither foot nor saddle was appropriate turned to some form of carriage transport. The jaunting car worked well enough in good weather but offered no protection from the Irish rain and wind. It was not until the development of the stagecoach that travel became less nightmarish. By 1737 you could travel by coach twice weekly from Dublin to Drogheda, Kilkenny and Kinnegad (if a purpose could be found for a journey there) and once a week to Athlone.

Since Belfast had steadily grown from a tiny fishing village, essentially a fiefdom of the Chichester family, to a substantial commercial centre in those years it was soon realised that some reliable system of transport between Dublin and the north was essential. The first regular stagecoach service between Dublin and Belfast was initiated on Thursday 27 April 1752. It ran quite successfully until 1754, when it ceased to ply beyond Newry. One of the reasons may have been the prevalence of highwaymen in south Armagh, for decades known as rapparee country. Belfast acquired a permanent link to the capital in 1788.

28 April 1680

The Royal Hospital

Old soldiers never die, says the song a little optimistically, but they do need looking after in age. Nell Gwyn, 'His Majesty's Protestant whore', is fabled to have suggested to Charles II (1630-85) the idea of a retirement hostel for old sweats. Thus, perhaps, the Royal Hospital in Chelsea was conceived and finally opened in 1695, a decade after the king's death. The Lord Lieutenant in Ireland, James Butler, 1st Duke of Ormond (1610-88), also motivated by Charles II, got there first, laying the foundation stone of the Royal Hospital in Kilmainham, south of the city, on Wednesday 28 April 1680.

Charles wrote to Ormond:

> ...And we do hereby give unto you full power and authority from time to time to issue and employ the same towards the building and settling an hospital for such aged and maimed officers and soldiers as shall be dismissed out of our army as unserviceable men, and for making provision for their future maintenance, in such way and manner as you shall think fit.

It was built to the design of Sir William Robinson (1645-1712), Surveyor-General of Ireland (1680-7) but the tower and spire were not added until 1701. It ceased to be used as a hostel in 1927 and it was the headquarters of the Garda Síochána 1930-50, until it was declared unsafe. But it was recovered from dereliction by the Office of Public Works (1980-4) to serve, at a refurbishment cost of £20m, as a National Centre for Culture and the Arts. On the three hundredth anniversary of its opening it became the Irish Museum of Modern Art (IMMA). Its permanent collection includes a collection of prints from British, German, Dutch and Flemish artists and fifty paintings donated by Sir Sidney Nolan (1917-92), the Australian artist of Irish descent.

29 April 1916

Surrender

On Saturday morning, 29 April 1916 Elizabeth O'Farrell, a nurse from Cumann na mBan, the female branch of the Irish Volunteers, left the GPO in Sackville (later O'Connell) Street carrying a white flag and a message from Patrick Henry Pearse to Brigadier-General William Henry Muir Lowe, the British army commander in Dublin, at the army's barricade in Great Britain (later Parnell) Street. The message read: 'The Commandant-General of the Irish Republican Army wishes to treat with the Commandant-General of the British forces in Ireland.'

Lowe demanded an unconditional surrender and at 15.30, Pearse, wearing a greatcoat and a Boer slouch hat, handed his sword to him. At 15.45 he signed the typed order to stand down:

> In order to prevent the further slaughter of Dublin citizens and in the hope of saving the lives of our followers now surrounded and hopelessly outnumbered, the Provisional Government present at Headquarters have agreed to unconditional surrender, and the Commandants of the various districts in the City and County will order their commands to lay down his arms.

This order had to be countersigned by James Connolly, as the Citizen Army recognised no leader but him: 'I agree to these conditions for the men only under my command in the Moore Street area and for the men in the Stephen's Green command.'

At 21.00 the Volunteers, apart from the garrisons in Jacob's and Boland's who at first refused to surrender, marched from Moore Street along Sackville Street to dump their arms at the foot of the five-year-old Parnell statue. The following fortnight saw the paced-out executions of the leaders of the Rising, the perceived harshness of which swung a majority of the populace who had at first execrated the Volunteers to support them in the coming struggles.

30 April 1919

'Religious or silly or indecent.'

Sir John Pentland Mahaffy (1839-1919), the quintessence of academic, witty and relentless anti-nationalism, was born in Switzerland on 26 February 1839 of Irish parents and educated at home in Donegal and in Trinity College, where he had a brilliant academic career and was ordained for the Church of Ireland. This last qualification enabled him to become a fellow of TCD in 1864. He became an authority on ancient Greece and even more ancient Egypt and essentially spent the rest of his life, academic and corporeal, in the college. He became a mentor to such like spirits as Oscar Wilde and Oliver Gogarty and compensated for his invincible snobbery with a deserved reputation for witty conversation, on which he wrote in *Principles of the Art of Conversation* in 1887.

He once described an Irish bull as always pregnant and, asked for the essential difference between men and women replied, 'I can't conceive.' Balked from the provostship of Trinity for ten years by the appointment in 1904 of Anthony Traill he once replied to the news of the latter's illness with, 'Nothing trivial, I hope.' His particular animus was directed against all aspects of national Irishness. He denied a platform in TCD to 'a man called Pearse' and criticised the work of the Gaelic League and the admission of Irish as a curriculum subject, saying that all Irish texts were 'religious or silly or indecent'. He was parodied, as were other Trinity dons, Traill and Atkinson, in Douglas Hyde's squib, *Pleusgadh na Bulgóide* (The Bursting of the Bubble). In it, spellbound by an tSeanbhean bhocht, they find themselves unable to speak *except* in Irish.

Knighted (illegally since he was a clergymen) in 1917, he proposed a Swiss-style federal solution to the Ulster question and died in the Provost's House on Wednesday 30 April 1919.

SUMMER

1 May 1932

Crimes and misdemeanours

The Monday session of the Dublin District Court had the usual mixture of small crimes and misdemeanours on 1 May 1932. The first was one of assault with a hatchet with an immediate counter-summons by the accused. Late on the Sunday evening Garda '65A' was on patrol in Meath Street, off Thomas Street West, when he heard cries of 'Police' and 'Murder' from neighbouring Earl Street South. He ran to the site and found James Browne lying in the hallway of one of the houses bleeding from a head wound and arranged for him to be taken to the Meath Hospital.

He later arrested Thomas Flannery, the assailant, who testified that between 11 o'clock and midnight James Browne had arrived at his hallway 'looking for a fight'. Mrs Flannery tried to intervene, asking him to go away. When he struck her she screamed and her husband came running down. He hit Browne with the hatchet on the head. Flannery claimed that the first assault came from Browne, who attended the court on the counter-charge, heavily bandaged. Both men were remanded on bail for a week.

Other cases dealt with included a pair charged with being drunk and disorderly on the previous Saturday night on the North Circular Road. Their solicitor successfully pleaded 'first offence' and they were allowed to put ten shillings each in the poor box. Joseph H. Wood of Mullingar was sentenced to one month with hard labour for the 'grave offence' of being drunk in charge of a vehicle and James Archibald and Joseph Croft, both of North Circular Road, were remanded on the charge of tampering with coinage. Croft admitted to treating a Free State halfpenny to pass it as a shilling with which he got cigarettes and eight pence in change.

2 May 1935

Aviation tragedy

To honour the embryonic Army Air Corps the Fianna Fáil government decided to hold a National Aviation Day in the Phoenix Park on 11 May 1935. The previous weeks were spent in intense rehearsal for a dazzling display of the corps' aeronautic ability. On Thursday 2 May, twenty-six-year-old Lieutenant Michael Kennedy, one of the pilots, crashed his Avro 626, hitting the ground at two hundred miles per hour. He and two fellow-officers, Lieutenant Johnston and their commander, Lieutenant Stapleton, were engaged in a demonstration of aerial gunnery against a ground target set up in Baldonnel Aerodrome, the corps base.

Johnston and Stapleton made their runs successfully and gained height again. Kennedy's plane failed to rise and crashed into the ground. The petrol tank exploded and flew like a fireball, landing two hundred yards away, and the plane was flung back about thirty-five yards from its first point of impact. The aerodrome fire appliance and ambulance were immediately mobilised but there was nothing they could do except put out the fire and recover the badly burned body, which was taken to St Bricin's Military Hospital for an inquest. It was already clear that death had been instantaneous, as even Lieutenant Kennedy's parachute had been completely burnt away. The other two planes circled the airfield and landed without incident.

The wreckage was also removed for inspection but no clear mechanical fault could be discerned. The seven cylinders had been found a considerable distance from the crash site. Eye-witnesses described how the three planes came in V-formation on their second run. The other two began to climb but Kennedy's did not pull out of its 'power dive'.

Tributes were paid to the dead pilot's popularity and a Requiem Mass was arranged for the Wednesday morning.

3 May 1916

The first executions

At 3.30am on the morning of Wednesday 3 May 1916 three leaders of the Easter Rising and signatories of the Proclamation of the Irish Republic were shot in the yard of Kilmainham jail. The official communiqué was terse:

> Three signatories of the notice proclaiming the Irish Republic, P.H. Pearse, T. MacDonagh and T.J. Clarke, have been tried by Field Court Martial and sentenced to death, The sentence having been duly confirmed the three above-mentioned men were shot this morning.

It was the first of a series of piecemeal and long-drawn-out executions that tactically achieved the aims of the participants, drawing attention to an Ireland 'unfree' and therefore 'never at peace', engendering a country soon united and militant and turning world opinion, especially American, against Britain. General Sir John Maxwell (1859-1929), who took over as commander-in-chief of the army in Ireland on 28 April and insisted on the executions, said on his arrival, 'I am going to ensure that there will be no treason whispered for a hundred years.' Was ever a man more mistaken.

More humane and more realistic was the attitude of General Charles Guinand Blackader, who chaired Pearse's court-martial:

> I have just done one of the hardest tasks I have ever had to do. I have had to condemn to death one of the finest characters I have ever come across. There must be something very wrong in the state of things that makes a man like that a rebel. I don't wonder that his pupils adored him.

Throughout the whole turbulent decade that resulted in Ireland's partial independence British authorities acted with a mixture of mean-spiritedness, pusillanimity and incompetence. The rot started with these dawn executions.

4 May 1963

Seizure of mail van

Early on the morning of Saturday 4 May 1963 a green mail van of the sort that came every night to collect the post from the last flight from London began its return journey to the central sorting office in Pearse Street. It was observed driving across the runway and then heading for the 'back' road to the airport through Ballymun at 12.30am. It was usual, for security reasons, for the driver to take this road, lying somewhat to the west of the main airport road. The man who told reporters that he had seen the van's departure also said that 'after what seemed like a very short time' an army officer came running into the terminal building with the news that the van had been held up less that a quarter of a mile along the road and driven off.

He reported that the driver had been pulled from the van, tied up and gagged and left lying by the side of the Ballymun road. He had managed to free himself and wave down the officer, who took him back to the airport and called the Gardaí. It was clearly a well-planned caper and suggested a degree of inside information about the timing and the route. From information obtained from the driver the Gardaí learned that the van had been flagged down by a man wearing a good approximation of a Garda uniform and two others seized the stationary van and, having tied up the driver, drove the van a short distance along the road before dumping him by the roadside. There were at least three men involved in the heist and the others followed the van in a black saloon car to where it was later discovered empty near the Boot Inn in the St Margaret's district.

5 May 1932

'A golden harvest'

The foundation stone of the Jesuit church of St Francis Xavier in Upper Gardiner Street was laid on 2 July 1829, the year of Catholic Emancipation, and completed in time for opening on Thursday 3 May 1832. Its classical façade was the work of its architect, Bartholomew Esmonde SJ (1789-1862), who had spent many years in Italy. It saw the funeral of the poet Gerard Manley Hopkins SJ (1844-89) and figured in James Joyce's short story 'Grace'. The centenary was celebrated with full ecclesiastical splendour on Thursday 5 May 1932.

The church was crowded well before noon, when Cardinal Joseph McRory (1861-1945), Primate of All Ireland, entered, wearing a striking long trailing scarlet robe, held up by two acolytes wearing white surplices and red soutanes. As he approached the high altar, gorgeously adorned with flowers and lit by a hundred candles, he blessed the capacity congregation on either hand. After the solemn High Mass came the sermon given by the Bishop of Raphoe, the Most Rev Dr William MacNeely (1888-1963).

He gave a brief summary of the work done by the Jesuit order in the Counter-Reformation that had earned them the soubriquet 'Soldiers of Christ'. He reminded his listeners that they had established Clongowes College, near Clane, in County Kildare in 1814 when the century-old anti-popery legislation had been repealed and the growth of the city gave them an important mission field. A few yards from the fashionable Mountjoy Square, the grand appearance of St Francis Xavier gave heart to the poor Catholics of Dublin who for so long had no social position. In fact their perhaps reluctant champion, Jonathan Swift, described their political position as 'the very definition of slavery'. His lordship ended his talk with the claim that the hundred years they celebrated had seen 'a golden harvest quietly and calmly reaped for Christ'.

6 May 1882

The Phoenix Park murders

One of the greatest setbacks in the quest by Prime Minister William Ewart Gladstone (1809-98) and Irish Party leader Charles Stewart Parnell (1846-91) for an agreed constitutional settlement of the perennial Irish question was the murder by a Fenian splinter group using twelve-inch surgical knives of Lord Frederick Cavendish, the new chief secretary, and Thomas Henry Burke, the Under-secretary, in Phoenix Park on 6 May 1982. The main target was Burke, who was strongly linked with the coercion methods of the previous chief secretary, William Edward Forster, known as 'Buckshot' Forster because he had the ball cartridges in the guns of the Royal Irish Constabulary (RIC) replaced with the less dangerous buckshot. (It was intended as a humane gesture but since the police subsequently used their guns more readily the humane element was lost.)

Parnell had been jailed in Kilmainham for encouraging boycotting and land agitation but under the terms of the Kilmainham Treaty, agreed by Gladstone and Parnell in March 1882, Forster was replaced by the more liberal Cavendish, agrarian reform halted the Land War and Parnell, publicly committed to peaceful campaigning, was released to lead a strong Irish Parliamentary Party. Four days later an extreme Fenian group, self-called the Irish National Invincibles, hacked Burke to pieces and slaughtered Cavendish in what would now be called collateral damage, as they strolled in the park near the Vice-regal Lodge.

The Irish Republican Brotherhood (IRB), as the Fenians preferred to call themselves, had played a part in the agrarian struggles but had acquiesced in the Kilmainham terms. The main body had nothing but loathing for the extremists and took no action when five of them were hanged. Public opinion in Ireland and especially in Britain hardened. The police set up a Special Irish Branch (still surviving as the Special Branch that deals with subversives) and Parnell was persuaded with the greatest difficulty to continue as leader. Many believed that the killings 'cost Ireland a further generation of slavery'.

7 May 1925

Prisons and prisoners

The report of the General Prisons Board for the year 1923-4 published on Thursday 7 May 1925 showed evidence of the existence of what these experts deemed a new criminal class 'composed of half-educated youths who would seem to have escaped from parental control'.

> There has grown up in the Free State a new class of criminal full of unfulfilled desires, youths who have been dazzled by sensational reports in newspapers of large sums of money obtained by organised robbery and they are thus seduced by the prospect of getting money really without having to work for it honestly.

The report also included figures of the prison population for the years 1914-23, The number of convicts showed a steady decrease from 1914 (52) until 1919 (23) but rocketed in 1920 (53) and 1921 (327) and decreased to 74 in 1923. One reason given in the report for the rise in those years was that 'immediately following on the suppression of the armed revolt the police forces were enabled to function more effectively'. Cases of drunkenness and committals also showed a decrease, ascribed to the 'high price of intoxicating liquors, with a reduction in the gravity of the liquors sold'.

The report also drew attention to the extensive damage to Free State prisons by internees 'in the last few years'. In 1923-4 a total of £10,000 (£480,000 today) was spent on repairs and structural alterations and the same amount on new equipment for Kilkenny and Kilmainham jails. Prison labour was used wherever possible. The report closed with a discussion about the need for appropriate occupation, especially for a large number of young able-bodied convicts for whom the usual options of tailoring, shoemaking and mat-making were unsuitable. It advised the setting-up of some system of vocational training to rehabilitate these prisoners and prevent their re-offending.

8 May 1916

More executions

General Sir John Maxwell aimed to make an example of the 1916 leaders in order to extirpate treason for ever in the country and Prime Minister H.H. Asquith (1852-1928) initially concurred, calling for punishment in 'the most severe way possible'. But the deliberateness of the executions was politically disastrous and helped win the originally scornful populace to the side to the rebels.

On Monday 8 May it was the turn of Con Colbert, Éamonn Ceannt, Michael Mallin and Seán Heuston. Colbert (b. 1893) had been a member of Na Fianna, the National Boy Scouts, run by Constance Markievicz, and during Easter Week had been in command of Watkins Brewery in Ardee Street. Ceannt (b. 1881) was born Edmund Kent in Glenamaddy, Count Galway. He was a skilled piper and worked as a clerk in Dublin Castle. He successfully commanded the South Dublin Union and was reluctant to accept the surrender.

Michael Mallin (b. 1880), one of the few leaders who had actual military experience, had been in command of the Citizen Army contingent in St Stephen's Green but moved it to the Royal College of Surgeons when the army occupied the Shelbourne Hotel. Seán Heuston (b. 1891) was a railway worker and organiser of Na Fianna. He led a contingent of the boys to bring arms from the *Asgard* to Dublin. In command of the Mendicity Institute, he was obliged to surrender in Wednesday 26 April. He was the only one of the four who had signed the Proclamation.

9 May 1959

Philately will get you anywhere

Shanahan's Stamp Auctions was a firm dedicated to the proposition that philately will get you anywhere. It was an adjunct of a well-established auctioneering firm in Dún Laoghaire that had been set up by Dr Paul Singer, a Jewish immigrant from Bratislava, in 1954. The firm bought rare stamps and sold them at monthly auctions. The idea appealed to a number of small-time investors and all seemed to go well. The firm had its own magazine *Green ISLE* (Irish Stamp Lovers Edition). Then early on Saturday morning, 9 May 1959, thieves made off with a cache of stamps valued at £460,000. These formed the Lombardo-Venezia collection and were to have been auctioned that day at the firm's premises in Upper George's Street, Dún Laoghaire.

It was soon discovered that the thieves had missed another cache of valuable stamps worth £35,000 due to be sold on 30 May and, wondering what to do with part of the loot, had ditched a suitcase holding £5000 worth in a laneway, where it was found by council workers. Singer reassured investors that all the stamps had been insured by Lloyds of London and that they should receive 25s/6d for every pound invested. But the robbery caused a panic and it soon seemed likely that Singer had been operating a pyramid scheme, paying interest out of money received for new investments. He was tried for fraud and sentenced to fourteen years, although acquitted on the instructions of a judge after a retrial. The foreman of the jury in the first trial was found to have a claim against Singer for £1375. Paul Singer and his wife left a for an unknown destination after the acquittal. His business partner, Desmond Shanahan, was sentenced to fifteen months.

10 May 1926

A flourishing theatre scene

In Dublin the week beginning Monday 10 May 1926 made it clear that, in spite of the Censorship of Films Act of 1923 and the agitation for a Censorship of Publications Act that would become law in 1929, the theatre flourished notwithstanding the prevalent contemporary Mrs Grundyism. The fare on offer was perfectly respectable and showed a generous variety of different kinds of excellence. The Gaiety had *St Joan* by local lad, George Bernard Shaw, with greater audience interest because she had recently been canonised. Certain less than saintly lines upset some who expected hagiography but the thirty-year-old Dorothy Holmes-Gore, who specialised in ethereal parts, got an ovation at the closing line: 'How long, O Lord, how long?' as Joan mourned the world's inability to accept saints.

The Abbey, after the February ructions at the opening nights of *The Plough and the Stars*, settled for a sure money-spinner, *Professor Tim,* by the unmitigatedly cynical County Antrim playwright, George Shiels ((1881-1949). With the acting talents of F.J. McCormick, May Craig, Eileen Crowe and Maureen Delany, it was popular theatre with a touch of class. The brassier Theatre Royal featured ex-jockey George Formby Junior, then three years married to his aggressive clog-dancing wife Beryl but before he had started cleaning windows or developed the banjolele. He was still the feckless 'John Willie' – the character invented by his then more famous father who had recently died – but on the way to becoming Britain's highest-paid variety artist.

The Olympia's revue, *Dublin Tonight,* saw the burgeoning of a local artist who was to be Formby's equal in talent and popularity in Ireland. This was Jimmy O'Dea, born in Lower Bridge Street and a qualified oculist who was about to become a full-time entertainer – and the pride of much more than the Coombe.

11 May 1953

The Ballets Jooss in Dublin

Kurt Jooss (1901-79) was a German ballet dancer, choreographer and founder of *Tanztheater* (dance drama). He was a pupil and colleague of Rudolf von Laban, who devised a new theory of dance and a system of notation that made it possible to record each movement in diagram. Jooss wanted dance to tell a story – he had no time for movement without a plot – whether comic or serious, with a strong moral content. He formed the Ballets Jooss in 1927 but because of his refusal to sack the Jews in his company when Hitler came to power he fled first to the Netherlands and thence to England, where he lived until 1949.

There was great excitement in Dublin critical circles that Jooss and his company were coming to the Olympia Theatre and would present some of the set pieces for which they had become famous. These included 'Pavane' a kind of Totenanz set in the court of Philip II of Spain, showing the sterile lifelessness of court life for those young and in love. The music was by Ravel and the costumes after Velasquez. 'Ball in Old Vienna' was much lighter and used Straussian effects to recreate the mores of the imperial city. 'Night Train' and 'Journey in the Fog' showed just how different was the work of Jooss and Laban from traditional classic ballet.

The first night house on Monday 11 May 1953 was disappointing, especially since it was felt that Ballets Jooss 'showed a precision, lightness and mastery of technique far in excess of anything that has been offered by other ballet companies that have been crowded out here in the past season,' as one critic observed. The counter-attractions of *Royal Spotlight No 4*, *Melody of Spring* in the Capitol and Shaw's *Mrs Warren's Profession* in the Gate proved too strong.

12 May 1916

The last to be shot

The executions of the 1916 leaders were carried out in a deliberately paced way over ten days, as determined by General Sir John Maxwell. In the words of Elizabeth, Countess of Fingall, it was like 'watching a stream of blood coming from beneath a closed door.' The last two leaders to die were James Connolly (b. 1868) and Seán Mac Diarmada (b. 1883) who faced the reluctant firing squads on Friday 12 May 1916. No one in Ireland seemed to have the authority to question Maxwell's methods and even the increasingly urgent objections of Prime Minister H.H. Asquith were largely ignored. The result was that no one could be sure that these killings would be the last.

Glasgow-born Connolly was, in a sense, the odd man out among the leaders; he was a socialist with all the determination and occasional naïveté of the doctrinaire and the only one with real military experience. He was badly wounded during Easter Week and held not in jail but in a room in Dublin Castle now known as the 'Connolly Room'. In spite of a doctor's opinion that he had no more than a day or two to live, the execution order stood. He was taken by ambulance to the Royal Hospital and thence to the yard of Kilmainham jail across the way. As he could not stand he was strapped to a chair and then shot, the last to go.

Seán Mac Diarmada, from near Kiltyklogher, County Leitrim, was in a sense the equivalent of Connolly in the IRB, although fifteen years younger; he was what might later be called 'hardline'. He was brilliant at organisation and misinformation and was essentially the mentor of Michael Collins, who shared his abilities. Although introduced to the IRB by Bulmer Hobson (1883-1969) in Belfast where he worked as a barman, he bypassed Hobson's authority to make sure that the Easter Rising would take place as planned.

13 May 1954

Aviator Fitzmaurice

On 12 April 1928 Colonel James Fitzmaurice (1898-1965) joined his co-pilot Captain Herman Köhl at the controls of the *Bremen*, a Junker D1167, and took off from Baldonnel airfield to make the first east-to-west transatlantic flight. Their only passenger was Baron von Hünefeld, the sponsor of the venture. They landed 36.5 hours later on a frozen lake on Greenly Island, off the coast of Newfoundland. Fitzmaurice had hoped to interest the Irish government in the project but all they required from him was to continue to train Irish air corps pilots in Baldonnel.

He returned to the subject in 1951 and three years later, on Thursday 13 May 1954, he spoke on 'This Trail-Blazing Business' at the monthly lunch of the Publicity Club in the Metropole Restaurant. He always had his eye on the harder crossing westwards and began appropriate research that, as he admitted, 'almost frightened the life out of myself'. There had been no great improvement in engine or aircraft design since the war and the science of meteorology could say little about a stretch of ocean the size of the Atlantic. As a decorated veteran of the RFC during the war he had loads of informed confidence about the project.

There was a plane in Baldonnel – a single-engined Martinsyde bomber – that had been converted as a passenger carrier and he was sure that he could load sufficient fuel to allow him to make a safe journey from Dublin to St John's, Newfoundland. But as he expressed it: Authority who 'knew so much more about the job than I did and…had always shown so much solicitude for my welfare, which had always been one of their tremendous worries.' The result was that a project which should have been a triumph for the Free State had to wait for nine years and the glory was then Germany's.

14 May 1951

A touch of sunshine

The Whitsun holiday of Monday 14 May 1951 was in Britain the second coldest ever recorded; the temperature there was 10°, a fraction colder than that of Christmas Day 1949. By remarkable contrast, Dublin had more than thirty hours of sunshine over the holiday period. Considering that Easter Sunday fell on 25 March, about as early as it could happen by ecclesiastical rules, the tropical weather of Pentecost was welcomed with a mixture of disbelief and enthusiasm by the 50,000 who left Dublin by trains and boats and planes, on wheels and on foot.

This exodus was compensated for somewhat by shoals of visitors who arrived by sea from Liverpool and Holyhead, the numbers in excess of 5000 requiring extra vessels to cope with the surge. More than 4000 tourists landed in Dublin airport and Aer Lingus announced one of its busiest Whitsun holiday periods with 1800 passengers flying out, a 25 per cent increase on the previous year's figures, mainly to destinations on the Isle of Man and Jersey.

Of those who preferred to stay in the fair city more than 11,000 visited the zoo on the Saturday and Sunday, not exactly a record but greatly in excess of previous Whitsuntides. The outlying resorts of Bray, Dún Laoghaire, Dollymount, Sandymount and Killiney were crowded with families, the parents determined in light of the miserable summer of 1950 to take the sun while they could. There were, however, few brave enough to try swimming in the cold Irish Sea. The hills were alive with the sound of walkers and for those less energetic there was racing in Baldoyle and an international friendly in Dalymount Park. The only sources of entertainment not greatly attended were the political rallies and party meetings. One touch of sunshine makes the whole world kin.

15 May 1961

Flight to the Congo

The African territory once known as the Belgian Congo became the Republic of the Congo on 30 June 1960 and twelve days later the Congolese government requested military assistance from the United Nations to maintain its territorial independence. On 28 July 1960 Lieutenant-Colonel Murt Buckley led the 32nd Irish Battalion there as part of the peacekeeping force. Irish troops were to stay in the Congo until 1964.

Reinforcements of weapons and ammunition were flown out from home in large Globemaster aircraft and early on the morning of Monday 15 May 1961 a plane loaded with NATO rifles and anti-tank guns took off from Baldonnel military aerodrome. Its cargo was to supply the 34th Battalion, the Irish UN forces in situ, and among its passengers were arms experts to instruct the soldiers in the use of these new weapons.

It was a typical Irish summer's day with heavy gathering clouds. The Globemaster took off without incident but at 3500 feet the propellor of number one engine began to give trouble. It was decided that the weather was unsuitable for a return to Baldonnel so the control tower of Dublin airport was alerted and full emergency measures were taken in preparation for the landing. The pilot had succeeded in feathering the engine and with three props working began the descent. Fire engines and ambulances followed the plane as it landed without incident.

It taxied up behind No 2 hangar and immediately army personnel, who had been informed of the emergency, imposed security arrangements while mechanics began to mend the propellor. The passengers, all wearing the blue berets that marked them out as UN forces, were asked to stand by in case the flight could begin again in the afternoon. They were later stood down, except for a few left to guard the plane overnight.

16 May 1945

'A small nation that…has never surrendered her soul'

On Sunday 13 May 1945 Winston Churchill (1874-1965), who had led Britain in the Second World War, made a victory broadcast. Understandably flushed with victorious euphoria he was lavish in his praise of the allies, including 'the loyalty and friendship of Northern Ireland', but less so when he turned his attention to 'Éire', suggesting that her neutrality was a betrayal. The reply of Éamon de Valera (1882-1975) came on the following Wednesday, in a broadcast from Radio Éireann. It was a masterpiece of restraint, generosity and consideration as well as a sharp rebuttal of Churchill's criticisms. That section of a wide-ranging speech that was clearheaded and realistic about the postwar prospects for Europe and Ireland was brief but incisive.

He began by being terribly understanding about Churchill's state of mind, for which allowances could be made 'in the first flush of victory'. Ignoring the implicit challenge, he said that he knew what response he would have made to such unjust and unfair criticisms twenty-five years ago: 'But I have deliberately decided that that is not the reply I shall make tonight.' With a lightning sketch of Ireland's wrongs at England's hands he found a frame that adequately expressed the national view, unusually united on this occasion.

The rebuttal was dignified but firm:

> Mr Churchill is proud of Britain's stand alone after France had fallen and before America entered the war. Could he not find in his heart the generosity to acknowledge that there is a small nation that stood alone, not for one year or two, but for several hundred years against aggression; that endured spoliations, famines, massacres, in endless succession; that was clubbed many times into insensibility but each time on regaining consciousness, took up the fight anew; a small nation that could never be got to accept defeat and has never surrendered her soul?

17 May 1926

'Grateful appreciation'

Seanad Éireann, the Irish Senate, has been a somewhat perplexing institution with its various and limited systems of election, its extremely limited power and the lack of clear public perception of its role. It had over the years a more interesting membership than the Dáil, with notables such as W.B. Yeats, Oliver St John Gogarty, Conor Cruise O'Brien and Mary Robinson, and always seemed to deal with aesthetic matters with greater ease and confidence than the lower house. A typical early event was the formal statement of acceptance of a donation by Cornelius Sullivan, a rich Irish-American lawyer who had been born in County Kerry.

Sullivan had succeeded in obtaining six portraits of distinguished Irishmen that had been offered for sale in New York and donated them to the National Gallery in trust for the nation. At a session of the senate on Monday 17 May 1926 the upper house took the opportunity of passing a resolution placing on record its 'grateful appreciation' of the donation. The portraits were of John O'Leary, the old Fenian who had such an influence on the young Yeats; Æ (George Russell), the mystic, poet, painter and apostle of the cooperative movement; Senator Yeats himself; Standish O'Grady, the novelist whose main theme was Ireland's epic mythological past; Douglas Hyde, founder of the Gaelic League and later Ireland's first president, and George Moore, the novelist and ironic chronicler of the Irish Renaissance.

The resolution was proposed by Gogarty, the Buck Mulligan of *Ulysses* and no mean litterateur himself, who said that behind the gift lay a great deal of power for the development of the country. To obtain the pictures in the face of public bidding in New York was no gratuitous operation. Colonel Maurice Moore, the novelist's elder brother, seconded the motion, which was passed by acclamation.

18 May 1931

Prima Pavlova

Anna Matveyevna Pavlova (b. 1881), possibly the most famous of all modern ballet dancers, died of pneumonia on Friday 23 January 1931 because the surgery that might have saved her would have meant the end of her career as a prima ballerina assoluta. She was not quite fifty. The Pavlova company continued its scheduled summer tour without its star and opened in the Gaiety Theatre on Monday 18 May 1931. The result was, as one critic said 'something akin to *Hamlet* without the prince' but some of the glamour and wisps of glory still adhered to a company that had Fokine as its original choreographer.

The opening performance was a sell-out and the audience stood to applaud for minutes when the final curtain came down. The highlight should have been Pavlova's breathtaking 'Dying Swan', with music by Saint-Saens, but wisely it was not attempted by any of the ballerinas. Instead they went en fête, opening with 'A Polish Wedding' with music by Krupsinski. As one observer put it: 'Reds, blacks, silvers and golds chased each other until the very theatre seemed to glow.'

Developing the Polish theme, the company presented 'Chopiana' based upon the mazurkas, waltzes, preludes and polonaise of the native son. Other composers featured were Gounod and Moussorgsky. From the press accounts of the opening night there was a mixture of sadness and bravura, while competent dancers persuaded that the glory had not departed. One critic in a moment of obscure enthusiasm suggested: '"Persian Dance" gave Cleo Nordi the possibility of proving that fluid angles might make cubism attractive.' The spirit of the missing star continued to haunt the theatre and there were many among the enthusiastic Dublin balletomanes who knew that the divine Anna's last recorded words were: 'Fetch me my swan costume!'

19 May 1798

'All that delirium of the brave'

Lord Edward Fitzgerald (1763-98) was the twelfth child of the Duke of Leinster and reared in Ireland in a strong reformist household. Joining the army he was wounded in America during the Revolutionary War and became an Irish MP, an ally of Grattan. He was strongly influenced by the ideals of the French Revolution and was cashiered from the army for advocating the abolition of hereditary titles. Impatient with the slow progress of constitutional reform he joined the United Irishmen and, as one with most experience, soon assumed headship of the military committee.

The preferred strategy was a French invasion but Fitzgerald's marriage to the illegitimate daughter of the Duke of Orleans, a noted 'aristo', was given as the reason for the refusal to cooperate of the Directory, the French administration at the time. The alternative was for the United Irishmen to rise at home. The movement was riddled with informers in the pay of the town-major, Henry Charles Sirr, who as head of the city police was in charge of anti-subversion. Fitzgerald managed to elude the swoop in Bridge Street that netted many members of the Leinster committee but with a £1000 price on his head it was not long until Sirr learned from a barrister called Magan that he was in hiding in a house in Thomas Street.

In the raid on his hiding place on Saturday 19 May 1798, although ill with fever, he defended himself fiercely, stabbing Captain William Swan, Sirr's assistant, and killing Captain Daniel Ryan, one of the attackers. He surrendered only after being shot in the shoulder by Sirr. He was taken to Kilmainham, moved to Dublin Castle and finally died in Newgate in Cornmarket of septicaemia from his untreated wound on 4 June. His arrest was the subject of a famous print by George Cruikshank, the illustrator of Dickens's early works.

20 May 1927

'Necessary to the maintenance of discipline'

Post Office workers in Dublin in the late spring of 1927 expressed their disapproval of their treatment by J.J. Walsh (1880-1948), the Minister for Posts and Telegraphs. At a meeting of the Post Office Workers' Union (POWU) on Wednesday 18 May 1927 a resolution adopted unanimously demanded his removal from any further connection with the department. On Friday 20 May, the proposers, seconders and supporters of the motion were suspended from duty indefinitely with immediate effect. The actual suspension was ordered by P.S. O'Hegarty (1879-1955), secretary to the department, in the absence of the minister and applied to Messrs Buckley (Dublin Postal), Hayes (Dublin Parcels), Fox (Dublin Central), Brady (Rathmines) and Miss Little (Dublin Telephones). When Walsh returned he approved the action as 'necessary to the maintenance of discipline'.

The POWU had objected strongly to recent actions of the minister in appointing three outsiders over the heads of senior qualified Dublin staff members and to a speech he made in which he suggested that the Dublin officials were guilty of malpractice. The facts that Walsh and O'Hegarty, both from Cork, had been friends since childhood, although not mentioned overtly, was known and privately commented on and that the speech Walsh had made was intemperate to say the least, were used by a deputation of members of the Executive Council of the Irish Free State to plead for commonsense, especially as William Norton, one of its members, was a senior member of the Labour Party and Secretary of the POWU. They met Walsh and President Cosgrave and, while agreeing that the call for Walsh's removal 'could not be tolerated', they won the right for the suspended members to be allowed 'to furnish an explanation'. There was a general air of people being let off the hook and the near certainty of reinstatement.

21 May 1957

'Starvation once again'

The general election of March 1957 returned the self-styled 'party of government' Fianna Fáil and dismissed the Fine Gael-Labour-Clann na Poblachta coalition to the opposition benches. De Valera and Lemass led the cabinet and among its new TDs were Charles Haughey and Kevin Boland, names of significance in the later history of the party. The country was in one of its recurring recessions – something that could, of course, be blamed on the previous government. The unemployment situation was dire. The first rushed budget by the new government removed food subsidies and the people took to the streets.

The main demonstration agency, the Unemployed Protest Committee, called a cleverly unusual demo for Tuesday 21 May 1957, a march to Leinster House by 3000 women – 'unemployed mothers', as they termed themselves. And since the word 'mother' implies children, there were many perambulators and lots of dramatically effective children in arms. When they reached Molesworth Street they found the gates locked and fifty Gardaí facing them in front and twenty behind them at the other end of the street. Some men made it to the gates on Kildare Street and called on TDs inside to come out.

As the crowd in Molesworth Street grow more impacted a sense of hysteria began to be felt. When a knot of people with a pram in their midst tried to push past a young Garda on the pavement the pram was turned on its side and for a moment it seemed as if there might be a scuffle leading to worse violence. The Garda apologised to the owner and good humour was restored. As the crowd moved to College Green the protesters sang to a well-known tune, 'Starvation once again; starvation once again. No bread, no butter, no tea, no sugar. Starvation once again.'

22 May 1953

Air Corps tragedy

A Seafire, a prop-driven fighter of the Army Air Corps No 1 Squadron, one of four engaged on a training flight on Friday 22 May 1953, was on its return approach to Gormanstown aerodrome when it suddenly dived into the sea. The pilot was Lieutenant F.J. Coghlan, a twenty-six-year-old bachelor, the only son of Captain and Mrs P.J. Coghlan of 150 Gracepark Road, Drumcondra. He had been commissioned in 1947 from the Irish Military College and had joined the Air Corps a year later. His plane had been one of six that had taken part in the fly-over in Dublin on Easter Sunday, nearly seven weeks earlier, to mark the opening of An Tóstal. The planes had flown over the Butlin holiday camp but no one had seen the crash.

When word of the incident reached Air Corps headquarters the Gormans-town chaplain went to Ben Head, the cliff that overlooks the location of the crash, and pronounced absolution. Boats were launched to search the waters round the site and they found the plane after some hours but there was no sign of the body. A patch of oil appeared about five hundred yards from the beach and the place was marked by a buoy. On the Saturday a fuel tank was washed ashore near the mouth of the Boyne, seven miles from the oil slick. A salvage party working from a trawler and motor launch all day failed to find the fuselage, in spite of help from a civilian diver.

It was another Gormanstown pilot who found the wreck of the fuselage on the Sunday at low tide. It lay in about twelve feet of water. It was hauled ashore after John Weldon, a Dublin Port and Docks diver, secured cables and when it came to the surface Coghlan's body was found inside.

23 May 1957

The Rose Tattoo

On 12 May 1957 Tennessee Williams's *The Rose Tattoo* was produced in the Pike, the small, avant-garde theatre run by Alan Simpson and Carolyn Swift. The theatre had been the first to stage Beckett's *Waiting for Godot* and Behan's *The Quare Fellow* and early English-language versions of plays by Sartre and Ionesco, so it was entirely appropriate to offer the work of one of America's leading dramatists. Because of its apparent disregard of the establishment both government and Church regarded the Pike's very existence as subversive, which in the prevailing Zeitgeist in Ireland it seemed to be.

The play, which premièred on Broadway on 3 February 1951, dealt with the life of Serafina Delle Rose, an passionate Italian-American widow in Louisiana, who is inconsolable on her husband's death but, learning of his affair, recovers some zest for life. One utterly shocking item was the mention of a condom, meant to fall out of the pocket of her new wooer. In the Pike production the act was mimed, sufficient to have Simpson arrested and imprisoned when Gardaí invaded the theatre on Thursday 23 May. The charge was that of showing a 'lewd entertainment' and in the storm of intellectual rage and mockery that followed from Becket, O'Casey and Behan, among others, it seemed as if the state was moving against a venture it could not control.

The case against Simpson provided much work for lawyers, arguing on such matters as to whether the instructions given to the arresting officer by his superintendent and his written statement were privileged or not. The case was finally thrown out by the Supreme Court more than a year later but the Pike never recovered from the crippling legal costs. It was in essence the last stand of the ultra-Catholic Censorship Board that gradually ceased to have any effective role.

24 May 1935

'Since the time of the Tans'

Although Fianna Fáil had attained a ruling majority by January 1933 the members were still regarded with suspicion and some fear by their adversaries, including the residual members of the previous administration, Cumann na nGaedheal. It was believed that Fianna Fáil deputies came armed into the Dáil chamber. It caused little surprise that on Friday 24 May 1935 a Fianna Fáil county councillor was charged with the possession of ammunition – one 0.303 bullet, six grenades and two detonators – without the necessary firearms certificate. He was Michael Newell, and his court was the military tribunal in Collins Barracks. He lived in Cnoc na nDruscacha, Galway, and since Irish was his first language, M.J. O'Brien, the prosecutor, began in Irish but reverted to English with the offer of an interpreter if required.

O'Brien described how when the Gardaí visited Newell's house on 24 January they found the bullet. They asked him if there was any more of the same material and got the reply that there was some 'since the time of the Tans'. He led them to a field and unearthed six grenades. Later that night he delivered the detonators (which from their rusty condition had lain there for some years) to the Gardaí. The grenades proved to be at least ten or twelve years old.

It was becoming clear that here was no case to answer and the credentials of the accused were impressive. He had been on active service in 1916 and applied for a military pension, was a Fianna Fáil nominee on the county council, president of the local organisation, served on both the old age pensions and agricultural committees and was a member of Galway Sluagh of the Volunteer Force. It did not take long for the tribunal to find him guilty of a technical offence but it announced that it would impose no punishments.

25 May 1921

Burning the Custom House

The War of Independence, begun in January 1919 as a series of guerrilla actions, had reached a pitch of brutality two years later. Indeed the last six months before the truce of 11 July 1921 were the bloodiest. Éamon de Valera, sensing that world opinion was turning in favour of the IRA and wishing characteristically to give its activities a moral basis, insisted in his capacity as príomh-aire (prime minister) of Dáil Éireann on declaring war on Britain on 11 March 1921. He disliked the inevitable nastiness of guerrilla warfare and longed for 'one good battle with five hundred men on each side'. The one example of such a confrontation turned out to be a propaganda triumph and a tactical and aesthetic disaster.

De Valera urged the burning of Gandon's masterpiece, the Custom House. It held the local government records and its loss would seriously compromise the working of the civil service. Michael Collins was strongly against the plan but it went ahead anyway. On the afternoon of Wednesday 25 May, about a hundred and twenty IRA volunteers made their way in small numbers to the site and at 1pm took over the unguarded building. The caretaker was shot dead when trying to call the police. The intruders scattered saturated cotton and petrol throughout the building and when a group of Auxies surrounded it they set it on fire.

In the action that followed five volunteers were killed and eighty taken prisoner. Collins's disapproval of the action from a military point of view did nothing to improve his relations with de Valera but it achieved its political purpose in bending Lloyd George towards considering a truce. The building continued to burn for eight days, gutting the entire interior. After the war the façade was faithfully restored, although some striking elements of Gandon's original were lost for ever. The Custom House now houses the Department of the Environment and Local Government.

26 May 1979

Rubbish on the streets

In 1979 the cleansing department of Dublin Corporation under normal conditions collected and disposed of around 3000 tons of garbage each week. That spring a number of industrial disputes caused the service to suffer disruption. A Corporation spokesman admitted on Saturday 26 May 1979 that they had not managed a complete cleansing operation since March and now the amount of uncollected refuse was somewhere between 10,000 and 20,000 tons. The current dispute involved the maintenance men at the depots. The result was that there was a severe shortage of working trucks and no collections could take place in the affected suburban areas, where unsightly piles of garbage were increasing each day. In the city centre, where the risks to health were potentially greatest, some collections of about 1000 tons a week were managed.

The presence of such organic waste was regarded as an eventual risk to health and a more immediate source of vermin infestation. Con Healy, the chief health inspector for the Eastern Board, reported a rush on the board's pest control services. Rats, with a reliable source of good unhealthy food so conveniently placed, were bound to increase in number and although the illnesses they could spread were serious, the likelihood of endemic disease in a normally sterile area was slight.

Healy urged all householders to become temporary waste-disposal operatives during the period of disruption. Noel Carroll, a Corporation official, could offer no professional help but asked for a DIY approach. He listed the various tip-heads where individuals might dispose of their domestic detritus: on the north side Dunsink Lane in Finglas and Balleally in Lusk; Ballyogan in Leopardstown and Friarstown in Bohernabreena in the south. Those with incineration facilities were encouraged to use them and there was a general call for commonsense about hygiene.

27 May 1954

Irish for post office workers

The question of the national language is one that has exercised Irish society ever since the founding of Saorstát Éireann in 1921 and continues to be a topic of enthusiasm for some and execration for others. The tongue used as a first language by a large majority for all practical purposes is English and while most Irish people look upon the language with benevolence, the sad fact remains that Irish, however effective as a means of modern communication and a convenient alternative private language abroad, it is not strictly necessary as a medium for the majority. It remains an official language, however, and something more than lip service should be paid by government agencies.

At the annual conference of the Post Office Workers' Union held in Dublin on Thursday 27 May 1954 a motion was tabled by the James's Street branch asking that only temporary officers born since 1921 be required to do an oral Irish test. S.S. O'Brien doubted that many people born before that date (apart from those from Irish-speaking homes) had ever heard a word of Irish spoken outside school. 'Many temporary officers only got into the service through the misfortune of being out of work.' Those who did 'scrape' through had no occasion ever to use the language after their appointment and the little Irish they learned was quickly forgotten. He emphasised that neither as a branch nor individually were they opposed to the revival but the present system did nothing to further it.

E. Leddy from the Blackrock branch said he knew people who had passed the oral test who did not give 'two hoots' about the language. He considered that the whole system was a farce. With general assent and a realisation among the delegates that the resolution would achieve nothing it was passed and forwarded to the authorities for consideration.

28 May 1779

Bard of Erin

The first child and only son of John Moore, grocer and wine merchant, who hailed form Kerry, and Anastasia Codd, the eldest daughter of a Wexford provision merchant, was born above his father's shop in 12 Aungier Street on Friday 28 May 1779. They could afford to give their son an excellent education, especially in the ancient classics, and after the Catholic Relief Act of 1793 became law he was permitted to attend Trinity College. There he met and became friendly with Robert Emmet, whose radical activities and revolutionary ambitions were an open secret. Once, when Moore played the tune for which he would afterwards write the words of 'Let Erin Remember', Emmet, who was fifteen months his senior, cried, 'Oh that I were at the head of 20,000 men marching to that air.'

Moore was no revolutionary but his genuine patriotism would perhaps do as much for 'Erin' in his English exile as the more dramatic heroes. He made no secret of his admiration for his college friend who died so cruelly in 1803. In the first number of the famous *Irish Melodies,* published in 1808, he wrote his most obvious verse tribute in 'O, Breathe Not His Name' and it is clear that 'The Minstrel Boy' and 'Lay His Sword by His Side' were inspired by Emmet as well. He also made Sarah Curran, Emmet's fiancée, eternally famous as the subject of 'She Is Far from the Land'.

Moore spent most of his life in England, the darling of Whig drawing-rooms, where his perennially cheerful mien and splendid tenor voice as he sang his own songs about harps that once, waters that met in valleys so sweet and the tear and the smile in Erin's eye eventually won his own country a modicum of English respect, cultural at least. He died in 1852.

29 May 1984

Drug trials

Niall Rush died on Tuesday 29 May 1984 in the privately owned Institute of Clinical Pharmacology. The young man, who had been undergoing regular treatment for a personality disorder, was taking part in a clinical drug trial and had been given a test injection of Eproxidine. He had been a regular in the institute, visiting it eleven times in the previous six years. The fee for taking part in the tests was £20. What had not been realised by the staff of the institute was that Rush had been on Depixol, an antipsychotic sedative, and had had a strong injection on the day before he was given the test drug.

The inquest into Rush's death was held over the two days 4-5 September 1984 and the jury returned a verdict of cardiac depression caused by the interaction of the two drugs. They also added a rider calling for the setting up of an independent review body to monitor drug testing and for the introduction of legislation to control the tests. After the inquest Kevin Rush, Niall's father, former Irish Ambassador to Luxembourg, said that although the death had been a great tragedy for his wife Kathleen and himself it would not have been needless death after all 'if something were done to protect other volunteers for the tests'.

Dr Austin Darragh, chairman of the board of the institute, emphasised that the volunteers who came to the clinic were not 'guinea pigs' but people who took part in trials that had benefits for everyone in the community. He too welcomed the call by the jury for a review of the screening process but observed that the case had shown the high standards with which trials were carried out. Barry Desmond, the Minister for Health, announced that proposed legislation would cover the jury's rider.

30 May 1932

The Far-Off Hills

In the list of Abbey dramatists, Lennox Robinson, the theatre's long-time manager and historian, is sometimes overlooked. Yet he wrote some excellent plays, both comic and serious that, like the plays of the Ulster playwright, George Shiels, could always be depended upon to make a profit when times were hard, especially in the 1930s. Neither a Synge nor an O'Casey and psychologically more satisfying and wittier than either, his knowledge of stagecraft was exemplary. His genial satire of small-town emotions, *Drama at Inish* (1933), is at once literary and funny, and such comedies as *The White-headed Boy* (1916) and *The Far-Off Hills* (1928) have safely preserved an older Ireland while retaining their viability as theatre.

The last named of these was chosen to mark the return of the Abbey company from their transatlantic tour. The author appeared on stage before the opening performance on Monday 30 May 1932. He hoped that the 'welcome back' aspect of the evening could be dealt with before the play should begin and he was warmly applauded. But any hopes he and the management might have had about the dreaded 'entry applause' were vain. As each well-known actor made a first entrance the action was held up while the audience greeted old friends. For Barry Fitzgeraid and his brother Arthur Shields, Hollywood fame was still more than a decade away and the peerless F.J. McCormick (Peter Judge) was just another ensemble player. Later Abbey 'names' – May Craig, Eileen Crowe, P.J. Carolan and Ria Mooney – had not yet achieved the cinematic recognition that led *Dublin Opinion*, the satirical monthly, to comment: 'There's another Abbey actor that was.'

The play, with its nearly blind paterfamilias, its three marriageable daughters (one of whom thinks she wants to be a nun) and a spate of matchmaking, is still playing somewhere in Ireland.

31 May 1941

Luftwaffe over Dublin

The long Whit weekend was in full swing as midnight revellers made their boisterous way home on Saturday 31 May 1941. Some, residents of Summerhill, suddenly became aware of the sound of an aeroplane flying low. They could see the searchlights, recently installed down by the docks, begin to lance the sky and some could tell from the broken hum of the engine and the black crosses on the wing and swastikas on the tail that it was a Luftwaffe bomber. It was not the first time that bombs had been dropped on Dublin; some had fallen on the southside on 2 and 3 January 1941, causing only a few injuries, but the crumps these residents heard of four bombs falling justly terrified them.

A 250lb bomb fell at the junction of North Circular Road and North Richmond Street, demolishing No 582 and setting the house next door on fire. All the occupants were rescued by firefighters from the Dorset Street station, still alive but badly injured. By now the largest bomb, the fourth, estimated as 500lb, had landed on the North Strand Road beside the Newcomen Bridge over the Royal Canal. It created most devastation and caused the greatest loss of life. The second, smaller, bomb fell in Rutland Place off Summerhill and the third, landing in the Phoenix Park, damaged the American Ambassador's house and Áras an Uachtaráin. Thirty-four people were killed, ninety injured and five hundred left homeless.

The raid seemed so inexplicable that all kinds of theories abounded: Éire wasn't neutral enough, RAF pilots flew captured Luftwaffe planes using captured German bombs (an explanation acceptable to Eduard Hempel, the German representative in Dublin). The probable cause was the jettisoning of lethal cargo by a plane the pilot of which was anxious to return safely to base.

1 June 1941

Collateral damage

Dubliners woke up on Sunday 1 June 1941 still bewildered and dismayed that their city had been blitzed with significant loss of life and many injuries. Then a comparatively trivial and not unconnected local event occurred that would have merited much greater coverage in the following day's newspapers under normal circumstances, adding to the sense of unreality that pervaded the city. As it was it had to take second place to such headlines as 'German bombs were dropped on Dublin' and make do with 'Dublin Houses Collapse' with the sub-head: 'Three Persons Killed.'

Two houses collapsed and a third partially fell in Old Bride Street just after 10 o'clock on the Sunday morning. The fatalities were Mrs Linskey (30), her five-month-old baby Noel and a pensioner, Samuel O'Brien (72), who had worked in Guinness's. They lived in No 46, an all but derelict tenement. The street, which was in the environs of St Patrick's Cathedral, and about a mile and a half from the site of the North Strand bomb, has long gone, replaced by urgently needed redevelopment; it is more than probable that they were badly affected by blast from that explosion. There was a report that the collapse had taken place shortly after a heavy lorry had passed through the narrow street but collateral damage (a term not known then) was almost certainly the cause.

Corporation officials immediately evacuated the nearest buildings and arranged for twenty-nine occupants to receive temporary accommodation in the Red Cross headquarters in Mespil Road. There were sixty officials on duty and they already had the task of placing four hundred and forty other refugees from North Strand. There was general relief when news came that a hundred houses in Cabra not due for occupation for another three weeks were being made ready for immediate use.

2 June 1954

The interparty government

The 15th Dáil was elected on 18 May 1954 and had its preliminary session on Wednesday 2 June, when the seventh government of Ireland was appointed. The parties in the uneasy coalition were Fine Gael, Labour and Clann na Talmhan (Party of the Land) which had been founded in 1939. The main cement was opposition to Fianna Fáil, the self-regarding 'party of government' that with sixty-five seats had failed to win an overall majority.

As the largest party, with fifty seats, Fine Gael nominated John A. Costello as Taoiseach (for the second time) and secured the departments of Agriculture, Defence, Education, External Affairs, Finance, Health and Local Government. Labour, with nineteen deputies, was given the office of Tánaiste in the person of the head of the party, William Norton, who had the Industry and Commerce portfolio. Labour also had Justice, Posts and Telegraphs and Social Welfare. Clann na Talmhan, with five TDs, was appropriately given responsibility for Lands.

The cabinet was notable (and unusual) in the politics of the time for the inclusion of a number of youngish men. Brendan Corish (1918-1990), Minister for Social Welfare, who would later lead the Labour party, was thirty-five and Liam Cosgrave (b. 1920), the son of the President of the Executive Council of the Free State, 1922-32, was two years younger. Both men had been toddlers when the Civil War, memories of which so bedevilled Irish politics, was raging. There was a gleam of hope that old bitterness might become assuaged, even though such well-known Treatyites as Richard Mulcahy (Education) and Seán Mac Eoin (Defence) were still to the fore.

A worsening balance-of-payments deficit and consequent new taxes, a renewed IRA campaign and a further population decrease led to a general election in March 1957 and a return to power of Fianna Fáil with seventy-eight seats.

3 June 1957

Manuscript Room

In the Fellows Garden in Trinity College there stands an elegant bijou building that was established as a magnetic observatory in 1837. Modern technology had made it redundant and it fell into disuse. Then someone had the happy thought that it would make an ideal manuscript room and its interior was refurbished by architect Ian Roberts with the collaboration of Dr H.W. Parke, vice-provost and librarian. On Monday 3 June 1957 the room was ready and in front of a large crowd the then Taoiseach Éamon de Valera, declared it open.

At the ceremony Dr A.J. McConnell, the provost, gave a quick sketch of the library's history. The magnificent Georgian building dated from 1732 and over two hundred years it had become a national treasure. The first extension, the new Reading Room, had been opened in 1937 by the head of the government and it pleased him that almost exactly twenty years later that same august person, holding the same high office, was present to open this next extension. There was no intention to use the annex as a place to display manuscripts or remove the college's treasures, such as *The Book of Kells* or *The Book of Durrow*. It was instead a place of research for scholars from all over the world.

The occasion gave McConnell an opportunity to advise the company that it was proposed to build a much bigger extension to house the facilities that a modern library needed to supply and that they would be appealing for financial assistance in the very near future. De Valera, who had been leading the 16th Dáil for only a few months, in his reply praised the college's collection of priceless artefacts, including *The Book of Armagh*, *The Book of Leinster* and *The Annals of Ulster*, but made no comment about finance.

4 June 1959

Anyone can drive a bus

Pub conversations, especially boastful ones, can lead the innocent or foolhardy into hot water. So Peter O'Shea, a twenty-five-year-old lorry driver from Ballybough Road, discovered to his cost on Thursday 4 June 1959 in the Dublin District Court. About three weeks earlier he had an exhaustive conversation with some visiting Englishmen about the driving of heavy lorries and buses. The strict rules about driving experience enforced by CIÉ, under which bus drivers had to have many years behind the steering wheel, were rubbished as nonsense.

When challenged, O'Shea admitted that although he had been driving heavy vehicles for five years he had never driven a bus. His friends immediately bet him that he couldn't drive a bus. He couldn't resist the challenge, walked to nearby CIÉ Clontarf garage, managed to find a bus with keys in the ignition and headed out the Howth Road with his challengers as passengers. He parked without mishap in Grace Park Road in Drumcondra. These events he related to the Garda who arranged for him to appear before District Justice Reddin.

He told the judge that he had been working in England and would return there if he could not find employment at home. He admitted that he had taken the bus 'on an impulse' and added that he had only a couple of bottles of stout. The judge was inclined to be lenient and while chiding him for his 'very foolish' behaviour wondered aloud why he didn't take a double-decker while he was at it. 'This was only a single-decker – I could drive it myself.' Admonishing O'Shea that it was time he grew up he fined him £5 'for taking a CIÉ bus from Clontarf garage without permission'. The court allowed him fourteen days to pay the fine or go to prison for two months.

5 June 1961

Rotarian Taoiseach Lemass

Seán Lemass (1899-1971), after years of faithful service to his leader and patient waiting in the wings, finally became Taoiseach on 26 June 1959. It was fitting, then, that two years later on 5 June 1961 – a Monday, Rotary's dedicated meetings day – he should become an honorary member of the Dublin Rotary club in the Royal Hibernian Hotel. In this he joined a list of distinguished honorary fellows such as President Eisenhower, King Gustav IV of Sweden, M. Henri Spaak of France, Mohamet of Pakistan and Sir Winston Churchill. At the induction, which was carried out by the Dublin president Walter S. Douglas, he was hailed by Grant Stockdale, the American Ambassador, as 'Rotarian Taoiseach Lemass'.

The induction happily coincided with the club's fiftieth anniversary and Douglas thought the acceptance of membership by a gifted statesman, who had paid tribute to Rotary in the past, showing himself sympathetic to its aims and indicating his recognition of the need for closer contact between all men of goodwill, was a fitting culmination to the anniversary celebrations.

Lemass, whose years of public service had given him an acute awareness of the need to drag Ireland, screaming if necessary, into modern life, was able to reassure the world that Ireland's image of a place not very efficient had largely vanished. He admitted that it still persisted in some places but that Rotary had played and still played an important role in banishing the myth.

Stockdale took the opportunity to announce that the building of the new United States embassy building would commence in a hundred and twenty days, a characteristic transatlantic usage to the ears of the Dublin Rotarians who quickly changed it mentally to 'four months or so'. He reminded the audience that their club was the first ever founded outside the North American continent.

6 June 1948

'Jolly mouldy bread'

On 15 May 1948 the bakers of Dublin went on strike to demand an increase in their weekly wage of 11s for van drivers and other workers, £1/7s for oven-men and £1/0s/6d for table hands. An initial offer of 9s by the Labour Court to a majority of the workers was rejected by the union negotiating committee. The employers, the Guild of Irish Bakers, the Dublin Master Bakers' Committee Branch of the Federated Union of Employers refused to advance the Labour Court award unless the government increased the bread subsidy or the price of a loaf or relaxed control of the industry.

When the strike, which lasted three weeks, began to bite, a number of Dublin TDs acted as liaison between the opposing parties and the final resolution of the dispute was achieved when Daniel Morrissey, the Minister for Industry and Commerce, set up a special conference of the employers' organisation and the strikers' trade unions. During the strike, bread rationing was suspended and people could buy bread and flour in any shop in the Dublin area, not just in the bakery that held their ration books. This order was re-established soon after the strike was settled on Saturday 5 June, when both sides reached a agreement; the workers got their rises and the bakers were allowed to increase the cost of a 2lb loaf by a farthing (a quarter of a penny). This was regarded as enough to cover the increased wage-bill of £100,000.

On Sunday 6 June, the oven-men and other workers who were required to ready the plant for production after the three-week gap reported to such long-established firms as Brennans and Johnston, Mooney and O'Brien (the second of which reached doubtful immortality in James Joyce's *Ulysses* as 'jolly mouldy bread'.) Normal supplies were available on the Tuesday.

7 June 1925

The venerable Matt Talbot

Granby Lane leads from Granby Place to Dominick Street and on the morning of Trinity Sunday, 7 June 1925, an ill-dressed elderly man was using it as a shortcut to St Saviour's Church, one of two churches where he usually heard Mass. He collapsed and died and as no one could be found to identify him his body was taken to Jervis Street Hospital. There it was discovered that he wore a heavy chain round his waist that was deeply imbedded into the flesh, another chain round one arm, a strong cord round the other and a fourth chain taut beneath his knee. The heavy overcoat he always wore hid the evidence of these austerities but the slits in his trouser's knees were made so that his kneeling vigils on the steps of St Dominick's or the Jesuit Church in Gardiner Street were on the bare stone.

Matt Talbot, (1856-1925), the man who died that day, had been a semi-literate alcoholic who at twenty-eight managed to pull himself out of the depths to lead a life more like that of early Irish monk than a Dublin labourer. In his Spartan flat in Upper Rutland Street off Summerhill his bed was a board with a wooden pillow from which he rose at 2am to pray and again at 5am to attend early Mass before going to work. This regimen he concealed from his fellow workers although they knew his lunch was dry bread and cocoa without milk.

Word spread and at the funeral of this 'unknown' on 11 June the streets were lined all the way to Glasnevin. Evidence of his exceptional piety led to his being declared 'venerable', the first of three stages of sainthood, by Pope Paul VI in 1975. A new bridge over the Liffey was named in his honour three years later.

8 June 1859

'A first-rate Irish newspaper'

The modern *Irish Times*, Ireland's leading newspaper of record, became the country's first penny daily on Wednesday 8 June 1859. It was not the first to use the name – there was a short-lived predecessor (1823-5) – and from Tuesday 29 March it had appeared on Tuesdays, Thursdays and Saturdays. It owner, the twenty-three-year-old Major Lawrence Knox, wanted an organ that would represent Protestant nationalism. He was a follower of Isaac Butt's Home Rule League and had stood unsuccessfully as a parliamentary candidate for the movement. In its first leader he wrote:

> Our intention…is to make *The Irish Times* a first-rate Irish newspaper, complete in its details, sagacious and consistent in its policy and faithfully reflecting the opinions of the most independent, intelligent and truly progressive portion of Irish society.

Knox died in 1873 and the paper was sold to the Arnott family, the owners of one of Dublin's major department stores. It radically changed its politics, becoming the essential voice of southern unionism and concerning itself with ascendancy affairs. Its total identification with Britain led to such usages as 'our empire', 'our forces' and 'our queen'. It joined some other Dublin dailies in calling for the execution of the 1916 readers.

This niche mentality persisted into the 1920s, the newspaper concerning itself with British rather than Free State affairs. Under the charismatic R.M. Smyllie (1894-1954), who took over when the firmly unionist editor John Edward Healy died in 1934, it became more realistically Ireland-centred. It was Smyllie who encouraged Flann O'Brien to write an at first bilingual column, the 'Cruiskeen Lawn', as Myles na Gopaleen, the true hero of Boucicault's *The Colleen Bawn*. The newspaper also began to develop a reputation for comprehensive cultural coverage, as an enemy of the censorship board and as a publication largely free from clerical influence.

9 June 2004

The female of the species

Judge Gerard Haughton presided over a busy session of the Dublin Children's Court on Wednesday 9 June 2004. Two cases stood out: an assault on a Garda by a seventeen-year-old girl and the effect of a seventeen-year-old's jumping from a moving car. Neither party could be named but in this case the female of the species was more deadly than the male. On 14 October 2003 Garda Caitriona Houlihan, attached to Fitzgibbon Street station in the north inner city, stopped the girl for a routine drug search and was immediately attacked. She was kicked so hard on the knee that she fell to the ground. The girl attempted to head-butt two other Gardaí and kicked Garda Houlihan again on the patella. She was off work for two weeks and unable to drive for months afterwards. She was still undergoing physiotherapy and might need surgery. The girl pleaded guilty to the assault and to the possession of a small amount of cannabis 'for personal use'. Judge Haughton, finding that she neither apologised nor showed remorse, sentenced her to two months' imprisonment.

The youth had been driving an untaxed, uninsured car in the car park of a hotel in Tallaght on 14 December 2003. A Garda had caught hold of the door handle and the lad had driven off. Seconds later he jumped out of the moving car, which continued to move until it crashed into a jeep parked nearby. In court he pleaded not guilty to criminal damage and dangerous driving but admitted driving without documentation. In mitigation he said he had been using the car to do errands for his family, which included his own child and alcoholic traveller parents. Judge Haughton banned him from driving for three years, imposed two months' detention and ordered a hearing on 1 July on the other charges.

10 June 1951

George Gavan Duffy

E very Irish schoolchild knows that the Young Ireland movement was founded in 1842 by Thomas Davis, Charles Gavan Duffy and John Blake Dillon. Some Irish schoolchildren know that after being sent to Australia on penal servitude Duffy became premier of Victoria province there and was knighted. Very few Irish schoolchildren know that his son, George Gavan Duffy, became president of the High Court of the Republic of Ireland after a distinguished public and legal career.

George Gavan Duffy (1882-1951) was born in Cheshire on 21 October 1882 and educated in Nice and Stonyhurst College. He qualified as a solicitor in England, becoming one of the partners in the firm of Ellis, Leathley, Willis and Gavan Duffy, while maintaining a thorough knowledge of Irish affairs. He was effectively dismissed by his partners because of his defence of Roger Casement in 1916 but by the following year he was called to the Irish bar. A personal friend and supporter of Arthur Griffith, he was an obvious choice as Sinn Féin candidate and MP for South County Dublin in the landslide 1918 general election. He was with Seán T. Ó Ceallaigh, the unofficial Sinn Féin delegate to the Versailles peace talks, but expelled from France on Britain's instructions.

An important delegate at the Treaty negotiations, he became Minister for Foreign Affairs in the new Free State administration but soon resigned because of the government's treatment of republican prisoners. He returned to private practice, becoming senior counsel in 1929 and a High Court judge in 1936. He played a significant part in the drawing-up of the 1937 Constitution, noted for his interpretation of Irish constitutional matters in the light of current Catholic teaching. He was also noted for his generosity to those too poor to afford legal fees. He died in Dublin on Sunday 10 June 1951.

11 June 1925

'The people of Burke'

W.B. Yeats was appointed to Seanad Éireann in 1922, appropriately as Ireland's greatest literary figure, an opinion confirmed by his being awarded the Nobel Prize for literature the following year, the first of four Irishmen to be so honoured. It was a deliberate move to involve a minority voice, although Yeats's nationalist credentials were authentic. He spoke for the Protestants who found little affinity with the overtly confessional and publicly pious state. He was opposed to the censorship of films and even more vigorously the threatened Censorship of Publications Bill that finally became law in 1929.

His most famous senate speech was the address he gave on Thursday 11 June 1925, attacking the government's refusal to allow divorce. There was no constitutional mechanism in the Oireachtas for such a bill, except as a private member's motion which need a first reading in both houses in order to proceed. The day was warm and as his long speech increased in passion observers noticed that he began to sweat and his sixty-year-old face grew red. It became an appeal, not so much for the right to divorce but for his own Anglo-Irish people, 'the people of Burke':

> I am proud to consider myself a typical man of that minority. We to
> whom you have done this thing are no petty people. We are one of the
> greatest stocks of Europe. We are the people of Burke; we are the people
> of Grattan; we are the people of Swift, the people of Emmet, we are the
> people of Parnell. We have created the most of the modern literature of
> this country. We have created the best of its political intelligence…If we
> have not lost our stamina then your victory will be brief and your defeat
> final, and when it comes the nation may be transformed.

12 June 1935

Refused to recognise the court

John Fitzsimons of McGuinness Square, a cabman, and Thomas McGrattan, a printer's helper, of Kenny's Cottage off James's Street appeared for a second time before the military tribunal, charged with membership of an unlawful organisation and with assaulting, resisting and wilfully obstructing Garda Joseph Egan. Fitzsimons was also accused of shooting at Egan, with intent to murder him, and of having illegally in his possession nine grenade cases, an instructional Mills bomb, an egg bomb and thirty-two necks for bombs.

In the 1930s de Valera had reintroduced trial by court-martial for cases involving quasi-military matters, especially those involving the residual IRA, and as a matter of course both men, as members of the organisation, had refused to recognise the court. The president of the tribunal directed that a plea of 'not guilty' be entered on their behalf. The story featured in all the Dublin papers on Friday 12 June 1935.

The attack had happened exactly one month earlier and with fingerprint evidence found on a bicycle at the scene of the attack and IRA material including mobilising instructions found in the houses of both the accused next day there seemed to be no doubt that Fitzsimons was the perpetrator. (It took five detectives to hold him down when Detective-Sergeant Henry MacNamara, the 'dabs' expert, was taking his prints.) Thomas Murphy, already sentenced to two years for complicity in the shooting, refused to testify when called as a witness, saying, 'As a member of the Irish Republican Army I refuse to give evidence against these men.' At this both the accused applauded.

Fitzsimons, found guilty of all charges, was sentenced to ten years' imprisonment, McGrattan got six months for refusing to give the Gardaí information and Murphy, guilty of contempt, was sentenced to six months to run concurrently with his existing sentence.

13 June 1988

'The Tart with the Cart'

On Monday 13 June 1988, as part of Dublin's millennium celebrations, Ben Briscoe, Lord Mayor, unveiled a statue to one of the most famous of all Dublin women, the fishmonger in excelsis, Molly Malone – she who wheeled her wheelbarrow through streets broad and narrow, crying 'Cockles and mussels, alive, alive-o.' The statue, designed by Jeanne Rynhart, showing a proud-breasted woman in her twenties and her laden cart (not a wheelbarrow), was installed at the bottom of Grafton Street. The official unveiling marked the formal adoption, to much rejoicing, of 13 June as Molly Malone Day, although Molly herself was later on unceremoniously displaced by a Luas track – part of a retrofitted link between the city's red and green lines.

It did not take long for Anon, that prolific Dublin wit and author, to devise appropriate subtitles for the piece: 'The Tart with the Cart', 'The Dish with the Fish', 'The Trollop with the Scollop(s)', 'The Dolly with the Trolley' and less specifically 'The Flirt in the Skirt'. Her low-cut bodice was ascribed to 18th-century fashions, the prevalence of contemporary public breast-feeding and more pertinently to the notion that though she may have been a fishmonger by day ('and sure 'twas no wonder/for so were her mother and father before') she was a prostitute by night.

Molly Malone is still such a part of Dublin's mythology that only the very brave would suggest that the subject of the song first published in Cambridge, Massachusetts, in 1883 was a fiction, a myth with no pith. Some assiduous researcher discovered that a Molly Malone, aged twenty-nine, had died on 13 June 1699 and was buried in St John's Churchyard, probably the same Ms Malone whose name is to be found in St Werburgh's parish records. *Si non è vero, è ben trovato*. It was enough for the members of the Millennium commission and the donors of the statue, Jury's Hotel Group.

14 June 1980

Rehabilitation of prisoners

Michael Keating (b. 1946) was a teacher turned Fine Gael politician (later deputy leader of the Progressive Democrats) and, as opposition spokesman on urban affairs, he spoke out on Saturday 14 June 1980 on the need to reform the prison system. As the Fine Gael frontbencher with responsibility for Human Rights and Law Reform he urged rehabilitation as a way of diminishing the prison population. He assured his listeners that rehabilitation was in no sense 'going soft on crime' but a way of avoiding recidivism. The current prison system was, he said, extraordinarily expensive, highly inefficient and clearly unsuccessful.

The key to rehabilitation was to give meaning to life and a sense of belonging and being loved to a person who had lost such feelings. The task was, then, to 'rekindle in a prisoner he feeling that he or she has a place in our special order, has potentially a contribution to make.' He urged the setting up of a programme by which many members of the prison population could deal with people 'in the community, in institutions or otherwise, who badly need the investment of time and attention of others.'

He visualised a programme on which carefully selected prisoners under careful supervision could work with old people or people of all ages suffering handicap. It could extend to youth education in the form of programmes designed to de-glamourise crime for young people and giving them insights 'about the pitfalls of growing up in today's society':

> The list of meaningful and important work is almost endless. No one will deny that the need for people to give of their time and commitment to others is increasing all the time. And in many of our prison population there is the resource which could meet – I stress under careful supervision – much of that need.

15 June 1931

North and west

In 1931 the Abbey Theatre produced the characteristically bleak Ulster play, *Mixed Marriage*, by St John Ervine (1883-1971), once the theatre's manager. Set in Belfast it chronicles the effect of sectarian bitterness in the troubled year of 1911 when Ulster readied itself for civil war. The possible mixed marriage is that of Hugh Rainey with a Catholic girl, Norah Murray, whose death during a sectarian riot climaxes the play. His father John, who had tried to calm the endemic violence, becomes an intensifier of the horror when, dismayed at the misalliance, he withdraws from a strike that had briefly united the two warring tribes. The actors were drawn from the golden age ensemble of the original Abbey players, especially F.J. McCormick, Arthur Shields (brother of Barry Fitzgerald), Maureen Delaney and Eileen Crowe, and if they did not quite manage the harsh Belfast accents their acting carried them through.

Following tradition there was a curtain raiser, this time possibly the finest one-act Irish play ever, *Riders to the Sea*, which became a short opera with music by Vaughan Williams. The central part of Old Maurya had been played magnificently by Sara Allgood (the elder sister of Molly, the original Pegeen Mike) seven years earlier and on the opening night, Monday 15 June 1931, Synge aficionados watching with beady eyes as Shelagh Richards essayed the part. Those seeing the play for the first time were impressed but old Abbey hands hankered for the lost Sara, now heading for Hollywood. Bartley, the sole surviving son, was played by Denis O'Dea and Eileen Crowe and May Craig his sisters. It was hardly fair to the naturalistic main attraction to couple it with a play elemental in every sense of the word. It was the Synge play that was given the headlines and the column inches in the press.

16 June 1904

'She'll never leave him.'

Now famous worldwide as the date on which all the events of James Joyce's novel *Ulysses* occur, Thursday 16 June 1904 was chosen by him as a tribute to his mistress, later his wife, Nora Barnacle. Possessed of a free spirit and a distinctive surname, she proved the ideal companion for the Dublin genius. The name pleased Joyce's father ('She'll never leave him.'); it was ornithological rather than marine in source, originally Ó Cadhain, *cadhain* being the Gaelic word for a barnacle goose. They had met six days earlier while walking in Nassau Street, she tall, confident, auburn-haired and with a Galway lilt to her speech, he with bright blue eyes and a yachting cap, taken by her to be a Swedish sailor.

They were at ease immediately and learning that she was employed in Finn's Hotel in Leinster Street, a continuation of Nassau Street, he arranged to meet her on Tuesday 14 June. He was grievously disappointed when she failed to appear but managed to make another appointment for the evening of the 16th. They walked out to Ringsend and there, as Joyce told her, 'You made me a man,' a reference to their first sexual encounter. By Tuesday 11 October, at the beginning of their more-or-less permanent exile, they were staying as man and wife in Gasthaus Hoffnung, 16 Reitergasse, Zurich, the significance of the name (meaning hope) regarded as a good omen. (When they returned to Switzerland in October 1915 they were even more gratified to find it was now called Gasthaus Döblin.)

Although the day of their certainty became the mise-en-scène for *Ulysses* one looks in vain for Nora as a character. But surely her unabashed sensuality is the prime source for Molly Bloom and the disparaging cry 'Oh rocks!' is shared by the two women.

17 June 1349

The Black Death

The great plague known as the 'Black Death' is thought to have originated among the Mongol troops in the Crimea in 1346. It spread inexorably, reaching Sicily in 1347 and Italy, France, Britain and Ireland in 1349. It was a combination of the three virulent strains: bubonic (characterised by swellings in the groin and armpits and fatal if not treated in between 0.3 and 0.75 of cases), pneumonic and septicaemic, both fatal. The bacillus was spread by fleas parasitic on rodents, especially the brown rat.

It is impossible to determine with any accuracy the number of deaths, the contemporary accounts being awefully exaggerated. 'A third of the world died,' said Jean Froissart (*c.* 1337-*c.*1410), the French chronicler and poet, probably underestimating the actual number of fatalities. There was extreme social disorder, with many assuming that the plague marked the end of the world. Pope Clement VI granted remission of sin to all who had died because there were no priests to shrive them. In Ireland, Dublin and Drogheda were afflicted first and it was reckoned that, by Christmas 1348, 14,000 had died in Dublin. The source of this information was Friar John Clyn, a Franciscan based in Kilkenny, himself eventually a victim. He believed that in Dublin there was hardly a house in which only one person had died.

He had written a chronicle beginning with the birth of Christ and his final entry on Wednesday 17 June 1349 anticipated his own death, also indicating that he hoped for some survivor who could continue the work:

> …lest the writing should perish with the writer and the work fail with
> the worker, I leave parchment to carry on the work, if perchance any
> may survive or any of the race of Adam may be able to escape this
> pestilence and continue the work I have begun.

18 June 1954

Death in the Coombe Hospital

On 11 May 1954 Catherine McElroy, a five-week-old baby of Kells Road, Crumlin, who was a patient in the Coombe Hospital, fell out of bed. She subsequently died on 14 June and an inquest was held in the hospital on 18 June to determine the cause of death. Dr D.A. MacErlean, the Dublin city coroner, concluded that he was satisfied that the hospital was in no way to blame for the death of the child and that the fall had nothing to do with the death.

Nurse Ann Bergin said that she had visited the ward about midnight on 10 May. All the patients were asleep except the baby's mother, who had Catherine asleep beside her. A short time later she was aware of a noise and, returning, found the baby on the floor. The mother said she had been rubbing the baby's back and it had fallen. When the mother took the stand her version was slightly different. She said that after feeding the baby she had fallen asleep and when she awoke Mrs Gough, another patient, was holding the baby, and that it was she who had found her on the floor. Mrs McElroy contradicted Nurse Bergin's statement that Catherine had fallen when she was rubbing her back. Sister Mary Kelly, however, conformed Nurse Bergin's version.

Dr J. Cullen of the hospital staff, who had performed the post-mortem, said there was no evidence of skull fracture and that death, in his opinion, was due to toxaemia following an inflammatory condition of the skull, one not caused by the fall. In further confirmation Professor John McGrath, former state pathologist, who had examined the body two days before the inquest, found no evidence of fracture. In spite of the apparent conflict of witnesses' testimony the jury found that the toxaemia from some other source had caused the fatality.

19 June 1957

Ronnie Delany in Santry

The brightest star in Irish athletics in the 1950s was Ronnie Delany (b. 1935), who won the 1500-metres gold medal in the summer Olympics in Melbourne in 1956. Then in his twenty-third year and already a worthy ambassador for Ireland, he was the appropriate choice to cut the first sod of the proposed sports stadium in Santry on Wednesday 19 June 1957. It was to be the home of Clonliffe Harriers Athletic Club and a significant initiative to supply a need for the city and country. He fellow launcher was the Lord Mayor, Councillor Robert Briscoe. Work was to begin on the first part of the project – a 440-yard cinder track – the first of its kind in Ireland.

Briscoe used the opportunity to welcome Delany home from his American university, Villanova, near Philadelphia, Pennsylvania. He said that both there and at home they 'looked forward to his contributing more and more to the honour of Ireland in the field of sport'. He greatly approved of the building of the stadium and said that when the idea was first launched he was one of the first subscribers and was happy that night to present a second cheque for £25. Among the officials present were J.P. Keane, the City Manager, G.J. Jones, the sports architect, who designed the stadium, and Clonliffe's Billy Morton, who initiated the project.

Both Morton and Delany were at pains to point out that the stadium was for general use – 'the schools and colleges can train here in the afternoon and we will have it at night'. The chromium-plated shovel that was used for the ritual breaking of the first sod had been donated by Bernard P. McDonough, an Irish-American shovel manufacturer who had contributed $1000 to the fund.

20 June 1951

Death on the roadside

John Dalton, a fifty-six-year-old unmarried farm labourer from Rathcreedon, west County Dublin, had been drinking on the night of 12 August and after midnight headed unsteadily for home. He was accompanied for part of the way by another walker, a young man, but not long after showing signs of fatigue he announced that he would go no further but would lie down to sleep. His unnamed companion did not quite know what to do next but then two men arrived from Newcastle and they discussed the situation. Eventually, as the night was warm and Dalton was clearly incapable of walking further they decided to leave him asleep on the grass verge. They went on their way and thought no more about the affair.

About fifteen minutes after midnight a man named McPartlin came cycling along the Newcastle road and was passed out by a car with only one headlight lit. He could hear singing as the vehicle passed and its speed was such that in his estimation it would not be able to negotiate a bend that was close by. When it reached the turn it was forced to mount the grass verge and immediately McPartlin heard a loud cry.

These facts were revealed by R.J. McLoughlin SC, the prosecution counsel in a charge of manslaughter brought against John Jordan, aged forty, a window cleaner of Marino Green, Fairview, on Wednesday 20 June 1951. He told the court that Dalton had died on the road between Rathcoole and Newcastle about an hour after being struck by a car that halted for a short time before being driven off. Neither Jordan, the driver, nor any of the other occupants made any attempt to render assistance. The hearing was adjourned until the following day.

21 June 1980

The teaching of religion

A measure of slowly changing attitudes in Ireland in the matters of education and religion was seen on Saturday 21 June 1980, in a statement by Monsignor John McCarthy, the chairman of the Catholic Primary Managers' Association. He was responding to the decision of the INTO (Irish National Teachers' Organisation) that the teaching of religion should be optional. He averred that there was a contractual obligation upon teachers to give religious instruction, as recently confirmed by leading counsel. The association through him respected the right of a teacher to opt out of teaching religion, on conscientious grounds, providing that he or she was willing to cooperate in ensuring that the subject was taught, for example, making a reciprocal arrangement with another teacher.

The statement was welcomed but it became clear that another issue lay at the back of both positions. This was the question of the INTO's boycott of meetings of primary schools boards of management because they disagreed with the representation of teachers there and with the system for the appointment of teachers to posts. The appointment of an extra person with educational expertise had not helped and in the opinion of the association the INTO required that the only members of an appointment board should be the chairman of the management board and the school principal.

It seemed to the monsignor that parents must be involved in selecting the people who would teach their children and equally that it would be unfair that the school 'patrons', who acquired sites and made contributions for buildings and maintenance, should have no representation. The dispute continued with accusations of intransigence on both sides. John Wilson, the Minister for Education, and Francis McKiernan, Bishop of Kilmore, both urged a resolution. All sides could clearly recall a time when teachers were appointed by the manager and that was that.

22 June 1948

The finest moment of his career

On Tuesday 22 June 1948 all the Dublin papers and many throughout Ireland carried accounts of the death of Dr Vincent O'Brien (1871-1948) Mus Doc FRIAM, late the night before. He was born in Dublin in 1871, the son of the organist in St James's Church, and studied music in the Royal Irish Academy of Music. He composed one opera and some choral works and set some songs but his greatest claim to fame was by association with more famous pupils and colleagues.

He was organist and choirmaster in the Pro-Cathedral in Marlborough Street, 1902-46, and it was to him that Edward Martyn turned when, after his interest in drama and the Abbey Theatre waned, he established the Palestrina Choir there that later became the Schola Cantorum of the Dublin diocese. He was an early adviser of John McCormack, who described how they met when he walked into the cathedral one Sunday morning and simply sang for him. In 1913 he travelled as McCormick's accompanist on his first world tour and appeared on McCormack's early gramophone recordings from 1914. O'Brien was the accompanist when his pupil sang 'Panis Angelicus' at the High Mass in Phoenix Park that marked the conclusion of the Eucharist Congress in 1932.

Advised by the Dominican sisters in Eccles Street that one of their pupils had a remarkable voice, he investigated and knew that he had found an Irish diva in Margaret Burke Sheridan (1889-1958). He contrived to find the money to have her attend the Royal Irish Academy of Music. On his retirement as the first music director of Radio Éireann (1926-41), where he conducted the first public concerts of the station's orchestra in the 1930s, he said that his participation in the High Mass at the Eucharistic Congress was the finest moment of his career.

23 June 1953

The third question

Edward Henry Malone was struck by a bus in Dawson Street on 30 June 1951 and killed. At the hearing of the case in the High Court brought by Malone's wife, Maud, against CIÉ (Córas Iompair Éireann) for damages, the jury found that the driver of the bus had been negligent but that the late Mr Malone had been guilty of contributory negligence. The case was dismissed in light of the jury's findings. An appeal was brought on Mrs Malone's behalf to the Supreme Court and Tuesday 23 June 1953 was the day judgement was given. The basis of her appeal against the verdict, which negated any hope of damages, was that the judge had not put the 'third question' to the jury. This legal term, which had been in use for more than a hundred years was, in effect: could the driver by the exercise of reasonable care have avoided causing the injuries from which Malone later died, irrespective of his negligence?

At the original trial the judge had decided that in view of the evidence before the jury there was no need to put the question and his directions to the jury had been perfectly proper in the opinion of the appeal judges. They found that Malone had stepped out into the road and run across the path of the swerving, braking bus. Allowing the third question might have allowed the jury to find in favour of the deceased and in the absence of evidence their findings could have been set aside. The three appeal judges – Lavery, Kingsmill Moore and O'Byrne – were in agreement that the trial judge was correct in not putting the third question and that the appeal should be dismissed with costs.

24 June 1927

Feather pillows

The War of Independence and the Civil War that followed continued to affect Irish life not only politically and psychologically but legally. On Friday 24 June 1927, an action of claim by W.J. McClelland, headmaster of Clonmel Grammar School, against Desmond FitzGerald, Minister for Defence, who had taken up the post only that morning, was heard in Dublin before Mr Justice Hanna. The claim was for £808/10s due to him under an implied contract and £200 for alleged breach of that contract. The case centred on the occupation of the school by Free State soldiers on 9 August 1922 and their use of it for a considerable time thereafter. Ninety-seven men (including officers) of the 2nd Dublin Brigade made 'full use of everything there' and McClelland arrived at his total by claiming 2s/6d per man per day.

The defendant, while denying culpability, brought £295/5s into court, offering it as sufficient to settle the matter. In the hearing that followed, the claimant's solicitors described how the military had taken over the whole school except for a few rooms allowed for the accommodation of himself and his housekeeper. Furniture was destroyed or used as firewood, feather pillows were stolen by the troops, who remarked that it was the only school in Ireland where the boys had such luxuries.

Witnesses from the Board of Works were called for the defence and they advised a rental of £3 a week during the occupation. The judge said he was anxious to be as generous as he could; he considered the sum suggested by the two experienced gentlemen from the Board of Works was not fair to McClelland. He therefore came to the conclusion that he would allow him £300 in compensation for the use of the building and £100 for the replacement of furniture.

25 June 1959

Seal of office

É amon de Valera became President of Ireland in his seventy-seventh year. It was the inevitable consummation of his life and in a ceremony on Thursday 25 June 1959 in St Patrick's Hall, the grandest chamber in Dublin Castle, the title was formally conferred. It was an appropriate setting, redolent of a different regime, with the royal blue carpet, the gilt column and furniture and the residual paraphernalia of the old Knights of St Patrick. The ceremony was timed to begin at 1 pm but the hall was nearly full by 12.30, with dignitaries of church and state.

Cardinal J.F. D'Alton was resplendent in crimson and the Dublin archbishop, J.C. McQuaid, followed in purple. By comparison the Protestant Archbishop of Dublin, G.O. Simms, was in black. The aldermen wore fur-lined scarlet robes, rivalled only by the army officers in full dress uniform. The president entered to a flourish of trumpets, accompanied by Seán MacEntee, the new Tánaiste, and took his place on the platform between the Taoiseach Seán Lemass and Seán T. O'Kelly, the former president.

Lemass made the formal statement in Irish that de Valera had been elected and asked the Chief Justice, Conor Maguire, to administer the prescribed declaration of acceptance of the office. He did so, also in Irish. De Valera read the declaration aloud and signed the document with a quill pen. As Maguire handed over the green box that contained the seal of office there was another fanfare from the trumpeters of the army band. Lemass then paid tribute to the one commandant of the Easter Rising who had been 'providentially spared' and wished him and his wife 'heartfelt good wishes for the years to come'. The new president made a short reply, the band played the national anthem and the twenty-minute ceremony was over.

26 June 1932

The Eucharistic Congress

The year 1932 was taken to be the 1500th anniversary of the coming of St Patrick to Ireland and in honour of the occasion Ireland was chosen to host the 31st Eucharist Congress. It was a time of the Free State's spiritual coming of age and in the eyes of many of the faithful a sign of benediction for the Fianna Fáil government. The exercises ran from 22-26 June and caused a state of unusual exaltation among Catholics and inevitable reaction from some Ulster Protestants who attacked pilgrim trains and buses on their return north. Nine cardinals, more than a hundred bishops, from places as far away as Danzig and Des Moines, and more than a thousand priests attended. Thousands of lay Catholics made their way to Dublin and houses throughout Ireland had the blue Congress encircled cross stencilled on their walls. Many boys born about this time were baptised Pascal in honour of the event.

On Wednesday 22 June, the congress began with Midnight Mass in every church in Ireland; on the Thursday – 'Men's day' – 250,000 men attended Mass in Phoenix Park; 'Ladies' Day' saw 200,000 women at the same site on the Friday. 100,000 children assembled in the park on the Saturday and the Congress closed triumphantly on Sunday 26 June, when at a Pontifical High Mass in the Phoenix Park an estimated one million people heard the great Irish tenor, John McCormack, sing 'Panis Angelicus' and listened to a relayed broadcast by Pope Pius XI as he gave the vast congregation the papal blessing.

As a kind of postscript, on the following Monday the Papal Legate, Cardinal Lorenzo Lauri, was made a freeman of the city, with the certificate of enrolment presented to him in an ornamental casket at a special meeting of the Corporation.

27 June 1953

The Queen of Tonga

One of the unanticipated highlights of the ceremonial parade to the coronation of Elizabeth II in 1953 was the presence of another queen, Salote of Tonga, who at 6'3" was unmissable as she rode along the Mall in an open landau in spite of heavy rain. At the back of her carriage stood a little Tongan boy in full exotic uniform whose impish smiling appearance caused an equal amount of appreciation. It is said that Noel Coward, the playwright famous for his rather daring wit, watching the parade from a VIP vantage point, was asked about the role of the miniature groom and replied, 'Her lunch!' The queen, her name the Tongan equivalent of 'Charlotte', was an overnight sensation and had a song written about her that made the hit parade, the contemporary equivalent of *Top of the Pops*. It was written by Edmundo Ros, Britain's leading practitioner of exotic rhythms, and nudged out the other coronation song 'In a Golden Coach'.

There was, then, considerable interest in the news that Salote was coming to Ireland. Saturday 27 June 1953 was her day in Dublin. She met Taoiseach Éamon de Valera in Government Buildings, visited Trinity College to view *The Book of Kells* in the company of Dr A.J. McConnell, the Provost, and was photographed with him for the newspapers. Her visit was of greatest interest to Irish Methodists, who were included in her list of guests, as the official religion of the Friendly Isles was Methodism, due to the efforts of Wesleyan missionaries in the early 19th century.

Other highlights of her tour were the Vale of Avoca on the Saturday afternoon, Killarney, where she spent the Sunday night, and Monday the rest of Kerry. Galway was scheduled for Tuesday and Connemara for Wednesday. She returned to London on Thursday 2 July.

28 June 1954

'The shaking hand of Dublin'

For many years in the last century a phenomenon known as the 'shaking hand of Dublin' caused extreme delight both to citizens and visitors. It was not a pathological condition but an index of bonhomie and cordiality. It belonged to Alderman Alfred Byrne (1882-1956), known universally as 'Alfie', and on Monday 28 June 1954 he was elected Lord Mayor for the eleventh time, beating his Fianna Fáil rival by twenty-two votes to twenty. The colourful title originated in his almost compulsive habit of shaking hands with any person he met in the street. He took his duties as first citizen very seriously, although not solemnly, seeming to incorporate in his personality all the geniality and friendliness of the Dublin of his time.

His father was a docker who died when he was thirteen. He worked as a theatre programme-seller and as a barman, and succeeded in buying his own pub in Talbot Street. He entered politics in 1909 and was a member of the Corporation from 1910. He was elected to the House of Commons as a member of the Irish Parliamentary Party in a by-election in 1915 but lost his seat in the 1918 general election that all but annihilated the party. In 1922 he became an independent TD in the Dáil and was returned at every subsequent election until his death in 1956, except for the three years 1928-31, when he was in the Senate. He was elected Lord Mayor for nine consecutive years, from 1930-9, and again in 1954.

At the inauguration for his tenth year of office he said that he did not believe that it would have been possible for him to be elected, that there were many members more worthy of the office and more capable of carrying out the work than he.

29 June 1913

Croke of Cashel

Thomas William Croke (1824-1902), known as 'Croke of Cashel' after his appointment as archbishop in 1875, was a strongly nationalist prelate, as stridently against Parnell after the adultery scandal as he had been strongly in his favour before it. He was the first patron of the GAA from its foundation in 1884 and in 1913, eleven years after his death, the central council of the association initiated the Croke Memorial Tournament to raise money for a suitable monument to his memory. The final, between Kerry and Louth, was played in the site that bears his name on 4 March that year. The two teams had notably different types of play, perhaps reflecting supposed county temperaments. The Munstermen tended to 'catch, swing and kick' while the north-easterners played a kind of soccer with low-level ground passing. At full time the 26,000 spectators – the greatest gate in GAA history – were displeased or relieved that the result was a draw.

The replay was fixed for Sunday 29 June and in the one hundred and seventeen days' interval the excitement began to affect many who had taken little interest in the campaign. The GNR, GWR and GSR, the chief railway companies, prepared forty special trains that carried more than 20,000 passengers to the Smoke. Special stands were erected and volunteers were asked to supervise stewarding. The gates were closed after 32,000 fans had crowded in and at least 3000 more, in true Croker anticipation, managed to scramble over the railway wall.

The two teams were level at half-time but the Kerrymen won easily by 2-4 to 0-5. The gate netted £2365 (equivalent to the purchasing power of £213,000 today) and one month later the committee was able to buy the grounds from the owner for £3500. It was intended to be called Croke Memorial Park, a title that was in fact never used.

30 June 1972

The Marian statue

The year 1954 was designated a Marian year and in the then very Catholic city of Dublin it was decided to assemble funds to erect a statue to the Blessed Virgin in memory of the success of the year devotionally. Many of the subscribers were dockers and although several other sites were suggested the very end of the Clontarf Bull Wall that marks the northern outer limit of the port of Dublin seemed highly appropriate. The years passed and by the beginning of the 1970s the sculptor Cecil King had completed his design. It consisted of three long shafts of pre-stressed white stone, surmounted by a white spherical globe and a ten-foot statue. The whole structure was at least a hundred feet high and would be lit up at night.

By the spring of 1972, with preliminary work already begun on the site, the Corporation refused to grant planning permission. An appeal was heard in the Custom House on Friday 30 June 1972 by C. Dardis, a Department of Local Government inspector. During the hearing it became clear that sites on the South Wall at the Pigeon House, on the Hill of Howth and on the Clontarf Road had all been rejected because of local objections. The Bull Wall had been approved by residents and had the blessing of Archbishop Dermot Ryan.

The chief objectors were the Dublin Civic Group, An Taisce and the National Monuments Advisory Council, generally agreeing that a monument of such vast proportions would be completely out of scale and harmony with its surroundings and 'an inappropriate intrusion on the nature of the coastline'. Dardis decided that he matter was for the minister to settle, no doubt totally unaffected by the fact that the structure was ready for assembly. The statue was formally launched nearly three months later, on 24 September.

1 July 1937

Fire in Bargain Kings

At some time between six and seven o'clock in the evening of Thursday 1 July 1937 a fire broke out in the storeroom of a city-centre branch of the general merchants known as 'Bargain Kings'. The store was at the junction of Capel Street and Mary Street and the flames caused a large crowd to gather at the scene on their way home from work. It was soon realised that two women who lived on the second floor above the shop were still in the building and at risk. They were Mrs Elizabeth Blake and her daughter Emily, aged seventeen and a half, and when they appeared at the window a tarpaulin was held stretched by some bystanders.

Emily eased herself off the windowsill, closed her eyes, jumped and landed unscathed in the centre of the makeshift trampoline. Elizabeth was not so lucky; she decided not to follow her daughter but to drop directly from the windowsill. As she later recalled: 'I struck something on the way down and I knew nothing more until I regained consciousness in a neighbouring house.' She had hit a projecting cornice and was taken to Jervis Street Hospital, where she was treated for leg injuries. She was allowed to go home a few hours later.

John A. Currid, the CEO of Bargain Kings, was on the premises when the fire broke out. Pearl O'Farrell, one of the shop assistants, had occasion to go the storeroom at the back and was met by a wall of smoke. At her screams Currid ran to her and found the room ablaze. He raced to phone the fire service and a tender arrived within minutes. It took three-quarters of an hour finally to extinguish the flames. Damage was estimated at several hundred pounds.

2 July 1935

Guilty as charged

Although the Civil War ended in May 1923 a number of IRA volunteers refused to accept the terms and remained disaffected even under the Fianna Fáil government of Éamon de Valera. Because of the existence of undeclared arms, cases involving declared members of the IRA were tried before military tribunals instead of civic courts. On Tuesday 2 July 1935 two youths, Michael Leonard of Windy Arbour and Edward Grant of Milltown, were charged with membership of an unlawful organisation and with the illegal possession of two 0.45 revolvers. Both refused to plead, Leonard making the usual formulaic response: 'We deny the right of a gang of British soldiers to try us.' The tribunal president directed that they should be entered in the record as pleading, 'Not guilty.'

Superintendent W. Mooney gave evidence of suspicion and arrest. He and Sergeant J.J. Molloy had been driving along Churchtown Avenue in Dundrum at 7.45pm on Wednesday 20 June, when he recognised the two accused. They left the car and proceeded on foot, stopping the two men. Mooney asked if they had attended an IRA rally that evening in Hazelbrook but neither would answer. When he searched Grant he found a full loaded revolver in his coat pocket. Molloy, searching Leonard, found that he was carrying a fully loaded Colt.

Leonard interrupted his evidence to ask, 'Were you responsible for the execution of six republicans in Galway?' and was told by the president to confine his questions to matters relating. When Chief Superintendent Reynolds confirmed that it was he who had authorised the arrest Leonard complained that they had not been allowed to wash and were given dog food to eat. The verdict of the tribunal was that they were guilty as charged and also of contempt of court, and it sentenced each to eighteen months' imprisonment.

3 July 1945

Graduate's complaint

Until 1970 the Lenten pastorals of 20th-century Dublin archbishops firmly placed a ban on the attendance of Catholics in Trinity College. There were several reasons for the refusal: the perceived danger to faith and morals, protection for the approved National University of Ireland and, it must be said, an instinctive assumption of control over the nature of third-level education for their flocks. In fact some Catholics were given a reluctant permission to attend for technical reasons such as lack of matriculation in Irish but in the sectarian climate of mid-century ecclesiastic politics the ban greatly diminished the number of native students who enrolled in the older college.

Outside the realm of religion, from time to time odious comparisons usually anecdotal, oral and confined to senior common rooms burst into the public realm, causing a brief meteoric splash in the local newspapers. One such was the settling of a libel action in the Dublin High Court before Mr Justice Haugh on Tuesday 3 July 1945. The action was brought by John Dufficy, St John's Road, Sandymount, who was a graduate of NUI and a member of convocation of University College Dublin. He had given an interview to a journalist in which he criticised his alma mater and seemed to praise TCD.

Dufficy insisted that he had not given permission to anyone to use his words in any public medium, although he can hardly have been surprised when an article headed 'Evening Students' Handicap: Graduate's Complaint' appeared on 18 May 1945 in *The Irish Times*. It certainly caused a deal of embarrassment but the case was based on lack of permission and not any personal injury. So the jury ruled, when Haugh explained the niceties of what the term 'libel' implied, awarding £500 and costs to Dufficy.

4 July 1836

The DMP

The Dublin Metropolitan Police (DMP) was founded as a local force on 4 July 1836. The force was almost indistinguishable from the London 'Met', established by Peel seven years earlier. Unlike earlier forms of policing the force was impartial and independent of the local authority. The organisation had its own particular set of regulations, promotion was usually from the ranks, the officers were free to marry without permission, had to be at least six feet in height and were not on the whole unpopular with the people in the areas of their jurisdiction, Dublin city and county and Wicklow. Unlike the Royal Irish Constabulary, which was a paramilitary force, fully armed, the DMP prided itself on its lack of weapons. It was assimilated into the Garda Síochána in 1925.

An early broadsheet ballad referred to their 'aspect stately' and the fact that they were 'drest from top to toe in blue, sirs/Their lofty heads a glazed top hat on'. (This headgear was replaced with the standard crested helmet later in the 19th century.) A later verse in the ballad suggests they were not entirely benevolent:

> *As I upon my beat was walking*
> *The prisoner that's here do you see/*
> *Had the impudence to look at me.'*
> *'Is that the case?' the inspector cries,*
> *While indignation lights both his eyes,*
> *'This charge I certainly can't o'erlook*
> *So put him forthwith into the dock.*

The force had an intelligence division, the first G-men, who proved their effectiveness throughout the Fenian campaign. Some members were able to supply useful information to Michael Collins during the War of Independence. The reputation of the DMP was at its lowest in 1913 because of the brutality of the attacks by some members on strikers during the infamous Lockout, when on horseback the 'unarmed' force used sabres to break up meetings.

5 July 1952

Summer storm

The island of Ireland and the province of Leinster in particular does not usually suffer extremes of weather but Sunday 5 July 1952 showed what nature could do even in the island of saints and scholars. The south-east bore the brunt, with a breakdown in telephone communications and severe flooding in Waterford. There was one tragedy: Thomas Hutchinson, a fifty-year-old father of two children from Killamick, County Laois, was on his way to Mass in Abbeyleix and took shelter from the torrential rain under trees. He died after a lightning strike. Also in the county five cattle were killed.

In Dublin the congregation were assembled for Mass in the church of SS Peter and Paul, Baldoyle, when the church was struck and the heavy stone cross was broken from the steeple and crashed through the roof of the vestry. It was almost unthinkable that a church on a Sunday morning with Mass about to begin should be a victim of a storm. Considerable damage was done to the church roof, as well as the vestry, although no member of the congregation, most of whom had run screaming from the sanctuary, had been injured.

The storm broke very early in the morning with relentlessly heavy rain and frightening thunder and lightning and so it continued for most of the day. The weather had been fine up until then and many Dubliners had made arrangements to spend the day at the seaside but that was now out of the question. The storm spread north, striking an electrical transformer near Portrane, cutting off supply to the town but not affecting the mental hospital. Some low-lying streets of the city were flooded but although the often indelible and odorous effects of domestic flooding afflicted some houses no loss of life occurred.

6 July 1946

Clann na Poblachta

Seán MacBride (1904-88), the son of Maud Gonne and John MacBride, who had been executed for his part in the Easter Rising, was prominent among a gathering consisting mainly of republican activists who met in Barry's Hotel in Dublin to form a new political party on Saturday 6 July 1946. The name chosen was Clann na Poblachta (Children of the Republic) and the very title was evidence of a perceived falling away from the ideals that had inspired the national struggle for political freedom.

The chief element in the party's manifesto was a call for 'a new standard of political morality in public life' and it drew attention to the weakening of the country by the 'forced emigration of its youth' and the enabling of a small section to 'accumulate enormous wealth'. The idea caught hold and in a short time there was established a network of branches nationwide. The party, with MacBride as leader, did well in local elections and secured ten seats in the 1948 general election. It was their intervention that weakened Fianna Fáil's grasp of the electorate and they were given two important cabinet posts, External Affairs for MacBride and Health for Dr Noël Browne, who did much to eradicate tuberculosis in his first years of office.

It was Browne's Mother and Child scheme, by which mothers and children under sixteen would have free medical treatment, that in essence broke the back of the party. The scheme was bitterly opposed by the Catholic Church, which was against state interference in family affairs, and even more vehemently by the Irish Medical Association. When MacBride sided with the Taoiseach John A. Costello in dismissing Brown, in obedience to Catholic teaching, it seemed to many a serious betrayal of the party's ideals.

7 July 1961

Smashing the gavel

Frederick Henry Boland (1904-85) became president of the United Nations General Assembly in 1960 after a stellar career in the senior civil service and as a diplomat. Although noted for his talent in negotiation and exemplary patience, the public highlight of his period with the UN (1956-64) was the occasion when he smashed his gubernatorial gavel trying to call Nikita Khrushchev, the Russian leader, to order. On Friday 7 July 1961 he flew into Dublin from New York on a five-week furlough. His arrival at the height of the Cold War, not long after the failed Bay of Pigs attempt by Cuban exiles to overthrow Fidel Castro, generated a lot of press interest.

He was as patient and forbearing as ever with the large crowd of reporters who interviewed him at the airport. There was only one 'no-comment' and that was on the question of Berlin and the fact that it was six weeks from becoming a 'walled city' in the worst possible sense, with Die Mauer about to cut its very heart in two. He was perfectly happy to discuss the many different spheres of activity of the UN, especially in the Congo and Kuwait, and at the diplomatic level in its fostering of international talks on nuclear disarmament. He personally was full of praise for its African influence and was especially glad to note that he had never met anyone who did not express the highest appreciation of the work of the Irish troops serving with the UN emergency force there.

Asked about the Khrushchev incident he smiled and revealed that when the incident became internationally known on television he had been sent a total of thirty-five new gavels and six or seven shillelaghs – perhaps a hint that the Irish club might be more effective next time.

8 July 1938

Joseph Patrick Kennedy

On Friday 8 July 1938 Joseph Patrick Kennedy, the recently appointed United States ambassador to the Court of St James, paid his first visit to Ireland. He was accompanied by his eldest son, Joseph Patrick Junior, for whom he had the highest possible ambition for an American, to become president of the United States. (That ambition perished in a plane crash over the English Channel in 1944 and the next son in line, John Fitzgerald, was groomed for succession.)

The party landed in Baldonnel Aerodrome after a short but 'bumpy' flight to be greeted by the US Minister to Dublin, John Cudahy, and Seán Murphy, Assistant Secretary to the Department of External Affairs.

The chief purpose of Kennedy's visit was to accept an honorary LLD from the National University of Ireland. He insisted to the Press that his visit was solely for this purpose but a diplomat with authentic Irish qualifications could hardly expect to be believed, especially one with Kennedy's connections. Éamon de Valera, resplendent in black and gold, presided as Chancellor of the NUI, as Professor T. Corcoran SJ declared that the ambassador was 'the organiser of great cohorts dedicated to civic service by sea and by land; he has ever been prompt in forward action at his country's call.' It would have been entirely inappropriate in the circumstances to hint at certain less wholesome aspects of the ambassador's earlier career.

After the conferring and a few words with the Chancellor, he left Merrion Square to be driven the two hundred yards to Government Buildings to meet de Valera again, this time in his political role as Taoiseach. His last duty before a dinner that night in the American Legation was a courtesy call on the seventy-eight-year-old Douglas Hyde, the new President of Ireland, in Áras an Uachtaráin.

9 July 1964

O'Casey according to John Ford

John Ford (born John Martin Feeney in Maine and not as he claimed, Seán Aloysius Ó Féinne in Ireland) was the ultimate Irish-American, better cast in the role then even John Huston. He made many excellent films, some of them classics, including *The Informer, Stagecoach, The Grapes of Wrath, My Darling Clementine* and *The Searchers,* and in a sense modified John Wayne and Maureen O'Hara, two favourite actors, into stardom. He filmed the ultimate blarney movie, *The Quiet Man* (1950), with them in Ireland and in 1964, at the age of sixty-nine, he returned to make a version of the life of Seán O'Casey.

On Thursday 9 July he was present at a press conference in the Shelbourne Hotel. The star of *Young Cassidy*, the Australian actor, Rod Taylor, was there, as were the co-producers Gianna and Graff, but not Jack Cardiff, who would take over and be credited with the direction. Ford made a stellar entrance in extremely casual clothes and sneakers and wearing a black patch over the left lens of his glasses. He battled with the press audience, who were enthusiastic but not uncritical of the project. The film was based upon O'Casey's six volumes of factionalised memoirs in which the protagonist is called Johnny Casside and has an approximately identical career to the Abbey playwright. The title of the film and the plethora of 'names' including Michael Redgrave (as Yeats), Edith Evans (as Lady Gregory), Flora Robson, Julie Christie, Maggie Smith, Siobhán McKenna, T.P. McKenna and Jack McGowran had to be included to meet the demands of the Hollywood money men.

The audience was wary of Ford's reputation for waspishness but were ultimately docile on learning that the other thirty-eight parts would be played by members of the great Irish repertory plus Shevaun, O'Casey's daughter, as Lady Gregory's maid.

10 July 1927

The Assassination of Kevin O'Higgins

Kevin O'Higgins was regarded as the most gifted and most ruthless of the ministers in the Cumann na nGaedheal administration that came to power after the Anglo-Irish Treaty. His was the vision that created the viable Free State but his vigorous prosecution of the civil war and his continuing opposition to the IRA as Minister for Justice earned him hatred as well as respect. He confirmed the reprisal execution of Republican prisoners in December 1922 as a member of the Cabinet, although with great reluctance: Rory O'Connor had been the best man at his wedding only a year before. O'Higgins's father was shot by an IRA unit in front of his family the following February, it was presumed in retaliation. By 1926 he had established the Garda Síochána as an unarmed civilian police and was clearly the next in line as leader of the party.

At 11.55am on Sunday 10 July 1927 halfway through his thirty-sixth year, he was killed on his way to Mass in the Church of the Assumption, Booterstown. The shots were fired as he turned the corner from Cross Avenue into Booterstown Avenue. Three anti-Treaty members of the IRA, Timothy Coughlin, Bill Gannon and Archie Doyle, shot him and as they ran away they fancied that they saw him raise his arm. Each ran back and shot him again in the head, heart and abdomen. Their stolen car was found abandoned in Richmond Avenue, Milltown. Coughlin was killed in 1928 by a police informer and the others, benefiting from de Valera's 1932 amnesty, were never charged. The IRA claimed that the murder was 'unsanctioned'.

O'Higgins remained conscious for a while before he died of his wounds. He was able to make a kind of oral last will and testament to Patrick Fleming, a neighbour from Cross Avenue, who cradled his head as he was dying. His last words were spoken to Fleming's brother, Ned: 'I die at peace with God and with my enemies.'

11 July 1921

'Forbearance and conciliation'

On 22 June 1921 George V opened the parliament of the new political entity, Northern Ireland, in Belfast City Hall and in the course of his speech, written mainly by Jan Christian Smuts, the Boer leader, and David Lloyd George, the British prime minister, he urged 'all Irishmen to pause, to stretch out the hand of forbearance and conciliation, to forgive and forget and to join in making for the land which they love a new era of peace, contentment and good will.'

The War of Independence is taken to have begun with the killing of two Catholic policemen at Soloheadbeg, County Tipperary, on 21 January 1919 and by the time of the king's speech four hundred and five policemen (including members of the notorious 'Black and Tans' RIC reserve force and the even more ruthless 'Auxies'), one hundred and fifty serving soldiers and around seven hundred and fifty IRA and civilians had been killed. It was essentially a guerrilla war, initially against soft targets, then with increasing ferocity on both sides. Attacks on towns like Balbriggan and Cork city by Tans and Auxies in bloody reprisals became commonplace.

Two days after the speech Lloyd George sent a letter to de Valera, President of Dáil Éireann, inviting him to attend talks. There was a deal of complex negotiation with de Valera imposing intricate conditions. The first step was the setting up of an agreed truce with terms worked out by General Macready, his aide Colonel Brind on the British side and Éamonn Duggan and Robert Barton on the Irish. This came into effect on Monday 11 July 1921. Richard Mulcahy, the IRA military leader, sent a general order to all units requiring them '...in pursuance of mutual understandings to suspend activities; active operations by our troops will be suspended as from noon Monday, July 11.'

12 July 1949

Hiding around the corner

At 10pm on Wednesday 12 July 1949 Douglas Hyde (1860-1949), the first president of Ireland, died, aged eighty-nine. He had been a leading figure in the Gaelic Revival, co-founder of the Gaelic League and Professor of Modern Irish in UCD. He had learned his Irish from 'the company of old countrymen' in his home county of Roscommon and was responsible for collections and translations of Irish poetry, tales, riddles and folklore. These appeared as *Leabhar Sgeulaigheachta* (1889) and *Beside the Fire* (1890) and had a clear effect on the work of Gregory, Yeats and Synge. He also wrote two important works of Gaelic scholarship, *The Story of Early Gaelic Literature* (1895) and *A Literary History of Ireland* (1899). His collaboration with Yeats led, in 1901, to the creation of *Casadh an tSúgáin* (The Twisting of the Rope), the first play of merit in modern Irish.

Hyde remained president of the Gaelic League until 1915 when, under the influence of Eoin MacNeill and Patrick Pearse, it ceased to be the non-sectarian, non-political organisation that he intended. He served as a Free State senator (1925-6) and retired from his university chair in 1932. He was persuaded to exchange his house, 'Ratra', for Áras an Uachtaráin in 1938 and died there.

His office entitled him to a state funeral but owing to the automatic obedience of the mainly Catholic Dáil members to the current ban against attendance at Protestant church services the only member of the cabinet present in St Patrick's Cathedral was Dr Noël Browne, the Minister for Health. The others stayed outside until the church proceedings ended. The absence was pilloried by Austin Clarke in his poem, 'Burial of an Irish President': 'Costello, his Cabinet, / In Government cars, hiding/Around the corner...'

13 July 1938

Baby farming

Mary Anne ('Mamie') Cadden, a qualified midwife, aged forty-seven, who ran a nursing home in 183 Rathmines Road, and Mary O'Grady, one of her staff, were charged in Naas court on Wednesday 13 July 1938, with abandoning a female infant aged about six weeks in Rosetown, Dunshaughlin, on 14 June. It was one of the highlights in Cadden's career as 'baby farmer' and abortionist that would later see her condemned to death as a murderer.

Cadden and O'Grady were arrested and cautioned in the home by detectives from Navan and Dublin and taken to the Bridewell. There both were picked out at an identity parade by independent witnesses as having been seen in Dunshaughlin at 9.20pm in a red motor car. The parade was conducted with protocol correct at the time: six women 'of the same dress and appearance' were found and the accused took their places in the line. Both were indicated by the placing of hands on shoulders. Asked that they be remanded in custody, Judge Reddin wondered if there was in existence a system for abandoning infants and granted the request. The two women were remanded to appear in Dunshaughlin on 26 July.

At the resumption of the hearing Cadden was sentenced to one year's imprisonment with hard labour. She was taken to be the dominant figure in the affair and her reputation as either an evil but unproved abortionist or an 'angel of mercy' for women in travail made her culpable in the eyes of the law. O'Grady, probably correctly, was taken to be very much her minion and, although given six months' hard labour, had the sentenced suspended during her good behaviour.

14 July 1944

Wonder drug

The informal use of mould as a healing agency had been practised for centuries but it was largely due to the pioneering work of the Scots biologist, Sir Alexander Fleming, that penicillin was engendered from the blue-green *Penicillium notatum* and developed as an effective antibiotic. By the 1940s it was freely used to cure war wounds and began to be made available for civilian use. On Friday 14 July 1944, in a joint statement, Robert P. Farnan, President of the Medical Research Council, and David Gray, the United States Minister to Éire, announced that a limited amount of sodium penicillin would be made available in Ireland. They emphasised that it was still not freely available commercially because of the needs of field hospitals but it was clear that civilian use would not be long delayed. Already production of the drug in America and Britain had been stepped up, so that its use for civilian treatment was steadily increasing.

The serum due from America was of the highest grade, in powder form, cream or in ampoules for injection. The pair was anxious to emphasise that research and tests were still ongoing and that two special teams of doctors in Dublin hospitals had gained considerable experience in the use of the drug through utilising Irish-produced penicillin agar prepared by two research workers, Oliver Roberts and Diarmuid Murphy. Results worldwide had been spectacular. Ten out of fifteen people suffering from the invariably fatal pneumococcal meningitis had been cured. Naval doctors asserted that it saved the lives of men with abdominal wounds on small ships or remote islands where quick surgery was impossible.

Its efficacy in the cure of gonorrhea and syphilis was well established and it had also proved therapeutic against nose and throat complications, eye infections, myocarditis and osteomyelitis. It really was a 'wonder drug'!

16 July 1938

Collision in Westland Row

At 7.45am on Saturday 16 July 1938 a train, auxiliary to the mail train going west, collided with the Greystones train ex-Amiens Street in Westland Row Station, injuring two firemen and causing general shock to many passengers. The injured men were James Harris (22) of 3 Daly's Terrace, Rathfarnham, who needed three stitches inserted in a cut over his left eye, and Albert Abbot (35), who had injuries to his right leg and sore ribs. After an x-ray that revealed no ribs were broken Abbot and Harris were discharged from Sir Patrick Dun's Hospital.

Five women, two sets of sisters, all from Ballaghadereen, showed evidence of considerable shock. However the three Misses Duffy and the two Misses Harkins were able to continue their journey home on a relief train that left two hours later from Westland Row. Because it was high season a relief train was required.

The actual collision happened on the bridge over Westland Row. The Greystones train was slowing down to stop in the station when it met the other train. Both engines were badly damaged fore and aft and buffers wrenched from the carriages behind them.

A porter from the Grosvenor Hotel across from the entrance described to the papers how he had heard a tremendous crash and when he rushed out to the street he saw a buffer and miscellaneous pieces of metal that had hit the street exactly where he had been standing a few minutes before. The crashed trains were clearly visible from the streets below. In spite of the early hour the street soon filled up with spectators, many of whom were residents of Westland Row. While a breakdown gang from the locomotive department cleared the line, trains were diverted to the up line.

15 July 1951

St Swithun sunshine

St Swithun was a ninth-century Anglo-Saxon bishop of Winchester and adviser to the Wessex kings. His name is still associated with a piece of medieval weather lore:

> *St Swithun's day if thou dost rain*
> *For forty days it will remain.*
> *St Swithun's day if thou be fair*
> *For forty days it will rain nae mair.*

If the belief has any meteorological value in Wessex it practically never applies to windswept Atlantic-exposed rainy Ireland. When it happens (rarely) that 15 July, the feast day, occurs in good weather it becomes copy for the press and especially in 1951, when it fell on a Sunday, there was not a copywriter who dared ignore the pluvial saint.

The east coast was bathed in Swithun sunshine and Dublin was crowded with visitors. The mean temperature in those pre-Celsius days was 66° Fahrenheit (18° for the Celsius fanatic.) The Belfast holiday, centred around the celebration on 12 July of the Battle of the Boyne, coincided, as did some of the Lancashire 'wakes' – originally religious vigils and the Glasgow Fair, celebrated in July since the twelfth-century tradition of the city going on holiday, somewhat as the quatorze juillet empties Paris.

The result was a welcome influx by train, boat and to a lesser extent by car and plane – Ireland was far from universal carriers in 1951. Over that weekend 1600 tourists arrived from Liverpool, 1000 from Glasgow, an equal number from the north by the Enterprise and 4750 from Holyhead, landing in Dún Laoghaire. There was a capacity crowd (30,000 people) in Croke Park to watch minor and senior Leinster hurling finals. CIÉ put on more than fifty special trains. As for the Dubs, they were remarkably patient as they queued in long lines for buses that would take them to Dollymount, Sandymount, Bray or the Dublin mountains.

17 July 1978

Extradition orders quashed

The Northern Ireland Troubles of recent years had an unfortunate habit of spilling south, politically if not always geographically. Extradition cases based on the 1965 act, drafted and passed years before their outbreak, could cause considerable legal difficulties, with occasional sharp differences between judges and resulting accusations of miscarriage of justice on all sides. On Monday 17 January 1978 two men from Donegal who were members of the IRA had their extradition orders quashed.

Patrick Joseph O'Hagan from near Buncrana was wanted on a charge of escaping from Magilligan Prison, County Derry, while serving a sentence for possession of explosives, causing an explosion with intent to endanger life and armed robbery. Francis Herron of Coneyburrow, Lifford, was charged with assaulting a woman in Strabane, County Tyrone. Because the offences were 'political' or 'connected with political offences' they were entitled to asylum under the act but not, as their counsels argued, liable for costs. Counsel for the Garda authorities disputed this argument, adducing a recent decision of the High Court opposing the granting of costs, since the authorities in the country were not in any sympathy with such activities.

Much legal argument with precise reference to High Court precedents followed and was further complicated by the possibility of the involvement of the Minister for Justice. Mr Justice Doyle, who had quashed the extradition orders, while admitting that it was hard to determine in which causes judicial discretion could be exercised, felt that in this case the nature of O'Hagan's offences were such that he could claim costs but Herron's assault on the Strabane woman by its nature injured another party, even if it was carried out as a punishment under orders from his superior officers in the IRA and carried out in pursuit of the organisation's aims.

18 July 1938

'Wrong-way' Corrigan

At 2.25pm on Monday 18 July 1938 Douglas Corrigan, a thirty-year-old aviator from Los Angeles, landed in Baldonnel Aerodrome in an aeroplane that was later described by Kenneth Behr, the manager of Floyd Bennett airfield, New York, as 'a terrible ship'. Corrigan had left Floyd Bennett at 5.15am New York eastern time the previous Sunday and headed, as he believed, for home. There was a suggestion that he had been forbidden to undertake a transcontinental flight in his plane because of its age, then nine years old. The fact that he flew east rather than west suggests that he had very little in the way of equipment.

He was smiling when he climbed out of the cockpit and explained to the crowd of army air officials what had happened. They took him off to the officers' mess, where he had a meal while someone phoned the American Legation. He was taken there on the order of John Cudahy, the US Minister. At his interview he was quite dismissive of the feat which, considering the paucity of instruments and the age of the plane, was in the words of Behr, 'the greatest flight we ever had'.

Already dubbed 'Wrong-way' Corrigan, the aviator was quite nonchalant about his return home on the same 'ship': 'All it wants is a little grease…' He explained that he used two compasses, one a Pioneer Straightway with which he set a straight course. Its setting was such that, although set for an east to west course, it could, through pilot miscalculation, actually have the machine fly west to east, and this was what happened. He had flown for eighteen hours above high-banked cloud and when he had vision realised that what he took to be the coast of California was actually the coast of Donegal. So he headed for Baldonnel.

19 July 1937

Aspro conspiracy

Benjamin Ridgeway, Marlborough Street, an employee of a wholesale pharmacy firm called May Roberts and Company, was accused before Justice Shannon on Monday 10 July 1937 of stealing a quantity of an analgesic called Aspro. He was one of four accused, the others being Thomas Doyle, Brighton Avenue, Clontarf; Edward Brady, North James's Street; and Bernard Cashin, Hardwicke Street. When all the evidence was heard the judge imposed suspensory sentences of six months' hard labour on Doyle and Brady and nine months' on Cashin.

The case of Ridgeway was more complicated, as it emerged that he seemed to be the victim of a conspiracy among his fellow workers. He had been in trouble with the local branch of the Irish Transport and General Workers' Union, the secretary of which was Doyle and which had Brady as a committee member. He had been called before the committee to answer charges of 'giving information to the firm' and although the management had wished to promote him to the level of packer they made certain to prevent it.

The evidence of the accused, if true, was damning: Doyle claimed he had seen Ridgeway purloin three dozen packets of Aspro tablets and that he had sold them to a shop. He also accused Ridgeway of asking him to steal more Aspro and bring them to Ridgeway's house. He said he had taken four three-dozen packets a week during the previous September and had received about £7 from Ridgeway. He further alleged that at a football match Ridgeway had introduced him to the man who was buying the tablets. As the other three accused had each pleaded guilty to theft the judge was inclined to reject their statements. He dismissed the charges and discharged Ridgeway.

20 July 1974

The Forty-foot

The Forty-foot swimming pool, really a deep, narrow inlet of the sea in Sandycove, was for many years a male-only amenity. It was used all year round by hardy annuals, often without bathing costumes. This freedom was eventually restricted to the hours before 8am but it remained a male preserve until Saturday 20 July 1974. Then a group of daring women calling themselves the Dublin City Women's Invasion Force insisted on using the pool. They had discovered that there was no legal basis to their exclusion.

The invading force came by land, sea and air, according to Nell McCafferty, the most vocal of the activists: Nuala Fennell and her family took possession of a rock, Mary D'Arcy by currach and Nell herself using an umbrella as a makeshift parachute. A crowd gathered quickly with male swimmers in a majority, some of them naked, as were some of the invaders. Chauvinists when challenged can turn nasty and some of the more vicious calls were specifically sexual, as were the physical gestures of some of barrackers.

In spite of the rearguard action of some local troglodytes the male bastion crumbled and fell. From then on women swam unconcernedly in the Forty-Foot, thus rendering the title of Mervyn Wall's elegant, witty 1962 monograph on the cove, *Forty Foot Gentlemen Only*, quaintly obsolete. That unpunctuated title was copied from an existent sign at the entrance but there was little gentility about the behaviour or the language of the objectors. Yet within the year men, women and children used it freely – those who could swim. The origin of the title remains obscure: called after the Black Watch regiment? greatest depth of the water? length of path from road to sea? It remains a superb amenity, the finest swimming hole in Dublin.

21 July 1927

A dangerous practice

A court case involving a motorcyclist, his pillion passenger and the driver of a car was finally settled in a Dublin court on Wednesday 20 July 1927 before Mr Justice Hanna and a jury and was an important story in Thursday's newspapers. The plaintiffs, Cornelius Locke of 51 Mary Street, a lift attendant in the Shelbourne Hotel, and Patrick Lambert, a boot maker of 6 Camden Place, claimed damages against John Callan, a commercial traveller of Tenure, Dunleer, County Louth, for personal injuries caused by the alleged negligence while driving a car in Balbriggan on 17 October 1926. In the collision when the car hit the bike Locke's thigh bone and left wrist were broken and Lambert's right hand was injured. Callan denied the charge and suggested contributory negligence on the part of the plaintiffs.

For the defence Peter Mulholland, who was a passenger in Callan's car, said that while the car was travelling he noticed a car sixty yards in front. (It belonged to a man called McMahon, the court was later told.) He claimed that the motorcycle 'shaved' that car as it passed and hit Callan's car between the front wheels, causing the driver a split upper lip and two broken teeth. He denied a prosecution statement that it had happened because Callan was in the process of passing out McMahon's car.

The judge's address to the jury dwelt on the dubious legality of being a pillion passenger, making it clear that he believed that it was a dangerous practice. They responded strongly in favour of the plaintiffs, finding that pillion riding was not dangerous, that the defendant was guilty of negligence, that the plaintiffs were not guilty of contributory negligence and that the occurrence was not the result of inevitable accident and awarded £750 to Locke and £175 to Lambert.

22 July 1943

Reynolds portrait

Thomas Patrick Bodkin (1887-1961) was a lawyer, professor and connoisseur of European art. He was the director of the National Gallery of Ireland for eight years, 1927-35, when he became Barber Professor of Fine Arts and first director of the Barber Institute in Birmingham. He retired in 1952. His report on the arts in Ireland, commissioned by the Taoiseach John A. Costello in 1951, led to the foundation of the Arts Council. His greatest personal triumph was the concordat with the National Gallery in London over the disposition of the picture collection of his uncle, Sir Hugh Lane. His honours included doctorates from both TCD and NUI, papal Knight of St Gregory and Officier de la Légion d'honneur, and after retirement he became a popular figure on radio and television, giving talks about painting.

On Thursday 22 July 1943 he successfully outbid all his rivals to buy a Reynolds for the Barber Institute, then four years old. His offer of £5100 for the master portraitist's picture of Richard Robinson DD, Archbishop of Armagh, was made at an open auction held by North of Grafton Street. Sir Joshua Reynolds (1728-92) was the supreme portrait painter in 18th-century Britain, first president of the Royal Academy and friend of Dr Johnson, Edmund Burke and David Garrick, all of whom he painted. The beautiful Emma, Lady Hamilton, was also a subject.

The nearest offer was £5000 from Lucius O'Callaghan RHA, considerably more than the £3000 that was all the National Gallery in Dublin was prepared to bid. The painting was a three-quarter-length portrait and measured 54in by 44in. It was part of the treasure of the Robinson family of Rokeby Hall, Dunleer, County Louth, and its subject as well as an ecclesiastic was the first Lord Rokeby. The Rokeby family library was due to be auctioned the following October.

23 July 1803

Emmet's rising

At about 9pm on Saturday 23 July 1803 Robert Emmet (1778-1803), later 'darling of Erin' unwittingly let loose an undisciplined, armed and drunken mob on the streets of south Dublin. It was to have been a rising against tyranny with help from forces outside the capital but the enterprise was dogged by ill-luck and incompetence. His plan was to attack Dublin Castle with a picked band of supporters and expect a promised insurgency from the areas recently involved in the 1798 rising. An explosion in Patrick Street in one of his arms depots caused him to bring forward the date by a week, even though the examination of the site by the town police was cursory and no immediate action was taken.

In a mood of what Yeats called 'delirium of the brave', Emmet donned the uniform he himself had designed: plumed hat, white breeches and green coat with gold epaulettes and with a number of trusted companions sallied forth into a town crowded with Saturday night revellers. The six coaches that had been hired to convey them from Thomas Street to the castle did not stop but were driven away after being challenged by a mounted army officer. The main party led by Emmet, having secured Thomas Street, was advancing along James's Street but its members were dispersed by a troop of soldiers from the barracks there. The expected aid from Wicklow and Kildare failed to materialise.

By now a mob of rioters who had obtained pikes and muskets went on the rampage. It was fortuitous that they surrounded the coach of the humane Lord Kilwarden, Lord Chief Justice, and his nephew, the Reverend Richard Wolfe, and spiked them to death, two of the total fifty deaths. Emmet fled to the mountains but was arrested on 25 August and executed on 30 September.

24 July 1802

Hunting Cap's revenge

Daniel O'Connell (1775-1947), the self-styled agitator, later justly called the Liberator, was *un homme moyen sensuel*, not untypical of the rackety Regency period of his young manhood. He admitted as much to his wife, who occasionally chided him about 'your female acquaintances before I knew you'. His name would continue to be linked with other women but Mary O'Connell (1778–1836), his cousin, became his wife and the mother of his eleven children, and there was no doubt about his devotion to her or the persistence of their affection. His reputation as a womaniser, indeed, may owe something to Kerry folklore, as appropriate to a paladin of his heroic stature.

Because of the hierarchical, almost tribal, nature of his upbringing a dynastic marriage was intended for him by his mentor and virtual father, Maurice O'Connell, his father's rich eldest brother, the sovereign of the tribe, known universally as 'Hunting Cap'. She was Mary Ann Healy, a plain but wealthy heiress from Cork. He might indeed have acquiesced in the match had he not, in attendance at the summer assizes in Tralee in 1800, met and fell in love with his pretty but penniless twenty-two-year-old cousin. Discovering that she was in the current phrase 'fancy free', he said, 'Will you engage yourself to me?'

The engagement had to be kept secret until he could find an appropriate time to tell Hunting Cap but in a characteristic burst of action he persuaded the parish priest of Tralee to marry them in secret. The ceremony took place on Saturday 24 July 1802 in the house of James Connor, Mary's brother-in-law, in Dame Street. By November Mary was pregnant and the news of the attachment could no longer be concealed from Hunting Cap, whose rage was fearful and vengeance swift, cutting O'Connell's patrimony by two-thirds.

25 July 1963

The Berkeley Library

In the 1960s the growth of numbers of third-level students necessitated the building of a new, larger library building in Trinity College. This was to be the Berkeley Library, named after the philosopher bishop and TCD graduate, George Berkeley (1685-1753). The provost, outlining the need, stated at the beginning of the campaign that nothing short of a large-scale new building would suffice. There was an acute lack of reading-room accommodation for the growing numbers of students and there was no longer room to house the steady flow of books that came into the college under the British and Irish copyright acts. The existing building dated from the early 18th century.

The TCD authorities had considered a plan to build in stages as money became available but this was abandoned on expert advice from 'other great libraries'. A design for a complete building that would accommodate 400 readers and find space for over a million books had been secured by an international competition that had attracted many entries. The cost would be met by the government doubling the amount raised by the college until it reached £640,000, the estimated total cost. (For a modern approximation that figure should by multiplied by a factor of seventeen.)

On Thursday 25 July 1963 it was announced that a donation of £30,000 by Mr Jack Morrison JP had brought the college within sight of success in meeting its target. The fund had been started by the Iveagh family, notable benefactors to the city, their riches coming from their ancestor's invention of Guinness. Their initial contribution of £60,000 formed a firm base that reassured other donors not that the cause was a worthy one, a reassurance they did not need, but that it would ultimately be successful. Preliminary site work had begun by the time the Morrison donation was announced, including the prospect of an underground link between the old and the new libraries.

26 July 1914

The Howth Gun Running

The event known as the Howth Gun Running and its bloody aftermath began in the early morning of Sunday 26 July 1914. It was a minor affair compared with the UVF landing of German weapons in Larne and other Ulster ports. Eoin MacNeill, one of the founders of the Irish Volunteers, had drawn attention to the condoned illegal importation by the northern unionists in an article in the Gaelic League journal, *An Claidheamh Soluis*, entitled 'The North Began'. An ad hoc committee of the Volunteers, consisting of among others MacNeill, Roger Casement, Darrell Figgis, Erskine Childer, Mary Spring Rice and Michael (The) O'Rahilly decided, partly for publicity purposes, to organise a similar enterprise, sending Figgis to buy arms and ship them into Dublin Bay in the *Asgard* and other small yachts.

Eight hundred members of the Volunteers, having picked up the rifles in Howth, marched into the city, where in Bachelor's Walk they were met by police under W.V. Harrell, the assistant commissioner, backed by a hundred soldiers of the King's Own Scottish Borderers. Darrell Figgis and Thomas MacDonagh engaged Harrell in conversation, thus enabling the dispersal of the arms. The stand-off encouraged a crowd of supporters to gather, who shouted at the soldiers. A single shot rang out, followed by a volley from twenty-one military rifles that led to the death of three people and injury to thirty-eight others.

In the enquiry report that followed on 4 September Harrell was dismissed for 'provocatively calling out the army' and Brigadier-General Cuthbert censured for allowing soldiers to be mustered without written order and for not having 'more scrupulously' considered their role in the affair. The result was an increase in support for the Volunteers and a hardening of attitudes in other aspects of the British administration.

27 July 1942

The half-ounce of tea

The Emergency, as the years of the Second World War were described with remarkable understatement, was a time both of scarcity and profusion. Bread, petrol, clothing, gas, sugar and tea were rationed; coal supplies were soon exhausted and turf was widely exploited as an alternative fuel. Anything that had to be imported was at risk and although Irish ships did what it could they were at the mercy of German U-Boats in spite of large indications of Éire's neutrality on all sides. Twelve merchant ships were lost in this way but Irish vessels successfully imported 712,000 tons of wheat, 178,000 tons of coal, 63,000 tons of phosphates, 24,000 tons of tobacco, 19,000 tons of newsprint and 10,000 tons of timber.

The sorest deprivation for the ordinary people was the lack of white bread and tea. The 'dirty brown loaf' that was the standard product of bakeries would not have borne analysis, and a couplet, given here in its politest form, expressed the heartfelt reaction:

> *God bless de Valera and Seán MacEntee*
> *For their loaf of brown bread and their half-ounce of tea.*

To general dismay, the tea ration had been reduced earlier in 1942 from one ounce to a half-ounce. It gave rise to frequent informal smuggling of tea south over the border and butter, eggs and liquor north. Irish mothers became, in the words of a topical cartoon caption, 'Wizards of ½Oz'. On Tuesday 28 July 1942 a Dublin woman was discovered to have drawn the tea ration for four people not resident with her. She was informed that she would not be struck off the books but because she had overdrawn her rations she would not receive her next quota of tea until she had caught up on the overdrawn period: two years and five weeks later, a date in September 1944.

28 July 1981

'A full-time criminal'

Three men charged with the attempted murder of a Garda and the armed robbery of £102,000 from the Bank of Ireland branch in Stillorgan Shopping Centre were found guilty of the crimes in the Special Criminal Court on Tuesday 28 July 1981. The incident had taken place on 30 December 1980 and the parties involved were Frank Ward (28), Knockmore Park, Tallaght, John Doran (27), Blackditch Road, Ballyfermot, and Anthony O'Brien (32), Emorville Avenue, South Circular Road. Ward, who described himself as a full-time criminal, had accused Detective Garda Tony Fennessy of using him as an informer since the previous August. This charge was rejected in toto and regarded by the court as a distraction from the main business.

Ward described how before Christmas Cornelius Sheehan had arranged with him to hide the money from the proposed bank raid. They buried a milk churn in a location in Glencullen and on the day of the raid Sheehan put him in position there and gave him part of his payment. Shortly before 4 o'clock a white Fiat car pulled up and a man carrying a machine-gun shouted his name. He told Ward to get into the car, saying they were 'up his arse'. The Fiat crashed a short time later and the occupants moved to a blue Datsun that also crashed at a Garda checkpoint. The raiders ran off, leaving Ward to face the Gardaí.

He said he intended to return any money he got to Fennessy, whose 'snout' he insisted he was. His payment from his involvement in the caper was to be £250 plus 5 per cent 'off the top'. Fennessy admitted professional acquaintance with Ward but denied previous knowledge of the Stillorgan raid. In view of the complicated evidence Mr Justice Hamilton, who presided, put off sentencing until 10 o'clock the following day.

29 July 1964

Them bones

In a city as old as Dublin, especially at the sites of the most ancient settlements, demolition of old buildings and excavations for new foundations can sometimes throw up remarkable discoveries. A gang of workmen sent to demolish a tenement behind the Four Courts Hotel in Dublin 7 uncovered a mass grave full of what seemed to be human bones. It was not until the tally exceeded about twenty that the workmen, led by Owen Duffy of Shelmalier Road, East Wall, sent for the Gardaí. The work was in preparation for the building of a banqueting hall for the hotel and already a number of finds had turned up. Duffy had found four spent bullet cases, an English farthing dated 1762, four English pennies and a shilling dated 1864.

Some of the skulls had what seemed to be bullet-holes and some showed signs of blunt-force trauma. Brendan O'Riordan, assistant keeper of Irish Antiquities, National Museum, was inclined to think that the finds might be of historical rather than archaeological interest and the date of interment could be determined only by reference to the buildings that had earlier existed on the site or by a fluorine or carbon test. He thought, however, that with bones so old the result might not be very accurate. The holes in the skull might be explained by an anatomist and since the remains were all those of adults, he tended to rule out a famine connection.

Local antiquarians offered alternative dating, one suggesting that the remains might date as far back as Clontarf (1014) as the site had been occupied by the Inns of Court from the 16th century and could scarcely have been a site for a mass grave. Others suggested a cholera epidemic or, more likely, relics of the 1798 uprising.

30 July 1961

The Asgard

The yacht *Asgard* made two historical Sunday landings, separated by forty-seven years, in Howth harbour. The first, on 26 July 1914, was the occasion of the importation by the Irish Volunteers of nine hundred guns and 29,000 rounds of ammunition as a formal challenge to the government who had seemed to condone the much more elaborate gun-running by the Ulster Volunteer Force (UVF). The sequel, with the killing of three people by the British army on Bachelor's Quay, made it clear just how different the reaction of the authorities to the activities of the two forces were.

The other landing, on Sunday 30 July 1961, was non-violent – in fact quite celebratory. Éamon de Valera, President of Ireland, led the reception party and to intensify the drama of the occasion the *Asgard* had been kept at anchor off Lambay Island since the previous Tuesday. She sailed into the harbour at exactly 3pm to become the centrepiece of what de Valera called 'a splendid, glorious and joyful' day. The yacht was moored at the pier in front of the lighthouse and the President inspected a guard of honour manned by the FCA under Commandant Edward Curry and was then conducted to the vessel. Its commander, Lieutenant Joseph A. Deasy, formally reported its arrival while the Army No 1 Band played.

In the course of his speech de Valera mentioned the participants in the original enterprise including Mrs Molly Childers, who lived in Glendalough. On behalf of the audience he sent a message through her son, Erskine, with the 'assurance that the great event in which she and her gallant husband took such a memorable part will never be forgotten by the Irish nation.' The ceremony concluded with the formal unloading of fifty Mauser rifles that were then shouldered by twenty of the original participants.

31 July 1893

Cunnradh na Gaidhhilge

On Monday 31 July 1893 a number of men gathered for a meeting in O'Kelly's Rooms in 9 Lower O'Connell Street. The invitations had been sent out by Eoin MacNeill and Douglas Hyde took the chair. The minute books preserved in the National Library in Kildare Street indicate that present were 'Chas Percy Bushe, Jas M. Cogan, Thomas W Elleker, Reverend William Hayden SJ, P. Hogan, Martin O'Kelly, John McNeill BA, Patrick O'Brien, Thomas O'Neill Russell. The circulars had invited them to consider the formation of a society to be called Cunnradh na Gaidhhilge, 'for the purpose of keeping the Irish language alive'. All had a public interest in the ideals of the League but the prime movers were Hyde and MacNeill, the latter's name just recognisable in the minutes.

MacNeill deliberately eschewed the word 'revival' as suggesting that life was already extinct, concentrating instead on 'preservation'. This echoed the name of an earlier venture, the Society for the Preservation of the Irish Language (SPIL) that had been founded in 1876 and had provided a kind of blueprint for the League. MacNeill who would later found the Irish Volunteers and edit *An Claidheamh Soluis*, the League's journal, had contributed an article to the *Irish Ecclesiastical Record* of December 1891 called 'Why and How the Irish Language Is to be Preserved.'

Hyde was the son of a Church of Ireland clergyman and was multilingual With W.B. Yeats he founded the Irish National Literary Society, the source of the Celtic Renaissance. He dedicated his life to Irish, translating much folk poetry and writing the first modern drama in Irish. Hyde's lecture of 25 November 1892, 'On the Necessity for De-anglicising the Irish People', convinced MacNeill that the time was ripe for an all-out effort to preserve Irish.

AUTUMN

1 August 1948

Clement Attlee in Dublin

Clement Attlee (1883-1967), the unobtrusive prime minister whose post-war Labour government established the welfare state in Britain, arrived in Dublin on Sunday 1 August 1948 at the start of a three-week holiday in County Mayo, to sign an Anglo-Irish Trade Agreement with the new Taoiseach, John A. Costello. It was due to be signed at 11am and was really an amendment to the 1938 agreement that was signed by Éamon de Valera and Neville Chamberlain. The terms of the contract had already been initialled by the relevant members of cabinet of both governments: Costello, Seán MacBride (External Affairs), William Norton (Social Welfare), James Dillon (Agriculture), Patrick McGilligan (Finance) and Daniel Morrissey (Industry and Commerce) from Ireland and Attlee, John Strachey (Food), Sir Stafford Cripps (Chancellor of the Exchequer), Harold Wilson (Board of Trade), Tom Williams (Agriculture), and P.J. Noel-Baker (Commonwealth Relations). The details mainly concerned cattle and poultry exports from Ireland and imports from Britain, mainly of coal and oil.

At the airport Attlee, who was accompanied by his wife and two daughters, was met by a deputation led by Lord and Lady Rugby, the UK representatives, and William Norton, the Minister for Social Welfare and deputy Taoiseach, but fielded all questions about trade or politics. He related that he intended to meet the president, Seán T. O'Kelly (1882-1966), and then drive west to stay in Melcombe House, Newport. Asked how he would manage three weeks without a telephone he laughed and said it would be 'just lovely'. He also intended to play 'some golf' and do a little unskilled fishing. As he left the terminal building he praised the airport: 'I think it puts ours to shame.'

The high level of diplomatic goodwill and agreement must have made Costello's announcement five weeks later of Ireland's leaving the Common-wealth and its establishment of a republic something of a surprise.

2 August 1946

Learner driver

In the days before L-plates, driving tests and dual-control cars, learning – and teaching – to drive could be at times hazardous. On the morning of 19 March 1946 Norma North of Fitzwilliam Place was behind the wheel of the car of Charles V. O'Donnell of Ailesbury Road, who was teaching her to drive. The car drove along Strand Road, Sandymount, and out the Merrion gates and proceeded along Merrion Road. While turning into Ailesbury Road the car collided with a cyclist, Dorothy A. Davison of Herbert Avenue, off Merrion Road. Her legs became entangled with the front of the car. O'Donnell extricated her and drove her to the Royal City of Dublin Hospital in Baggot Street, from where she was allowed home after treatment.

Nearly five months later, on Friday 2 August, O'Donnell and North appeared before District Justice O'Grady on charges under the Road Traffic Act. Noel Hartnett, O'Donnell's solicitor, submitted in defence that his client, sitting beside North, had control over the handbrake, foot brake, clutch and accelerator; North merely steered the vehicle. It gave rise to a nice legal point as to who exactly was the driver but no definitive legal answer was offered. O'Donnell admitted that it was his error of judgement that caused the accident as they turned into Ailesbury Road, although North remained in the driving seat.

The judge imposed fines on both parties: on O'Donnell £5 for dangerous driving, £5 for having allowed North to drive without insurance, 10s for having no driving licence and 5s for having no rear mirror. A further charge of employing North to drive his car was dismissed. On North £3 for aiding and abetting O'Donnell in the dangerous driving charge, £5 for driving without insurance cover and 10s for driving without a licence. A charge against her of driving 'without due consideration' was dropped.

3 August 1933

'Brutal conduct'

An inquest on Thursday 3 August 1933 heard evidence of a lack of humanity and public-spiritedness on the part of two motorists at the scene of a fatal accident. Liam Nolan (junior), a fourteen-year-old boy, received injuries that led to his death in Booterstown, Blackrock. He was the son of a hotelier who lived above the premises in Pearse Street before moving to Heytesbury Street. He was a pupil in St Enda's College, Rathfarnham, and had just come back from a course in Irish in the Connemara Gaeltacht. He and a friend decided to go on their bicycles to the swimming pool in Blackrock. On the way he thought it a good idea to hang on to the back of a passing lorry for greater ease in traction, a common device for young cyclists in the days when motor traffic was sparse.

The driver of the lorry had to swerve to clear the lines for a passing tramcar and young John was thrown off his bicycle. The lorry driver was unaware of his hanger-on and had to be told to stop. Some passers-by tried to stop two cars for assistance but the first one did not stop and the second drove off again at the sight of the boy's condition. A motorcycle combo did stop and the now moribund boy was taken to hospital. The medical evidence showed that James had died of shock and haemorrhage as a result of the accident.

Dr J.P. Brennan, Coroner for South County Dublin said that the callous conduct of the motorists who failed to help must be condemned. The jury returned a verdict of accidental death, exonerated the driver of the lorry from all blame and also condemned the brutal conduct of the two motorists.

4 August 1945

'The issueless predicament of existence'

On Saturday 4 August 1945 Samuel Beckett (1906-89), then known more as a quondam French lecturer and personal friend of his late fellow-exile James Joyce than the laureate of humorous lack of communication and glorious verbal inadequacy, wrote a review of an art book for *The Irish Times*. He was thirty-nine, had had a tough war in France and would have to wait ten years to see the English version of *Waiting for Godot* reach the stage. The book, *Jack B. Yeats: An Appreciation and an Interpretation,* by Thomas MacGreevy (1893-1967), brought together two giants of the Irish art world – the artist, brother of the more famous W.B., and the author, art critic, poet, Joyce's executor and future director of the National Gallery of Ireland. MacGreevy also wrote on Nicholas Poussin, famous now as the painter of *A Dance to the Music of Time,* that gave Anthony Powell the title for his fictional duodecalogy.

The review was sober and generally appreciative. Beckett knew something of the book's history, MacGreevy having failed for seven years to find a London publisher. A typical sentence in a continuously astringent piece reads: 'It is difficult to formulate what it is one likes in Mr Yeats's painting or indeed what it is one likes in anything...' The reviewer does not quite approve of MacGreevy's emphasising the national aspects of Mr Yeats's genius, claiming him as fit to be judged on purely aesthetical grounds: 'He brings light as only the great dare bring light, to the issueless predicament of existence, reduces the dark where there might have been, mathematically at least, a door.' The prose was of a higher quality than even Ireland's leading paper was used to, at times requiring a greater concentration than usual but well worth failing to find its absolute meaning.

5 August 1984

Prison matters

An attack on a prison officer on Saturday 4 August 1984 and another on an inmate of Mountjoy Prison two days later seemed to have a sinister link. As Patrick Hayes, an assistant chief officer of the 'Joy', was driving home around 8.20pm on the Strawberry Beds Road, Lucan, he was forced to stop his car when confronted by three masked men. They beat him with iron bars, then drove off. Next day the Gardaí appealed to the public for information, asking especially motorists, cyclists and pedestrians who were in the neighbourhood of Lucan, Clonsilla and Chapelizod between 7.30 and 8.30pm to contact them at Lucan Garda Station. They were particularly anxious to talk to a couple who visited the station soon after the assault.

A prisoner who was shaving in his cell in Mountjoy at 4pm on Monday 6 August was not aware that an intruder had entered the cell. It was during an unaccustomed 'recreation' period because of the relaxation of rules on the bank holiday. His assailant slashed him on the back, the deep cut requiring eighteen stitches in A&E in the nearby Mater Hospital. On his return to the prison he was locked in the B base section – the punishment section – for his own protection. He had committed the most heinous of all prison sins, giving information to the 'screws'.

That night Stephen Delany, the general secretary of the Prison Officers' Association, suggested that the slashing (and the fact that the prisoners knew almost immediately what information the informant had conveyed) was somehow linked to the Hayes attack and a threat received by another officer in his home in Kells. As later became clear, the background of all this unease was an ongoing struggle between the POA and Michael Noonan, the Minister for Justice, about prison overcrowding.

6 August 1937

The old adversary

The Royal Dublin Society's horse show was first held with little stir in April 1864 but it survived the cataclysm of subsequent Irish history to become the highlight of the late summer season. By 1937 the city and the state had sufficient self-confidence to value the show as one of the greatest of the year's events and as an index of this confidence the Irish Free State Army jumping team on Friday 6 August that year secured the Aga Khan trophy outright, having won it for the third year in succession. This victory put Ireland in the forefront of the world of horsemanship.

The first round netted the Irish team fifteen faults and when the second round began a silence descended upon the Ballsbridge arena that was deafening. But when the last member of the team had a faultless round the cheers from the crowd drowned the official announcement that with only two faults in the second round Ireland seemed certain to lead the field. The final fault score showed how decisive her victory was: Ireland – 17; France – 41; United States – 51; Netherlands – 54; Switzerland – 57. Belgium had been eliminated during the second round. Great Britain did not feature in the final table because the team had been disqualified for a breach of the jumping rules.

The crowd numbered 43, 913, an advance of 1599 on the 1936 fourth-day total and 9114 on that of 1935. At the parade of the various national teams it was noticed that when the English group arrived the spectators joined enthusiastically in singing 'God Save the King' and cheered the old adversary with nearly the same enthusiasm as they bestowed on 'The Soldier's Song' when Team Ireland entered the field. The news that England had been disqualified was greeted with genuine disappointment.

7 August 1942

False pretences

Mrs Annie Blackmore, 'Wynston', Churchtown, after three days of appearance in the Dublin District Court was on Friday 7 August sent for trial to the Criminal Court on multiple charges of attempting to obtain money by false pretences. Over the three days, evidence of many cases, some settled out of court, was presented before District Justice McCann. Mrs Blackmore's many claims for compensation were made against suppliers of food, insisting that she been injured by foreign bodies in their products.

Frank Forshaw of 'Aliens', Orwell Road, Rathgar, testified that he had received a letter from Blackmore complaining that a piece of steel in bread bought from him had injured her mouth. Wheat crumbs and a tiny piece of metal were included in the envelope. Nora Sexton, who ran a bakery in Meath Street, received a similar letter from the defendant complaining of a cut tongue. She, like Forshaw, turned the matter over to her insurance company. Other allegations included injury from a brass pin found in a steak bought in Dame Street, glass in a cake, a piece of steel in a Hafner's sausage, chips of enamel in a tin of peas and worms in oatmeal.

Payments of £2 or £3 were made without prejudice in out-of-court settlements by several Dublin firms but the Yorkshire Insurance Company called on a surgeon to examine Blackmore. He could find no trace of injury anywhere in her mouth. The surgeon hired by General Accident and Life made a similar report. Annie Fitzpatrick, a witness who lived opposite Blackmore in Drimnagh in 1941, said that she had made no mention of injuries but did complain of finding the worm in the oatmeal. In the light of the cumulative evidence the judge had no hesitation in returning her for trial.

8 August 1923

The Gardaí

The first Irish police service was established as an unarmed force by the Provisional Government of the Free State on 21 February 1922. It replaced the eighty-three-year-old Royal Irish Constabulary (RIC) and the Irish Republican Police (1919-22). Its first member was Patrick Joseph Kerrigan from County Mayo and its first commissioner was Michael Staines, also from Mayo. It was intended at first to replicate the RIC as an armed force with jurisdiction outside the capital.

The first six months were problematic, with unrest leading to a mutiny in August 1922. Kevin O'Higgins, the then Minister for Home Affairs, dismissed Staines and appointed Eoin O'Duffy to reconstitute the service as an acceptable unarmed force. It was Labour TD Cathal O'Shannon (1893-1969) who proposed the name Garda Síochána (guard of the peace) and this was incorporated into the Garda Síochána (Temporary Provisions) Act that became law on Wednesday 8 August 1923. The bill provided for the creation of a 'force of police of police to be called and known as "The Garda Síochána"'. Section 22 of the act was held to have renamed the existing force. It was later to take responsibility for policing the capital when it assimilated the DMP in 1925.

Its initial strength of 4000 was increased by the Garda Síochána Act (1924) to 6300, consisting of one commissioner, five supervising officers, twenty-seven chief superintendents, a hundred and fifty superintendents and inspectors, 1200 sergeants and 4918 Gardaí. Another Garda Síochána Act of 1958 provided for the recruitment of women into the force. Total membership on 31 May 2014 was 12, 954, with one deputy commissioner, eight assistant commissioners, forty-one chief superintendents, one hundred and forty three superintendents, two hundred and sixty-two inspectors, 1825 sergeants and 10, 674 Gardaí, the office of commissioner then vacant. The figures for women (November 2009) were in the same order: one, three, ten, twenty-three, two hundred and fifty nine, 2741 – a total of 3014.

9 August 1944

Galway of the Races

Galway Race Week began with less ceremony in 1869 when it was a two-day event in Ballybrit, beginning on the last Monday in July each year. Like Topsy it growed from that unambitious beginning into one of the big dates of the Irish year. Robert Lynd wrote glowingly about it in 1912 but in August 1944 it incurred the displeasure of the rather disapproving Bishop of Galway, Dr Michael Browne (1895-1980).

Browne was in many ways the epitome of the Irish prelates of the period, endlessly energetic in building sixty schools, thirty churches and a new cathedral that many found architecturally unpleasing. He was also notorious for his outspoken comments on public affairs, which led to frequent controversies. He referred to Trinity as 'a centre for atheist and communist propaganda', complained inaccurately that Seán O'Faolain's lively journal *The Bell* was full of rancour towards the Church and generally arrogated to it many aspects of Irish life that seemed to a majority to belong to the government.

In 1944, apparently shocked by the 'pagan revelry' of race week, he caused a letter to be read at all Masses in his diocese on Sunday 6 August (printed in all the national papers the following Wednesday). It was a typical crosier-wielding episcopal effort, a preaching to the converted but a cause of mirth to the roisterers:

> The scenes of rowdyism and drunkenness, to mention no worse, which
> took place in this city in the last few days have offended and alarmed all
> decent and God-fearing Christians.

He was, of course, perfectly right in his condemnation and many of his flock heartily approved of his censure but like so many other actions of the Church at the time it was ineffective and served only to increase the popularity of the event.

10 August 1961

Record attempt

On 6 May 1954, at a running track in Oxford, Roger Bannister, a twenty-five-year-old medical student, managed to run the mile in just under four minutes. He was aided by two athletic friends, Chris Brasher and Chris Chataway, who acted as pacemakers. His time of 3min 59.4sec has since been reduced by 17sec but it remains an ideal standard for all middle-distance runners. Using modern measurement the achievement is the equivalent of a speed of 24.14km/h. During the next decade many other runners attempted to emulate the achievement of Herb Elliott, who set the record in 1958 at 3min 54.5sec.

Ireland's leading middle-distance runner was Ronnie Delany, who had won a gold medal over 1500 metres at the Melbourne Olympics in 1956. On Thursday 10 August 1961 at the Clonliffe Harriers international athletic meeting in Santry Stadium (of which he was the patron), he made a supreme effort to beat Elliott's time. He ran a brilliant race, easily surging past the opposition in the last lap of the mile and causing the crowded stadium, keen to see records broken, great excitement. He had not seemed to make any effort in the early stages and when Ken Wood and Graham Everett took the lead he had begun to edge forward.

It soon became clear that Wood had moved out too soon and Delany began his famous surge, which took him easily past both his opponents. His strange leg-movement that journalists called his 'famous kick' took him over the finishing line but his time of 4min 4.2 sec was almost ten seconds too slow. Another famous athlete of the period, Gordon Pirie, was one of the visiting celebrities, who completed his three-mile run in a respectable (if no record) 13min 31.6sec. Pirie ran barefoot 'because lately running shoes seem to blister my feet'.

11 August 1943

Compulsory Irish

Examination results produce either elation or despair among teachers as well as candidates. This response was heightened in the summer of 1943 in the case of compulsory Irish in which a forty per cent mark was necessary to attain the Leaving Certificate. The results in the Irish examination announced on 11 August were not good and a chorus of complaint greeted their publication. Teachers in general felt that a great injustice had been done in the setting and marking of the papers. They said that the standards set were too high and the result an increase in failures and a decline in honours awards. Words such as 'scandalous' were used with particular reference to the Irish paper, which for the second year had been set and marked by 'university professors', who were accused by irate teachers of not being fully aware of the needs of students carrying five or six other subjects.

They also complained that too much attention was paid to tiny aspects of texts involving details that the average pupil would not advert to. There was, they said, no sense of appreciation of the significance of the pieces of literature as a whole. The papers of earlier years – those by the Department of Education – had been better suited for purpose. The fact that the results were generally poor should have been a warning sign that the Irish paper had failed in its purpose of selection and grading. There were many examples of students who had done well in all their other subjects and achieved only thirty per cent in the compulsory Irish. None of the teachers actually expressed dissatisfaction with the fact that no certificate could be issued without the necessary but there was an implicit air of questioning as to whether there should be any compulsory subjects.

12 August 1942

Thrilling aerial experience

The first airmail and passenger flight between Dublin and Berlin took place in 1932 and as a memorial of that leap forward a square wooden box labelled with this information was carried on the initial flight of every new route inaugurated by Aer Lingus. Ten years later, on 12 August 1942, in a courageous gesture, a new Dublin-Limerick air service was inaugurated. At a few minutes after 1pm a four-engined de Haviland express airliner touched down in Rineanna (now Shannon) Airport. The passengers were Major G.J. Carroll, general manager of Aer Lingus, Seán Ó hUadaigh, director, J. Cannon and J.P. O'Brien of the Irish Tourist Board, Senator Seán Campbell, Rory Henderson, C.E. McConnell and the Irish Movietone cameraman, Joe Evans.

They were met by D.J. O'Malley, Mayor of Limerick, J.J. Berkery, Limerick city manager, and other public representatives. Speaking for the citizens of Limerick, the mayor described the occasion as unique and expressed warm thanks to the directors of Aer Lingus for starting the new service, the significance of which could be gauged by the level of newspaper interest. It was an important boost to the reputation of the city that would now be known internationally. Ó hUadaigh, speaking on behalf of Seán Leyden, the Aer Lingus chairman, said that, thanks to the enterprise and foresight of the government, Rineanna Airport was second to none. It impressed and surprised aviation experts all over the world and was capable of meeting any future demand.

The plane took off on its return flight for Collinstown with Mayor O'Malley and his wife as guest passengers. O'Malley said that although he had flown all over the continent, to see his native soil from the air was his most thrilling aerial experience. His wife said simply that the flight was delightful.

13 August 1914

Redmondites embark for war

Britain declared war on Germany on Tuesday 4 August 1914, after the Kaiser's troops marched on Brussels. The declaration came almost as a relief to the Liberal administration, who feared that the Ulster Volunteer Force (UVF) was about to start a civil war in the North and believed that the officer class might refuse to move against their 'brothers' in Ireland. Better a complicated dance of guns and diplomacy 'somewhere over there' than a messy struggle in their own backyard. And besides it would all be over by Christmas. (They could not have known that the Christmas would be that of 1918 after seventeen million fatalities.)

With commendable speed an army was mobilised in Ireland when Carson and Craig delivered the UVF to Kitchener, even though, like true-born Irishmen, they detested each other. John Redmond (1856-1918) was soon persuaded to offer his National Volunteers to swell the 'contemptible little army' although that was not the purpose for which Eoin MacNeill had first called the movement into being. The first batch of Redmondites was equipped and ready to embark from Dublin docks on Thursday 13 August 1914, a mere nine days after the declaration of war. Recruitment had been brisk throughout the country, but especially in Dublin, and now the streets were lined with cheering wellwishers.

There were recruits from both traditions and all joined in to render 'God Save the King' and 'Rule, Britannia'. The band played 'Garryowen' and 'St Patrick's Day' and both spectators (who were momentarily classless, showing a mixture of all trades and professions) and recruits joined in the singing. Handkerchiefs were waved from shops and office windows and, although many women wept by the dockside, they had the consolation of knowing that for the first time in years they would have a steady income in the form of a soldier's pay.

14 August 1984

The Hop Store

Guinness stout has been made in Dublin in the St James's Gate brewery since 1759 and, now owned by Diageo, it is still the largest supplier of stout in the world. An important part of the plant was the Hop Store located in Rainsfort Street, a substantial building that, no longer required for the process, became a visitors' centre for the throngs of tourists anxious to discover the primary source of the famous black stuff. On Tuesday 14 August 1984 parts of the building were officially opened as an artistic centre by the city's new Lord Mayor, Michael O'Halloran. The transformation was not complete on that day; the ground floor was still a kind of junk room full of wooden crates, traffic cones and Corporation bollards and the attic was empty except for an intermittently noisy water tank.

The new vestibule had a staircase constructed of wood and steel and at its foot Brian Slowey, the managing director of Guinness, welcomed the Lord Mayor and congratulated him on the 'exciting event'. The firm had been one of the sources of finance for the conversion, along with the government and the EEC (as it was then known). The project had not met with universal approval; its many-windowed glass front had been attacked nightly by vandals until the contractors installed screens. There was a threat that Rosc, the four-yearly art exhibition called after the Irish word 'vision-image', due to be held that year in the Hop Store, might be used as a protest opportunity.

At the opening Dr Peter Walsh, one of the distinguished guests, caused some laughter when he opined, 'It won't be the Guinness Gallery and it won't be the Guinness Museum. It will be the Guinness Hop Store where...' here he paused, '...where's there's always something interesting going on.' A good summing-up.

15 August 1649

'An astonishing mercy'

In the summer after the death of Charles I in January 1649 most of Ireland remained in the hands of the Confederation (of native Catholics and Royalists), with only Dublin held by the Parliamentarian forces. The Marquess of Ormonde gathered his troops in Rathmines to take the city and deprive the enemy of the last port open for invasion. Colonel Michael Jones, the Dublin commander, carried out a surprise attack on 2 August while the Confederate forces were still assembling and scattered them, killing around 4000 and taking 2517 prisoners.

Oliver Cromwell, not yet the Lord Protector, although heading that way and already Lord Lieutenant of Ireland (the only commoner ever to hold the post) had begun his expeditionary preparations on 14 July 1649. News of Ormond's defeat greatly cheered him. With his customary assurance and Biblical language he described it as 'an astonishing mercy, so great and seasonable that we are like them that dreamed.' His first journey abroad saw him in the words of his chaplain, Hugh Peters, 'as sea-sick as ever I saw any man in my life'. All this was forgotten when he safely landed his 9000 foot and 4000 horse soldiers and £20,000 (£2.3m today) in cash.

His arrival in Ringsend was greeted with cheers from the large crowd that had gathered and the welcoming firing of cannons. Both he and his men were convinced, because of Rathmines and a propitious if stormy crossing, that their mission was godly. Cromwell wished to wipe out any residual Royalist support and also carried, perhaps unaware, a visceral determination to avenge the strongly overstated massacre of Ulster planters in 1641. His mission of 'the propagating the Gospel of Christ' involved the slaughter in Drogheda, Clonmel and Wexford that followed within a year and Ireland's oldest and foulest imprecation was firmly rooted.

16 August 1937

'Open to criticism and censure'

Two significant dates in the early history of Saorstát Éireann were those of the establishment of Radio RN, the national radio network in 1926 – the 'RN' a literal rendering of Éireann – and the Censorship of Publications Act in 1929. If Radio Éireann, as was later written, did not clash much with the censorship board it was due to an even more swingeing internal censorship. The main objection to the official decrees was that they were the bluntest of instruments, banning with equal fervour the most extreme form of rancid pornography and the most sober works of literary criticism because they dealt with the works of banned authors.

The radio service fulfilled admirably its charter as a public service medium, within the limits of a confessional state. Typical of the high intellectual content of some of its programmes was a series of lectures on *Great Writers of Today* and on Friday 16 August 1937 Frank O'Connor, one of the country's finest (and banned) writers was scheduled to give a talk on D.H. Lawrence and James Joyce.

The broadcast was cancelled and a number of reasons was offered for the decision: the script had not been submitted five days in advance; since Lawrence was dead and *Ulysses* had been published fifteen years earlier neither author could be called a 'writer of today'; the talk, 'although suitable for an intellectual or critical audience, was not suitable for general dissemination.'

One is still shocked at the broadcasting authorities' dishonesty and craven fear of leaving 'themselves open to criticism and censure', as they stated in the response. The truth was that O'Connor, already a controversial figure, was unafraid to speak plainly, Lawrence wrote, perhaps over-emotionally, about sex and Joyce had not yet become the country's chief cultural icon and tourist goldmine.

17 August 1878

Buck Mulligan

Oliver St John Gogarty (1878-1957), the Dublin Corinthian iconised as 'stately plump Buck Mulligan' by James Joyce in *Ulysses,* was born in Rutland (now Parnell) Square on Saturday 17 August 1878. He was educated in a variety of Jesuit institutions including the Royal University and TCD, where he qualified in medicine and became an intimate of John Pentland Mahaffy, Professor of Ancient Greek and later Provost, and Robert Yelverton Tyrrell, Professor of Greek. His period as co-tenant with Joyce of the Martello Tower in Sandycove was quite short. They were of different temperaments: Dedalus intense, acerbic and convinced of greatness; Mulligan confident, flamboyant, athletic – the 'plump' was more euphonious than accurate – verbally nearly as dextrous as his friend. Both were self-consciously classicists.

Gogarty soon became known for his unpublished witty and bawdy verse and his expertise as a leading ENT surgeon. His house in Ely Place became a kind of salon, its prestige enhanced by having George Moore (1852-1933) as a neighbour. Moore named the self-defrocked priest in his novel *The Lake* after him. He reputation as a 'buck' increased with the coming of his butter-coloured Rolls Royce, his aeroplane, his escape from republicans as a strong supporter of Arthur Griffith and the Treaty by swimming the Liffey ('just going through the motions') and his appointment as a Free State senator and organiser of the Tailteann Games.

He found the Ireland of the 1930s intolerably church-driven and puritanical, describing his bête-noire de Valera in the Senate as 'our Celtic Calvin' and privately as 'a cross between a corpse and a cormorant'. When his book of unreliable memoirs *As I Was Going Down Sackville Street* (1937) led to litigation in 1939 he left Ireland for good, living mainly in America and continuing to write. He died on 22 September 1957. His deepest feelings were adumbrated in his poem. 'Non Dolet' which concludes: 'But with the Strivers leave the Strife/ Nor after Caesar skulk in Rome.'

18 August 1951

Art adviser in Kerala

Margaret ('Gretta') Gillespie was born in Boyle, County Roscommon, in 1878 and in 1903 married James Cousins, a minor figure of the Irish Literary Renaissance, author of the play *The Racing Lug*. He was a self-educated intellectual born in Belfast in 1875 and joined enthusiastically in his wife's agitation for women's suffrage. She found imprisonment in Holloway for six months on an admitted charge of throwing stones in Downing Street 'a living hell'. She had a further year in jail in Madras in 1932, even though she was the first woman magistrate to be appointed in India, for speaking at a proscribed meeting against British special powers and the incarceration of Mahatma Gandhi.

The couple had become theosophists in 1908 and with no prospect of the vote for women they left Dublin for India, where they both played a significant part in the slow but ultimately successful campaign for Indian independence. This contribution was recognised by Pandit Nehru, who sent Gretta 15,000 rupees to help her recovery when, after an accident in 1943, she was let paralysed. James, once known as Séamus Ó Cúisín, was an educationist, academic and art adviser to the government of Kerala. Author of more than a hundred books, he founded the first art gallery in India.

The pair combined their literary talents to write a joint seven-hundred-and-seventy-page autobiography, *We Two Together*, describing their eventful lives and world travels. It was published in 1950 by Ganesh in Madras and happily a copy made its way to the desk of the literary editor of *The Irish Times* who printed a review by H.R. Chillngworth on Saturday 18 August 1951. It did not meet with his full approval: he noted redundancy in later chapters but relished the account of the literary life of their (and his) younger Dublin days.

19 August 1949

Gold cigarette cases

Mrs Frances Shirley Barkley (28) of no fixed address in Dublin was sentenced on Friday 19 August 1949 to four months' imprisonment for the theft of gold cigarette cases, one valued at £175 from Messrs West of Grafton Street, the other worth £60 from Messrs Weir & Company in the same street. She had devised a simple but effective scam that succeeded because of her confident attractiveness – she was a beauty specialist by profession.

W. Conway, prosecuting, described how on 17 June of that year Mrs Barkley had persuaded a salesman called Murtagh that she was the sister-in-law of Ernest Barkley, one of Messrs West's regular customers. She asked to be shown on approbation a gold cigarette case, specifically an Asprey. She accepted the case he offered and left with it, having signed an undertaking to return it on 20 June. She then moved on to her next target, Messrs Weir & Company, where she obtained the second case from a salesman called McGahey by reminding him that she was an old acquaintance, whom he recognised as 'Miss Martin of Chapelizod'.

The scene then shifts to the Dún Laoghaire-Holyhead steamer, where a customs officer discovered Messrs Weir's case in the luggage of Mr McGill, Barkley's companion. The case was confiscated but the pair was allowed to proceed. Three weeks later, on 12 July, they sold Messrs West's gold case to a jeweller in Regent Street in London for £140. On 21 July Barkley was arrested in Dublin. Her solicitor, H. Good, told the court that Barkley had had a very profitable cosmetic and perfumery business with a yearly turnover of £45,000. As the business began to fail her partner had absconded, leaving her to pay the debts. In her desperation she devised the scheme with the full intention of paying back the money.

20 August 1963

The death of Hazel Mullen

Shan Mohangi was a South African from Natal studying medicine in the Royal College of Surgeons. He lived in a flat in 95 Harcourt Street, above a restaurant called the Green Tureen where he worked as an assistant chef. It was in the oven there that he tried to dispose of the dismembered body, including the severed head, of his girlfriend, Hazel Mullen. He himself was twenty-three and, among the inevitable speculations as to motive, two prevailed: he fell into a rage when she said she wanted to end their relationship or she had died during an attempt at an abortion. Hazel, from St James's Lodge, Crinken, Shankill, was almost sixteen and had worked in the printing department of the Bank of Ireland as well as being a part-time model. She was last seen at 12.30 on Saturday 17 August 1963, when she finished work, and her mother reported her disappearance to the Gardaí. It was the odd odour in the kitchen that caused the search to be made.

At six minutes past eight o'clock the following Tuesday evening, 20 August, Mohangi was driven to the Dublin District Court and there charged with murder. He was remanded in custody until Tuesday 27 August, when the charge was changed to manslaughter, for which he was sentenced to seven years' imprisonment. He served four of these before being deported to Natal. There he changed his name to Narantuk Jumuna and began a successful career as a businessman and a politician. On 23 March 2009 he was forced to withdraw as a candidate from the election for the KwaZulu Natal provincial assembly scheduled for 22 April when his early history was revealed. He was removed from the list by Hanif Hoosen, the secretary-general of the Independent Democrats.

21 August 1937

From the frying-pan into the fire

The besetting problem of life in cities is what to do about vehicular traffic, both a help and a hindrance to mobility and commerce. It is not just a modern phenomenon: the Romans had to ban it during the hours of daylight. Although by twenty-first century standards, Dublin traffic before the Second World War was sparse, it still presented a problem to traders. On Saturday 21 August 1937 the managers of shops in Grafton Street were up in arms against a new traffic code that was about to be imposed.

Some of the measures were thought to be too drastic and, as always in such cases, the opposition claimed that 'they would not only fail to achieve their end but would be detrimental to business interests.' They included the introduction of a system of one-way traffic with unilateral limited parking (twenty minutes) on alternate days. This dismayed firms such as Switzer's and Brown Thomas, whose managers declared that their windows would not be seen from the other side of the street and, although twenty minutes was an insufficient time for shopping, the parked cars would still cause a serious obstruction 'in such a busy thoroughfare'. The present congestion was caused by stationary vehicles and slow-moving horse traffic. The only answer in their view was to 'abolish all parking'.

The bigger stores had been driven to open alternative doors (Switzer's round the corner in Wicklow Street, Brown Thomas in Duke Street) but parking even in these side streets had vitiated the scheme. The proprietors' concern for their potential pedestrian shoppers led them to argue rather heatedly that 'many of their customers had found it difficult to approach the pavement to alight'. The reiterated general consensus was that the new moves would 'be nothing more than a transfer from the frying-pan into the fire'.

22 August 1984

Working overtime

Margaret O'Brien, a prison officer in Limerick, became pregnant in 1984 and looked forward to having her baby in February 1985. The early days of the pregnancy were difficult, with much nausea, requiring sick leave from 13-26 June. On her return she was required to work a twelve-hour day. In the week beginning 21 April she worked sixty-eight-and-a half hours, which with lunch breaks counted as seventy-two hours of continuous duty over a six-day period. She asked for and obtained a temporary injunction in July excusing her from working overtime for one month. The injunction expired on Wednesday 22 August 1984.

On that day she appeared in the High Court in Dublin seeking to restrain Michael Noonan, the Minister for Justice, from requiring her to work overtime on the grounds that she was worried about her health, about which her husband shared her concern. She was represented by David Byrne BL who made it clear that he was appearing for Mrs O'Brien personally and not on behalf of the Prisoner Officers' Association.

James Connolly BL, appearing for the minister, suggested that the case depended not on the plaintiff's medical condition but on the conditions of her employment and held that it the matter should have been settled internally at administrative level. In Limerick jail there existed an 'unavailablity book', which 75 per cent of the female staff had signed. The effect of this was that any system of voluntary overtime was impossible to organise and the case had been brought as part of concerted industrial action. Justice McWilliam brought the argument to a close by granting the injunction on the grounds that Mrs O'Brien had 'a good arguable case' but he emphasised that he was not setting a precedent in making his decision.

23 August 1961

The Amerigo Vespucci

'In 1492/Columbus sailed the ocean blue,' as many American children learn at school. In 1499 Amerigo Vespucci sailed the brine and realised that the New World discovered by his fellow countryman was a continent in its own right. From his written accounts of what he found, a name was devised by Martin Waldseemüller, a German cartographer, for his discovery. It was known thenceforth as America, based on the Latinate form of Vespucci's first name.

The Italian nation has taken a just pride in those who discovered these lands and in the 1960s its chief training ship was named *Amerigo Vespucci*. She and an accompanying battle cruiser, the *Raimondo Montecuccoli*, sailed into Dublin on Wednesday 23 August 1961 on a courtesy visit. Like other training vessels she was a three-masted, full-rigged ship. It has always been a naval tradition that, although the age of sail is a distant dream, a mariner is not worth his salt until he has shinned up masts, hung about the crow's nest and done his stint afore sail. The 4000-ton naval academy had five hundred and fifteen hands on board, of whom three hundred and fourteen were ratings and a hundred and sixty-four officer cadets. The establishment comprised thirty-one officers and four instructors under the command of Rear-Admiral Giuseppi Roselli-Lorenzini.

Both ships arrived off Dún Laoghaire at about 8.30am and the *Amerigo Vespucci* exchanged a 21-gun salute with Dún Laoghaire East Pier saluting base. They docked in Alexandra Basin at 10am and were boarded by the Italian chargé d'affaires and the naval attaché. The senior Italian officers later visited the Chief of Staff, the OC of the naval service, the Lord Mayor and the chairman of Dublin Port and Docks Board. After a day of many other courtesy calls the officers attended a cocktail party in the Shelbourne Hotel.

24 August 1943

Butter emergency

Éire, during what was called the Emergency at home and the Second World War further afield, suffered many scarcities as all but the most essential imports were unavailable. Coal was scarce, petrol even scarcer, tea practically unobtainable. Yet she could rely on her native resources: meat, dairy products and alcohol. A steady amateur smuggling of tea and white flour to the south from Northern Ireland and reciprocal traffic of eggs, butter (the allowance there was two ounces per person per week), meat and liquor to the north made life a little bit easier. Another Irish solution to an Irish problem.

When, on Tuesday 24 August 1943, it was announced in the Dublin papers that, while not actually forbidden, the serving of butter in hotels and restaurants was to be restricted, the news was greeted with a mixture of dismay and incredulity. Most private city dwellers managed perfectly well on their ration of half a pound per head but the prospect of a lunch or dinner out without butter was unthinkable. The government order was uncompromising: no butter would be served at meals consisting of two or more courses at which meat (or fish) and a vegetable were served. Government inspectors from the Department of Supplies would visit hotels and restaurants to make sure that the order was being obeyed. Furthermore, each menu had to carry the message: 'It is illegal to serve butter at luncheons and dinners.'

From October the production of surplus butter would end and from then to May 1944 the country would be dependent on the accumulated reserve stocks. The current monthly consumption of 48,000 cwt (2, 438, 513 kg) was 1000 cwt (50, 802 kg) in excess of expectations.

25 August 1963

Princess Grace

Grace Kelly (1929-82) was a rich, beautiful and competent film actor whom Alfred Hitchcock made into a star with films such as *Rear Window* and *To Catch a Thief*. Because she was Catholic and Irish-American she was, after Jackie Kennedy, whose fame she predated, the best-known and most popular American female with the Irish. When her stellar career was terminated on her marriage to Prince Rainier III of Monaco in 1956 there was real regret, yet a sense of a fairytale ending in her marrying a genuine prince. And there was always the possibility that she would one day yield to one of the many demands that she return to the screen. Her royal career was eagerly followed by the media, as was her premature death in a car accident after a stroke in 1982.

At 19.05 hours on Sunday 25 August 1963 she and her five-year-old son, Prince Albert, landed in Dublin at the start of a three-week holiday in Ireland. She was greeted with cheers as she came down the steps of the plane, dressed in a tight-fitting turban and a light pink woollen travelling coat. Her husband arrived at the airport an hour later with their eldest daughter, the seven-year-old Caroline, the staggered arrivals caused by the current practice of not having both parents travelling on the same flight. Asked about their plans, the princess said that they did not intend to travel very far: 'We are here for a rest and a quiet time.' The prince, who was an eight-handicap golfer, had arranged to play in Portmarnock and in Hermitage Golf Course, near Carton House, Maynooth, where they intended to stay.

The weather was abysmal, with continuous rain, but many people turned out to greet what was almost an official procession with Garda squad cars leading the drive through the city and motor-cycle escorts on both flanks.

26 August 1913

The Lockout

At 9.40 on the morning of Tuesday 26 August 1913 there was a great deal of bustle as crowds of people were making their way to Ballsbridge to the Horse Show. They were at first puzzled and then annoyed to discover that from College Green to the GPO in Sackville Street there was an unbroken line of abandoned tramcars. Up to two hundred motormen and conductors (they had that luxury in those days) had begun a strike organised by the Irish Transport and General Workers' Union, a union founded by James Larkin (1876-1947) to try to ameliorate the working conditions of the city's labourers, some of whom lived in 'the worst slums in Europe'.

Larkin's chief adversary was William Martin Murphy (1844-1919), who headed the Employers' Federation and claimed that he had no objection to his workers organising but refused to countenance membership of the ITGWU, – 'a disreputable organisation' headed by 'an unscrupulous man' with personal ambitions. He announced that as head of the Dublin United Tramway Company he would provide £100,000 to put down Larkin's 'terrorism'. He had support from the Dublin Castle authorities, who could call upon the Dublin Metropolitan Police. Of the company's 1700 workers, seven hundred came out on strike but the DMP and the non-strikers soon restored the service.

On 3 September members of the Employers' Federation locked out their workers and within a few weeks more than 100,000 Dubliners faced starvation. Relief ships were organised to bring in supplies to the needy but when starving children were being brought to England for care the organisers were accused by the ill-informed and absent Archbishop William Walsh (1841-1921) of proselytising. When food supplies from outside ceased early in 1914 the workers capitulated but although Larkin's ITGWU was seriously depleted in numbers Murphy was not able to break it.

27 August 1946

Impeccable crash landing

At approximately 9.30pm on Sunday 16 June 1946 Aer Lingus flight EI-ACA took off from Shannon on a scheduled trip to Dublin. About five minutes later, when the plane was still only three miles west of Sixmilebridge, the fuel gauge of the starboard engine indicated a failure of power. The appropriate single-pressure procedure was put into operation by the crew, a cross-feed valve to feed fuel to the stricken engine was switched on but the engine did not recover. There was no alternative but to return to Shannon and, coming in from the south, make a crash landing. This was successfully achieved with no loss of life and only minimal injuries.

The findings of the Inspector of Accidents' preliminary investigation were published in Dublin on Tuesday 27 August and included a detailed account of the incident. The starboard engine had fallen away but no one on board noticed and the pilot eventually touched down in a field five hundred yards beyond the approach road to the airport and slid a further two hundred and fifty yards before coming to rest. In the landing the port engine hit a tree and it too caught fire. There was no panic and the only injuries sustained were minor cuts and bruises by those members of the crew without safety belts. All aboard walked to safety through the main door without a hint of panic.

The report stated that no blame could be attached to any member of the crew, whose behaviour throughout had been exemplary, and that the crash landing of the plane without loss of life was impeccable. The fire in the starboard engine, the immediate cause of the accident, was due to a leak in one of the pipelines in the engine nacelle but the cause was now undiscoverable. No further enquiry was considered necessary.

28 August 1922

Pallbearers

The document quoted below contains a handwritten list of the pallbearers who had the mournful task of carrying the body of Michael Collins, Commander-in-Chief of the army of the infant Free State. He had been shot on Tuesday 22 August, in an ambush by anti-Treaty forces in Béal na mBláth, on the road from Macroom to Bandon in his native County Cork. Because of disruption to the road network as a consequence of the Civil War, his body was brought by sea from Cork and lay in state on the capital's City Hall for three days before removal to the Pro-Cathedral in Marlborough Street for Requiem Mass on Sunday 27 August.

The country was still reeling from the death ten days earlier of Arthur Grffiiths, its elected president and one of the architects of the Treaty that ended the War of Independence. Griffith had died from a cerebral haemorrhage. The assassination of Michael Collins was an almost crippling blow that greatly increased the nation's grief and was to have an incalculable effect on future history, especially respecting the North. Thousands paid their respects in City Hall and the Pro-Cathedral was crowded for the funeral service on the Monday. As Collins held the rank of general the funeral would be a military one with regimental trappings, and rehearsals were held in Portobello Barracks on the Saturday at 4pm and the Sunday at 12 noon.

The instructions and names of the personnel were listed in the official document:

> The pallbearers will parade outside Pro-Cathedral at 10.40am. At 10.55 they will march into the church to take up positions on each side of the catafalque and will act as Guard of Honour during Mass.

The pallbearers were: Major-General Tobin, Commandant-Generals Cullen, Ahern, Dalton, O'Connell and Dolan and Captains Byrne and Rylands.

The body of the hero was taken on a gun carriage from Marlborough Street to Glasnevin Cemetery on Monday 28 August 1922, through densely crowded streets.

29 August 1933

Car radios

Regular broadcasting in Ireland began on 1 January 1926 as 2 RN but it was not until a high-power station was established in Athlone, the most central location possible, to coincide with the Eucharistic Congress in 1932, that programmes were receivable countrywide. The service became known simply as 'Athlone', even after 1938 when the name was officially Radio Éireann. A luncheon in the Metropolitan Restaurant on Tuesday 29 August 1933, arranged by the firm of Charles F. Huet, the chief distributors of wirelesses in the Free State, announced the existence of a novel development, a radio set in a motor car.

Carlton Dyer, the managing director of the Philco Radio Company, told the company that at the Motor Show that year the manufacturers would equip their models with aerials: 'The day is not far distant when radio will be accepted as part of a car in everybody's mind.' It was a brave statement and the day envisioned was in fact far distant, with radios in homes far from universal and car ownership even less prevalent. There were a lot more 'optional' extras with greater priority and the little matter of the Second World War also delayed the fulfilment of Dyer's dream. The same cosmic retardation applied to his other promise of television 'within a few years'.

Dyer severely criticised 'Athlone' for breakdowns and faults. These had lost it a lot of income from sponsored programmes – as commercials were then more decorously called. The fault lay with inadequate technical equipment and under threat from such firms as his of 'not putting any more money into this station until its faults were rectified,' he believed that his criticisms were being acted upon and by September 'we shall be able to put on Philco programmes every morning'.

30 August 1968

Abbey workshop

On Friday 30 August 1968 at the Abbey playwrights' workshop there were four men of the theatre, each with a different expertise. Lacking the immediacy of a performance they could do little more than advise out of their own experience of all aspects of dramaturgy. The workshop's title was not meant to limit participation to writers who had had plays staged in the Abbey but given the location of the symposium it was not inappropriate that three of the contributors had strong Abbey connections: Gabriel Fallon, a member of the board, Tomas Mac Anna, artistic director, and Hugh Leonard, who wrote many Abbey pays. Alan Simpson, the fourth member, who had founded the Pike as an alternative venue, would soon become an Abbey man himself.

Fallon began by rejecting Lennox Robinson's figure that of play scripts received 75 per cent were duds, instead making it 90 per cent. He insisted that the dramatist needed three qualities, intense love of theatre and life, extraordinary application and guts. Leonard urged a more agnostic, existential approach to theatre in the hope of losing parochialism. MacAnna's contribution on 'Theatre in the Round' was inevitably technical and it was left to Simpson, a war-scarred veteran who introduced plays by Beckett, Behan and Tennessee Williams to an overtly scandalised Dublin, to be challenging.

His talk. 'Play Doctoring, Re-writing, Adapting and Rehabilitating' was the most practical and controversial contribution, debating the primacy of author, actor and director. He opined that the earlier plays of Tennessee Williams had been models of discipline but as he became more famous his work became less disciplined. He speculated that the three plays that made O'Casey's name may very well have been reworked in rehearsal and that some of his later plays were unstageable. He believed that Behan's *The Hostage* was considerably modified by Joan Littlewood and her actors but that the author had acquiesced in the changes.

31 August 1959

The first fair rose

In an island dedicated to festivals the ritziest is unquestionably the event known worldwide as 'The Rose of Tralee'. There at the very end of summer – autumn if you use the Celtic calendar – smart young women with greater or lesser claim to Irishness entertain with chat and minimal performance as they strive for the coveted title and its bonuses. The first Festival of Kerry was held in 1957 but Dan Nolan, chairman of the festival committee, felt it needed a better focus. Visiting New York he had a profitable chat with fellow-Kerryman, Brian K. Sheehy, who had been president of the 'B&P' (the Kerrymen's Patriotic and Benevolent Society of America). They fastened on Tralee's greatest international claim to fame, the song 'The Rose of Tralee', especially as sung by Ireland's premier tenor, John McCormack.

It was a song of lost love – as Chesterton wrote of the Irish: 'And all their songs are sad.' – but it was the nucleus they needed. It was written in 1849 by William Mulchineck, a Protestant supporter of Daniel O'Connell, to commemorate his dead Catholic love, Mary O'Connor, but it was the hook on which they could hang their ever more successful festival. On Monday 31 August 1959 in the Ashe Memorial Hall, under a canopy in the shape of a red rose weighing two-and-a-half tons, five postulants for rosaceous fame from New York, London, Birmingham, Dublin – and Tralee – paraded before a panel of judges including Michael Mulchinock, the great-grandnephew of the poet.

The contestants were chosen – all daughters of one or two parents born within a specific area in Tralee Urban District – from almost a hundred competitors in regional finals. The winner, the first ever modern Rose of Tralee, was the Dublin Rose, nineteen year-old Alice from Trimleston Gardens, Booterstown, the daughter of a Tralee-born civil servant, Thomas O'Sullivan.

1 September 1935

Death suspicious and unsuspicious

The last weekend of summer in 1935 was marred by three untimely deaths and two possible accidents. At 6.45am on Sunday 1 September, a Civic Guard, as members of the force were then known, found the body of Leo Keegan from Windsor Avenue, off Fairview Strand, on a seat in Fairview Park. By his side were two bottles that had contained disinfectant. The Garda, who was on night duty, immediately informed Clontarf Station and Keegan's body was taken to the morgue, where an inquest would later be held.

The second body was taken from the sea at the Bull Wall, Dollymount, at 4.30pm on Saturday 31 August. The body, identified later as that of Leo Poynton from Tallaght, had been seen floating at the end of the wall by A. Yale, a Clontarf man, but a strong wind made it impossible for him to reach it. The body was finally brought ashore by a man called Appleyard, who had been out sailing. It too was taken by the Gardaí to the morgue to await an inquest.

The other death deemed 'unsuspicious' was that of Thomas Edward Davis of Alverston, Ballymun Road, who collapsed while walking along Burgh Quay on the Saturday and was dead on arrival at Mercer's Hospital. William Whelan, a man of about sixty from Lower Dominick Street, off Parnell Street, had been found unconscious with head injuries by a workman in East Wall early on the Saturday. He was detained for observation in Jervis Street Hospital.

The last victim of Saturday misadventure was John Curley from Liverpool, who was one of a party of six hundred people on an excursion to Dún Laoghaire. He slipped and fell on board the specially commissioned *Cambria*. An x-ray in St Michael's Hospital, Dún Laoghaire, showed that there had been no fracture.

2 September 1933

A frieze of misery

The cases before the Dublin District Court on Friday 2 September 1933 painted a not uncharacteristic frieze of misery and minor misdemeanour. Two children, aged four and five, had been found wandering in a distressed condition, exhausted, cold, hungry, dirty and barely clothed, on an informal caravan site in Green Lane, Terenure. The report was made by a SPCC inspector called Johns, who visited the old caravan that was the children's home. Someone had sent for the 'cruelty man', to use the term current at the time.

The caravan was dirty, smelly and buzzing with flies. There was no food, except scraps in the linnet's cage. The children, named Smith, were taken to the police station in Terenure where they were cleaned up and fed. Sergeant Coghlan was sent to the site, where he learned that the parents, Thomas and Esther Smith, were regarded by their campsite neighbours as 'of the rough type' and consequently snubbed. The Smith parents did not arrive until 11 o'clock. They insisted that there were plenty of clothes but the children would not keep them on and that there was plenty of food. The mother told a jumbled story about three other children who had been taken from them and 'sold to a Protestant home.' The judge remanded them in custody and placed the children into what passed for care in those Spartan times.

The case of Glynn Quinn and James Hewson, two stowaways found concealed in the SS *Kenbane Head,* was considerably less painful, if more mysterious. They had boarded the ship in Montreal on 17 August and were arrested on arrival in Dublin. Quinn was local and vouched for by his uncle but Hewson's relatives could not be found and there was some doubt as to his nationality. Both men were sentenced to seven days' imprisonment.

3 September 1959

Eamonn Andrews and RTÉ

Eamonn Andrews, in his heyday the highest paid broadcaster in Britain, was appointed chairman of an advisory committee of four to prepare for the launch of what would become Radio Teilifís Éireann on Thursday 3 September 1959. Michael Hilliard, Minister for Post and Telegraphs in the Fianna Fáil government of the day, also appointed three relative unknowns: E.B. McManus, already a member of the Television Commission, Commander George Crosbie, director of the *Cork Examiner*, and a solicitor from Naas, County Kildare, P.P. Wilkinson.

All had experience of public service but Andrews, who had come from sports journalism through sports commentary to general broadcasting, was the star. An amateur champion middleweight boxer, he gave the live commentary immediately after winning the title bout and with an agreeable mid-Atlantic accent and a natural broadcasting ability rose to the heights of fame as chair of the Sunday night peak-time quiz programme *What's My Line?* and the wielder of the famous red book in *This Is Your Life*.

The minister announced that he would arrange for the supply of studio and transmitter sites and equipment. In answer to an unasked question, Andrews said he happily accepted the post that would bring television to Ireland but that the appointment would not entail giving up his present work for the BBC. It would not interfere with his work for some time in the future and it would be too difficult to say what the position might be when Irish television had begun. The work should take up only part of his time and it was for this reason that he had refused the full-time position of inspector-general of the Irish Television and Radio Authority. The BBC had offered 'advice and assistance' and he could continue his work in London, travelling back to Dublin as often as necessary.

4 September 1979

Rehousing Dublin

Inner-city degeneration in 1970s Dublin had reached crisis proportions. Rehousing was continuing but many dwellers were reluctant to leave their old homes. In their anxiety to remedy a serious social problem the Corporation did not always take such matters into consideration, being concerned primarily with providing houses, irrespective of location. True inner-city Dubs were understandably reluctant to go to live in what they considered vast soulless peripheral estates miles from their native places.

The trouble was that the houses and flats they inhabited were in many cases very expensive to repair and refurbish; it made better economic sense to clear both the sites and the tenants and build new houses 'in the country', as the suburban sites were designated. On Tuesday 4 September 1979 a meeting of the Corporation's special committee for the inner city convened to discuss a report 'in a Dublin evening paper' in which the Reverend Patrick Dowling, the administrator of the Pro-Cathedral parish, was reported as claiming that the Corporation was 'using unjust psychology' against his parishioners, specifically that one of the weapons they were using was to leave them in dilapidated flats and deprive them of essential services. He also said that decisions were made without consultation: parishioners did not know when they would be asked to leave for a 'totally alien area in the suburbs'.

Reaction was mixed but largely negative: Councillor Frank Sherwin described the reported claims as 'bloody nonsense'; Christopher Geoghegan, the principal officer, insisted that over half the residents had been relocated to areas of their own choice. Tony Gregory, chairman of the committee, thought there might be some substance in the Fr Dowling's comments. The committee admitted that there were problems and recommended to the Corporation the speedy implementation of the three-stage plan already put forward.

5 September 1931

De Valera's newspaper

At the beginning of the 1930s there were two leading dailies, the *Irish Independent* that unabashedly supported Cumann na nGaedheal, the government party of the time, and *The Irish Times* that was still a Protestant if not totally unionist paper. What was clearly missing was a paper to represent the views of the anti-Treatyites, now readying themselves for government as Fianna Fáil, under Éamon de Valera. The new paper to be called the *Irish Press* had been registered in 1928 and now in the early autumn of 1931 was about to hit the news stands.

De Valera had raised funding in America during the 1920s and the paper's launch on 5 September, a Saturday, was deliberate as a significant part of its sports coverage dealt with the next's day's All-Ireland Hurling Final between Kilkenny and Cork. Up until then the GAA had not featured greatly in the existing papers but they soon found it expeditious to emulate the new champion. The presses were ceremoniously started by Margaret Pearse, later to be a senator, the mother of the 1916 heroes, Patrick and Willie. The first editor was Frank Gallagher, who had helped edit the *Irish Bulletin,* the mouthpiece of the Dáil, during the War of Independence, and his five-year stint established the paper on a sound footing.

At its peak the circulation of the *Irish Press* reached 200,000, with notable coverage of the Irish language, and its nationalist verve helped towards a greater 'greening' of its rivals, notably *The Irish Times.* Its diarist, Benedict Kiely, writing as Patrick Lagan, established a literary reputation that reached a golden age when its editor, Tim Pat Coogan (1968-87) appointed David Marcus as literary editor and gave him the space for New Irish Writing, the best 'little magazine' that never existed. The paper ceased publication in 1997 after experiencing management problems.

6 September 1942

Leonine sparring contest

On Sunday 6 September 1942, for the third time in as many weeks, visitors to the Zoological Gardens were entertained to a friendly wrestling match between a nine-months-old lioness and an amateur trainer. What made the event an unusually spectacular occasion was the fact that the lioness's sparring partner was just eight years old. The leonine tussle began three months before when Ken Ryan from Stillorgan went with a number of other children to meet Flame, the zoo's prize cat. Flame came over and nuzzled Ken, who responded without fear.

Within a few days they were wrestling happily, playing tig and rolling on the grass, just like any boy with a lively pet. It seemed that lion taming wasn't all that big a deal. Yet when any other person tried to approach, the pussy cat snarled like a grown-up lion. Each time young Ryan came, Flame was able to pick him out of any crowd. He was missing for a period of six weeks during the school summer holidays and on his return Flame came bounding over to meet her special friend.

The zoo superintendent, Mr C. Flood, admitted that it took him several days to get on terms with Flame but Ryan seemed to be absolutely without fear. When he was interviewed at home he confessed that his only previous experience with animals was the care of his forty tame rabbits. He told the reporter that he was also on friendly terms with an older lioness, called Stephanie, and Sarah, the elephant, but he had never wrestled with either of them. No one could fully explain the odd affinity of boy and beast, although Ken's total lack of fear had undoubtedly played its part.

Ken did not try to explain and smiled when he was asked about a future career.

7 September 1937

Tragedy and farce

Totus orbus agit histrionem (the whole world plays a part) was the supposed motto of Shakespeare's Globe Theatre, usually approximated by Jacques's line: 'All the world's a stage' in *As You Like It*. If real drama is sought away from the painted stage, the courthouse is the modern Globe for both comedy and tragedy. On Tuesday 7 September 1937 two greatly differing dramas were rehearsed in Dublin's Central Criminal Court. The attempt of two men to rob a bungalow in Glenageary ended in farce while an alleged suicide and murder were successfully averted.

Robert Farrell (26), of Robert Street off James's Street, had been found in the Grand Canal near Rialto Bridge, about three feet from the bank, while two feet away floated his child. They were helped out of the water and he carried the child in his arms to his home. Garda Monaghan, who was alerted by bystanders, went to the house, where he sent for a ambulance. The child seemed unaffected by the experience but Farrell was in a state of shock. He was later accused of attempted murder of the child and of suicide.

Patrick Carroll of Congress Gardens, Glasthule, and Matthew Doyle of 66 Eden Villas, Glasthule, tried to obtain money by menaces in The Bungalow, Spencer Villas, Glenageary. The owner, Miss Hope Haddock, described in court how a man with a 'dirty handkerchief…up to his eyes and what appeared to be a toy revolver in his hand' forced his way in, shouting, 'I want your money.' He pushed her back into the room, pointing the gun, and so they stood for five minutes. By now Elizabeth Haddock, her sister, and a friend, Eileen Moran, had come to her assistance and chased him from the house. He and his accomplice were arrested the next day.

8 September 1944

A phenomenal rush of tourists

By the autumn of 1944 it looked certain that the Nazis' power would crumble and in Éire, as the country called itself then, the prospect of peace alerted the main tourist agencies to the fact that once the hostilities ceased there would be, as they described it on Thursday 8 September, a 'phenomenal rush to this country…and we must not be caught napping.' This apparently calculating attitude was based on a reasonable extrapolation from their wartime experience. Then Éire was a neutral country showing few of the scars of battle and outsiders flocked when possible to Dublin and the south where the cities were brightly lit, there were meat, eggs and dairy products aplenty and, even if tea had become an epicurean rarity and the bread somewhat suspect, the restaurants were doing great business.

They had already calculated that the only rival tourist centre was Scotland, which intended to spend £30m pounds on the industry and had more lochs and higher mountains. Travel restrictions would soon be lifted and they considered that with ships arriving in Dún Laoghaire and Belfast they could well expect an influx of 11,000 tourists weekly. As an official from the Thomas Cook agency expressed it: 'Good food, cheap beverages, a change of scene and freedom from the war atmosphere will bring people from across the water by the hundred thousand.'

Part of this manifesto was directed at the government, implicitly urging it to release petrol for buses and fuel for trains. With regard to potential travellers from Ireland, the tendency for the Irish to go on pilgrimage was not ignored by the agencies. Lourdes and Rome, unavailable as destinations since 1939, were about to enter the field and, although the relevant consulates could give no guarantees, all systems were ready for when permission came.

9 September 1945

Reviving 'the dying soul of the Irish nation'

The sudden death of Thomas Davis from scarlet fever on 16 September 1845 deprived Ireland of one of her leading cultural and political figures. He complemented the work of Daniel O'Connell in recreating an Irish nation. It was entirely appropriate that a hundred years later a week should be given over to a celebration of his centenary. On Sunday 9 September 1945 more than 10,000 people, representing many different organisations, paraded through Dublin to mark the opening of the Thomas Davis and Young Ireland movement centenary week.

The procession was led by the Lord Mayor, Alderman P.S. Doyle TD, followed by members of the Corporation in full ceremonial robes, accompanied by the Number 1 Army Band. Their route was from the Parnell Statue along O'Connell Street, Westmoreland Street and Dame Street to City Hall. An earlier party representing the Old IRA and representatives of Dublin Trades Council and affiliated unions marched through Lord Edward Street, Winetavern Street and crossed the Liffey twice to assemble in Parliament Street, opposite City Hall. Members of the Local Defence Force lined the streets, a necessary marshalling because of the crowds of the spectators that included many American and other overseas servicemen, some recently demobbed. To add to the festive air fourteen bands took part, including several groups of girl pipers.

A platform had been set up outside City Hall and when the various strands had taken up their positions Éamon de Valera, the Taoiseach, the Lord Mayor, members of the Urban District Council of Mallow, County Cork, Davis's birthplace, and prominent figures in Ireland's political life appeared, to inaugurate the celebrations. The Lord Mayor made a short speech before laying a wreath on Davis's statue, reminding the throng that it was he who had 'revived the dying soul of the Irish nation'.

10 September 1953

Bob Hope in Dublin

Leslie Townes Hope ('Bob' in his seventy-two-year-long showbiz career) died at the age of a hundred in 2003 and since his death his reputation has suffered. Yet he had a genuine comic talent, playing the opportunistic, venal coward, with such mottos as 'Brave men run in my family' and seen at his best in the series of 'Road' movies – six in all – in which he teamed with Bing Crosby and Dorothy Lamour. He continued to appear at troop concerts in all spheres of action for fifty years, often placing himself in danger, especially in Korea and Vietnam.

He depended heavily on gag-writers, his serious innate lack of ability making the expected 'unrehearsed' ad libs something of a trial. His right-wing politics did not endear him to liberals, who tended to exaggerate his mean-spiritedness with employees, but his timing was excellent and has capacity for survival was matchless. In 1953, in his fifty-first year, he was in Ireland and travelled to Dublin on Thursday 10 September. Arriving at what was then Amiens Street Station on the Great Northern Railway he was greeted by a crowd of fans. He was accompanied by the MGM star Gloria de Haven and on the spot agreed to a characteristic act of kindness.

He was to do two nights with two shows each night in the Theatre Royal and when Mrs L. Bishop approached him during a press conference in the Metropole Ballroom to ask him to present a cheque for £500 pounds, collected by the parents of children suffering from cerebral palsy, to the director of the Irish National Clinic, he said, 'I shall be only too delighted.' It was known that he had already raised more than $250,000 for the same good cause and he made the presentation to great applause at the 9 o'clock show that night.

11 September 1952

Death on the tracks

Peter Timmons, a sixty-four-year-old from Belton Park Road, Donnycarney, was employed as a plate-layer by the Great Northern Railway Company. On 29 August 1952 he was struck by a train and killed and twelve days later, on Thursday 11 September, Dr D.A. MacErlean, the city coroner, presided at the inquest. Timmons was walking on the down line in the direction of what was then called Amiens Street Station when he was seen to stoop and drive a wedge into a sleeper base with his heavy hammer, apparently completely unafraid. Then with his hammer on his shoulder he crossed to the up line because he was aware of a passenger train coming from the station. He was at once hit by a diesel coming from Howth.

Maureen Likely from Howth, who was sitting near the front of the diesel, said she could see a man balanced on a sleeper, seemingly unaware of the oncoming train. She could only watch as the train sped on and saw that at the point of impact the figure did not move. The driver left the controls to look out the window but returned to his cabin and continued his journey to Amiens Street. The post-mortem was carried out in Jervis Street by Dr Stella Whittey and she gave the cause of death as laceration of the brain and noted that there were head injuries and fractured ribs and right forearm.

The driver of the diesel was not called to give evidence but J. Murtagh, his solicitor, revealed that he and Timmons had been close friends. Before the jury retired the coroner admonished them that they should not express any opinion on the question of negligence on anybody's part. They found in accordance with the evidence presented that Timmons had died after being hit by the 9am Howth train.

12 September 1979

The Dublin Theatre Festival

The Dublin Theatre Festival was founded by Brendan Smith in 1957. He had persuaded Bord Fáilte to sponsor it, with the intention of stimulating tourist interest when the peak summer months were over. Smith was an actor, playwright and founder of the Brendan Smith Academy of Acting, saviour of the Olympia Theatre. The festival brings to the city the best available international theatre and balances that with the production of Irish drama. Smith ran the festival for more than twenty years and it is still one of the leading theatre events in the world.

On Wednesday 12 September 1979 Smith called a press conference to announce details of the twenty-first festival, which would open on 1 October, the last day of the papal visit. (John Paul II's own record as a playwright seemed to augur well.) The total cost would be in the region of £235,000, of which around £100,000 had been secured from sponsorship commitments. This, plus an expected 75 per cent seat occupancy, should keep the festival within the financial boundaries but it still sought further grants from the Arts Council, Dublin Corporation and the county council.

Hugh Leonard, who had had fourteen plays in previous festivals, was having the première of *A Life,* a touching play, with its germ in his great success, the autobiographical *Da,* in the Abbey. The Peacock would have a dramatisation of *Deoraíocht* by Pádraig Ó Conaire and later Maeve Binchy's first full-length play, *The Half-Promised Land.* When Brendan Behan first wrote *The Hostage,* the play that made him famous for all the wrong reasons, he used Irish and called it *An Giall.* Now it was to appear again in the Damer Hall. Plays by Joe Orton, Simon Grey (to be directed by Harold Pinter in the Olympia), Desmond Forristal and Jim Sheridan were also scheduled.

13 September 1984

Mount Jerome Cemetery

Mount Jerome Cemetery in Harold's Cross, south of the city, has been a burial ground since 1834. Until 1920 it was an exclusively Protestant site but now, with its attendant crematorium, no distinction of sect is made. It hold the mortal remains of 300,000 people and part of that list is a kind of roll-call of the city's artistic, political and professional leaders. There lie, for example, the mortal remains of William Rowan Hamilton, who proposed the theory of quaternions, the writers Æ, Sheridan Le Fanu, J.M. Synge, William Carleton and Maeve Binchy, the father and mother of Oscar Wilde, Thomas Davis, the Young Irelander, and Jack B. Yeats, the artist.

After a century and a half the cemetery (essentially a private enterprise) was in financial trouble and a liquidator, Ray Long, was appointed. On the night of Thursday 13 September 1984 he announced that the cemetery would be unattended from the next day. He said that closure was inevitable because the owners had not been able to acquire necessary further land. It meant that the gates would close and the twenty-three staff would be made redundant. The company directors had tried to initiate discussions with the government and the Corporation but nothing happened. Now the place would have to close because of its susceptibility to vandalism.

Fred Hanna, one of the directors of the company, said that they had been seeking financial backing from the state for years and they could not allow the company to run up such large debts. By winding up they could pay their creditors in full. Alan Shatter TD urged the Office of Public Works to assume responsibility for running the cemetery. Later that year it was acquired for Massey & Co, funeral directors, who have run it since then.

14 September 1949

DIY houses

For years after the ending of the Second World War there was a shortage of new housing. In 1948 ten skilled Dublin workmen combined their talents to build their own houses. Five – Bernard Brown, James Barry, Peter Dunne, Oliver Purcell and Michael Gibney – were carpenters; Bernard Woods was a plumber, Frank Fletcher an electrician, John Durney a fitter, Hector Ludlow a costing-clerk and Patrick Woods a builder's foreman who was soon made chargehand. The speed and success of the venture was attributed to the alacrity with which the nine others 'carried out his instructions without question'.

The idea came to two members of the party, Gibney and Brown, when they read in the papers that the Corporation was prepared to offer free sites to those who could build their own dwellings. They joined forces with the other eight and acquired sites in Collins Avenue, Whitehall. Each put up £100 and, with plans drawn up by an architect, applied for a government grant of £275. Work started immediately and the building was done in their evening hours of leisure, sometimes working the night through. The finished houses had two reception rooms with folding doors and French windows that opened on to the garden. Repayments of Corporation loans, ground rent and rates amounted to twenty-five shillings a week.

Michael Keyes, the Minister for Local Government, arrived on Wednesday 14 September 1949 to declare the houses open. He was full of justifiable approval of:

> ...the most praiseworthy answer of human enterprise to the difficulties of the time. Local authorities will welcome the offers of this kind from your association and the others which are following the same lines. Obviously the most healthy condition of affairs is that in which individual enterprise and initiative provide everything required.

15 September 1977

Civil Rights protest

On the afternoon of Saturday 6 August 1977 a number of protesters, some from the Irish Civil Rights Association, blocked the traffic at the top of Grafton Street. It was a deliberate choice, intended to cause he maximum disruption to the city's commercial life. As District Justice Ó hUadaigh remarked in court on Thursday 15 September, it was chosen 'because a large number of people would be coming from public houses and men and their families would be shopping.' He strongly rejected the claim that the protest was peaceful, saying, 'It was on the fringe of anarchy and could not be tolerated.' Since, too, they no longer had 'an alien government' the protestors had a mistaken view of their rights.

There had been violence and Gardaí had been assaulted; the judge found eight people guilty of obstructing the pubic highway and of intending to cause a breach of the peace – criminal acts. He imposed jail sentences on seven men and fines on eight. There were shouts of: 'You Fascist Pig of a Free State Justice' and 'We will be back.' Their supporters in the public gallery began the anthem, 'We Shall Overcome', in which the prisoners joined as they were taken down.

The charges were mainly of malicious damage and assaults on Gardaí. John Doherty of Synott Place, Dorset Street, was sentenced to two terms of twelve months. Martin Walsh of Ballyfermot Road got three months for malicious damage, fourteen days for assaulting a motorcyclist and a total of £12 in fines. Seán Doyle from Ballymun got nine months suspended. Tiernan McGarry of 'Sráid Chaoimhín Íocht' (Lower Kevin Street) and Michael Ryan of Effra Road, Rathmines, each got three months, Patrick O'Connor from Baldoyle two periods of six months and Ciaran Farrelly from Ballymun twelve months for assault.

16 September 1933

Attempted Robbery in Inchicore

The Hibernian Bank had an independent existence from 1825 until 1958, when it was taken over by the Bank of Ireland. Its Inchicore branch was the scene of a not very successful bank raid on Friday 16 September 1933. Two young men carrying revolvers, James Jones (21), 6 New Road, Clondalkin and Thomas Ryan (19), 128 Upper Dorset Street, entered the bank at 2.40pm, demanding money. The manager, Mr Coulter, and Mr Butler, his chief cashier, both refused to comply. The latter seized a heavy office stool and flung it across the counter, hitting one of the raiders on the forehead. He staggered and seemed to stoop down.

In the confusion Coulter bent low behind the counter and was able to scuttle out a side door into the street. Fortuitously he met an acquaintance who was able to drive to Kilmainham Garda station and report the incident. By the time Coulter got back to the bank the armed men had disappeared. Making sure first that Butler was all right he rang the detective branch in Dublin Castle and waited for the Gardaí who arrived within a few minutes, soon followed by a team of detectives. Although Butler's desk was covered with 'many thousands of pounds' none was taken.

Shortly before 3.30pm Sergeant McGrath of the Lucan station noticed from his seat on the top deck of a Chapelizod bus two men running from a lane to catch the bus at the next stop. He arrested them and had them detained in the local station where they were interrogated by Chief Superintendent Byrne and Superintendent Peter Ennis of the detective branch. The Gardaí found the jettisoned guns near a car abandoned in Ballyowen, Lucan. The men were returned for trial in the District Court the next morning.

17 September 1959

The Eblana Theatre

Busáras, the main bus terminal in Dublin, was opened in Store Street to less than public delight in 1953. Its modernist appearance pleased the architects of the period but it was some time before the plain people of Ireland took it to their hearts. On Thursday 17 September 1959 its basement became the site of a small but very influential theatre. Eblana, its name, was taken as a Latinate form of Dublin (although some have disputed this) and it became a house for experimental drama and the work of novice playwrights.

It was officially launched by Lord Killanin, the chairman of the Dublin International Theatre Festival, who revealed that the seating had been put in that day, a mere five days before the first presentation, Synge's last unfinished play, *Deirdre of the Sorrows.* He used the occasion to praise the foresight of the chairman of CIÉ, Todd Andrews, for including the space for a theatre in the original design for the station, then 'Dublin's most contemporary building'.

The auditorium was fan-shaped, had a sloping floor and could seat an audience of two hundred. Its front seats were 20ft below street level, so that the theatre was below the Liffey water level at high tide. Killanin's remark that the theatre was on a floating foundation confused his listeners but he reassured them that it meant that it was free of the main structure and therefore free of vibration and other noises. It had no wings and lighting control was at the back of the auditorium, making it unique among Dublin theatres that had to gauge the effect from the side of the stage.

The Eblana closed in 1995; the space was gutted and is now used as a left-luggage depot for the station.

18 September 1946

Faulty tyre

At an inquest held in St Michael's Hospital, Dún Laoghaire, by Dr J.P. Brennan, Coroner for County Dublin, on Wednesday 18 September 1946 the jury found 'that the cause of the crash was sue to a faulty tyre in the lorry, which, in our opinion should have been replaced some time previous to the occurrence.' The dead person was Daniel McGrath (49), Oliver Plunkett Road, Monkstown, an employee of Dún Laoghaire Borough Corporation. He had been killed when the refuse lorry in which he and his colleagues were travelling crashed into a tram standard. Three other workmen travelling in the lorry were injured.

Garda J.L. Conner, Booterstown, in evidence stated that the left front tyre was torn on the inside and appeared to be flat. When he arrived three men were lying on the road in front of the lorry, unconscious and bleeding, and McGrath, who appeared to be dead, was lying against the standard. Dr John Maher, house surgeon, said that death would have been instantaneous. The lorry was examined by Garda experts from the Carriage Office and Garda J. Flanagan reported that steering and brakes were in good condition. He had found a cut in the left front tyre that had been caused by the collision but there was an older tear that could easily have caused a blow-out: 'There were two cuts in the tyre, one caused by the accident, one which caused the accident.'

Thomas Maher, who worked as a driver and mechanic, testified that a fortnight earlier he had fitted a new tipping gear to the lorry and that the brakes and steering were in order. He had found no fault with the tyres and suggested that the damaging cut could have been caused by glass in one of the dumps. Sympathy was offered to the dead man's family.

19 September 1951

The ultimate humiliation

Patrick Kavanagh (1904-67) lived in Dublin from 1939 until his death twenty-eight years later. During the 1940s and the 1950s, often in poor health and poverty, he scraped a living by casual journalism. He had the almost obligatory rite of passage of Irish writers of the time when his extended poem, *The Great Hunger* (1942), probably his finest single piece of work, and his novel, *Tarry Flynn* (1948), were banned by the zealous Irish Censorship Board. As a writer he was undoubtedly very talented but tended to accept offers of help and work with less than gratitude.

One of his sources of appreciation and practical help was John Ryan, painter, editor, memoirist and Joyce enthusiast. He owned and edited the literary journal *Envoy* (1949-51) in which he published Kavanagh's poetry as well as the work of Brendan Behan and the American expatriate, J.P. Donleavy. He was a member of the Irish Cultural Relations Committee and arranged for the hard-up Kavanagh to undertake a lucrative lecture tour in the United States. Frank Aiken, the Minister for External Affairs, refused to authorise the grant for travelling expenses. No reason was given but it was assumed that Kavanagh's personality, occasional alcoholic episodes and the recent banning of his novel had coloured Aiken's attitude.

On Wednesday 19 September 1951 Ryan wrote the minister a letter of resignation, releasing it simultaneously to the Dublin newspapers. He described how the tour (including the subvention for travel expenses) had met with unanimous approval at a general meeting of the committee. He chided Aiken for his refusal to give reasons for his stance, contrasting it unfavourably with similar cases he had approved. He deplored his belittlement of Kavanagh and finished with '...I know that the ultimate humiliation will not be his.'

20 September 1803

Darling of Erin

At about half-past one on Tuesday 20 September 1803 the twenty-five-year-old Robert Emmet was taken in chains from his cell in Kilmainham jail by carriage in a circuitous route to Thomas Street, crossing the Liffey in Islandbridge and back again over the Queen's Bridge. The journey through a crowded and silent city had taken nearly an hour and a half, a decision probably made by Major Sirr, the chief of police, for security reasons. There, in front of the forty-year-old St Catherine's Church, a scaffold had been erected. Emmet was helped to the platform and the noose put round his neck; blindfolded, he was given a handkerchief to drop as a signal that he was ready.

He seemed to hesitate, as if hoping that the promised help from Wicklow might even then rescue him. Asked twice by the hangman if he were ready, he replied that he was not but a third refusal was cut off. After he was declared dead the executioner cut off his head with a butcher's knife and holding it by the hair declared to the crowd: 'This is the head of Robert Emmet, a traitor.' The cherished detail of dogs licking the blood that seeped through the planks and of women dipping their handkerchiefs in it may well be true, as it was of other similar occasions – but 'bold Robert Emmet, the darling of Erin' was already assumed into Irish hagiography.

Emmet's speech from the dock was a fine inspiring example of national rhetoric, his romantic involvement with Sarah Curran when he risked his life for love was almost operatic in its romantic fervour and the brave idealistic pointlessness of his rabble revolution claimed him as another hero for old Ireland, another young man whom, in Yeats's phrase, excess of love bewildered until he died.

21 September 1977

Flawed legislation

In a interesting case involving an apparent clash between the courts and the government, Mr Justice D'Arcy made an order in the High Court in Dublin on Wednesday 21 September 1977 directing Sylvester Barrett, the Minister for the Environment, to show cause why road traffic service vehicle regulations made by him should not be quashed. The judge directed that the order also be served on Anthony Hederman, the Attorney-General. It was a prime example of the dictum that the full significance of legislation cannot be realised until it has been tested in court.

The case involved John Collins, Claremont Court, Glasnevin, a family man with five children who, having been unemployed for sixteen months, decided to begin full-time employment as a taxi driver and purchased a Ford Cortina first registered in January 1977. He obtained a small public service licence in March but was told that he could not use his car for the purpose until he had obtained a PSV licence for it and that the only period available to him was 1-14 September 1977. He went to the carriage office on 1 September but was told that under recent regulations he could not apply until September 1978.

Gabriel Warde, Collins's solicitor, advanced several grounds for declaring the regulations null and void including natural justice, constitutional rights, actions beyond the minister's power as conferred on him by the act and imposition of restrictions by the state, almost wholly without notice. It meant that the minister was shutting all newcomers out for a year. When questioned, Collins said that he had obtained £1000 on a trade-in for his old car and had taken out a bank loan for the remaining £2000. The judge took little time to make the order as it was clear that the legislation was flawed.

22 September 1940

Hollywood's golden age

The Emergency, Ireland's take on the Second World War, was 385 days old on Sunday 22 September 1940 and already the isolation and the scarcities of tea, sugar, fruit, coal and petrol, were beginning to have an effect. There was, however, no blackout and peat stockpiled throughout the country was keeping the home fires burning and the trains running, if at reduced speeds. And to cheer up a depressed population there were plenty of films of sufficient variety to suit most tastes. In retrospect it was Hollywood's golden age and in the cinemas of Dublin there were showing that week, among many examples of stock material, some authentic film classics.

Best of these was John Ford's brilliant filming of *The Grapes of Wrath*, John Steinbeck's stark novel of the Great Depression in America. It won him an Oscar and Jane Darwell, known to later film goers as the 'feed-the-birds' lady in *Mary Poppins*, won best support. It was one of Henry Fonda's best films and was booked for a season in the Metropole. In the Adelphi was *My Son, My Son*, a film based on the worldwide bestseller *O Absalom* by Howard Spring, the title coming from Kind David's lament over his son in the Old Testament. The agonised father was played by the Irish actor, Brian Aherne, who also led in *Captain Fury* in the Astoria, Glasthule.

There were three other classics available that same week that hold their place in the canon. In the Regal was Patrick Hamilton's *Gaslight* with Anton Walbrook and Diana Wynyard. The Grafton had *Broadway Melody of 1940* with music by Cole Porter, dancing by Fred Astaire, George Murphy and Eleanor Powell and choreographer Busby Berkeley's most extravagant chorus effects. *Pinocchio*, possibly Walt Disney's finest film, was going to run and run at the Capitol.

23 September 1977

Home from exile

The management of the Abbey Theatre, eleven years after its return to the street after exile in the Queen's Theatre, was finally persuaded to enlarge and make more commodious the greenroom, where the cast could prepare and unwind before entrances and after exits. In Shakespeare's time it would have been called a 'tiring' room but the original accommodation for 'tiring' in the new Abbey was inadequate.

The newly enlarged facility was formally opened on Friday 23 September 1977 by the sixty-seven-year-old Cyril Cusack (1910-93), then the doyen of Irish theatre. Although not one of the original Abbey company, his breadth of experience in all aspects of drama (including film and television) made him the most appropriate person for the task. Regarded as the best Fluther in Seán O'Casey's *The Plough and the Stars* since Barry Fitzgerald's original portrayal in 1926, Cusack was also a donor. He brought with him a bronze bust by Jacob Epstein of George Bernard Shaw, who had written *The Shewing-Up of Blanco Posnet* especially for the theatre, and a personal collection of about a hundred books about theatre.

The bust was placed on a plinth in the corner where, on shelves especially provided, the Cusack library would sit. The donor was on a week's break from acting Fluther in the National Theatre in London's South Bank and in his short presentation speech mused in a characteristically philosophical way on changes in acting technique. The production of *The Plough* in which he was appearing at the Olivier had no curtains, no proscenium arch, no footlights and almost no make-up, so different from his early barnstorming days. In his peroration he said he still preferred 'the proscenium containing is own eternity, footlights reflecting their very own reality and the greenroom its tabernacle of tradition'.

24 September 1948

Keats and Chapman

John Keats, the finest of the Romantic poets, died in 1825, aged just twenty-six; George Chapman, the Elizabethan and Jacobean dramatist and translator of *The Iliad* and *The Odyssey* of Homer died in 1634, well into his seventies. Their only previously known connection is Keats's famous sonnet 'On First Looking into Chapman's Homer' in which he admitted that he had never breathed Homer's 'pure serene' until he 'heard Chapman speak out loud and bold'. Yet by the magic of literature they were brought together and shared many paronomastic adventures in the sparkling gallimaufry that was 'Cruiskeen Lawn'.

One of the dazzling features of *The Irish Times,* the regular column was the creation of the even more dazzling Brian O'Nolan (aka Flann O'Brien) using one of his other aliases, 'Myles na Gopaleen', and it ran from 1940 until 1966. The two poets made contemporaneous by the relentless imagination and punning capacity of the columnist featured regularly. On Friday 24 September 1948 Myles na Gopaleen recounted the case of Chapman having fallen madly in love with Keats's young niece. Knowing that the young lady was insanely interested in art and artists he posed as a 'neurotic surrealist'. At once fascinated by the prospect, she agreed to a secret tryst in Chapman's studio.

Once there he explained with equal manic fervour that he painted people, not pictures of people – in fact used human skin as his medium. Although somewhat nervous but resolutely dedicated to art in all its forms she allowed him to apply paint decorously to her upper back. He released her only after her solemn promise to return for another session. That evening, concerned about the situation, she sought out her uncle to ask if he was a man she could trust. 'I think,' replied Keats, 'he has designs on you!'

25 September 1979

Security for the Papal visit

John Paul II's pastoral visit to Ireland lasted from Saturday 29 September to Monday 1 October 1979. During this time he celebrated Mass in Phoenix Park, travelled north to Killineer, near Drogheda, where he pleaded for peace in Northern Ireland, went to Galway to say Mass for 200,000 young people, on to Knock, Maynooth and finally Limerick. On site he travelled in a specially designed vehicle enclosed with bulletproof glass, almost immediately christened the 'Popemobile'.

It was one of a number of security measures deemed necessary by the Garda Síochána in spite of a certain amount of public impatience and even annoyance. The full details were announced by Superintendent Peter McGing of the Garda Public Relations Office on Tuesday 25 September 1979. Certain sites were going to be designated as 'high-security' zones and all entering them would require official accreditation documents, including photographic identification; this rule would apply even to invalids in wheelchairs and to ministers of the government and members of the hierarchy.

All possibilities, even the extreme one of someone planting a bomb or otherwise attempting to injure His Holiness, had to be considered. People going to the public sites could expect to be 'frisked' and have their picnic bags examined. Foreign visitors, including journalists, would be checked by their own police forces and Interpol. Photographers had been refused permission to use light planes or helicopters to take pictures of the scenes because of the dangers of collision and the potential consequences of a crash on the thousands of people present – not to mention the possibility that a subversive group might use the excuse of aerial photography to attack from the air. Finally the Gardaí intended to have placed a five-mile radius traffic ban that would be strictly adhered to about any centre where a papal event was taking place.

26 September 1978

Wood Quay

Wood Quay is a riverside area of Dublin bounded on the north side by the Liffey, on the west by Winetavern Street, on the south by John's Lane and on the east by Fishamble Street. The Corporation acquired the site between 1950 and 1975 and then announced it as the location of their new civic offices, although it was an area of Viking settlement, one of the finest in Europe. Fr F.X. Martin OSA, Professor of Mediaeval History in UCD, aware of its archaeological importance, was the leading figure in a Save Wood Quay crusade that grew exponentially as battle lines were drawn. The protests took the form of occupation of the site and a huge protest march on 23 September 1978.

The immediate result was an order from the government to the Office of Public Works (OPW) the following Tuesday to place a further indefinite stay on work on the site. It was an interim move and did not please the campaigners, who wished the site to be preserved as a national monument and a fresh location be found for the civic buildings. There was relief that, at least, the bulldozing of the precious artefacts had temporarily ceased. The Irish Civil Rights Association described the decision to postpone what they called the destruction of Wood Quay as 'totally inadequate'.

The campaign failed ultimately in spite of 'Operation Sitric', a twenty-day occupation of the quay in June 1979. It was named after Sigtrygg, the Hiberno-Norse king of Dublin 989-1036, and a wide spectrum of politicians, academics, writers, poets and artists took part. The stays of execution allowed archaeologists and volunteer assistants to collect and preserve the Viking artefacts. It also had the more permanent effect of startling the sleepwalking Irish into heritage-consciousness.

27 September 1977

Flying equal

The first flight by Aer Lingus was from Dublin to Bristol in 1936. It took forty-one years for the company to appoint their first female pilot but it was the second airline in Europe to introduce women pilots. Grainne Cronin was a twenty-two-year-old third-year Arts student in University College, Dublin, when she was accepted as a trainee pilot on Tuesday 27 September 1977. She had worked as an air hostess from the previous February and was now about to join twelve other successful applicants on a week-long induction course in Dublin airport.

This preliminary step would be followed by a fourteen-month basic flying course in the Oxford Training school in Kidlington, north-west of the city. Those who qualified would then do a six-month advanced training course at home in Dublin, before taking up flying duties as second officer. Grainne thus became Ireland's first woman pilot. She had held a student's pilot licence since August 1976 and had flown her father's Piper Cub under supervision. He was still a senior pilot with the company when she piloted her first Boeing 747 the following January.

Captain Grainne Cronin retired as a pilot on 25 May 2010, after thirty-three years of service, and it became clear from the press release that she was part of an aviation dynasty. Her father Felim and her sister Caroline were also commercial pilots, her two daughters, Alana and Louisa, held private pilot licences, the latter then having completed her training as a commercial pilot – and her husband was also a pilot. Since the struggle for flying equality – *per ardua ad aequalitatem*, to adapt the RAF motto – there was no pioneer more elegant or more courageous. And possibly the reddest of red-letter days was 2 August 1988, when she captained the first all-female crew on a flight from Dublin to Shannon.

28 September 1959

Dangerous treatment

Patrick Pearse Coghlan, a 42-year-old insurance agent, of Brighton Square, Rathgar, drowned in the Quarry Pond, Quarry Road, Crumlin, on Saturday 26 September 1959. The inquest was held in the morgue in Londonbridge Road the following Monday. The coroner, Dr J.P. Brennan, had some words to say about treatment of patients by unqualified practitioners. In finding that death was due to drowning he observed that this was the second occasion in as many months that it had been his unfortunate experience to hear evidence of such treatments.

As the hearing proceeded it became clear that Coghlan was suffering from some form of mental illness. Bridget Coghlan, his wife, told the court that he had been attending psychoanalysts in Monkstown four days a week for at least four years and recently had got into the habit of seeing them at night as well. In spite of this his condition had steadily worsened. He was deeply depressed and refused to discuss the treatment, saying mysteriously that he broke one of the rules but could say nothing 'as it was all still secret'.

On the Saturday morning he was so physically ill that his wife sent for the doctor and when he arrived she began to explain about his treatment. He interrupted them, saying bleakly, 'They're all dead out there now,' before walking out to his death. She was convinced that the psychoanalysts had her husband completely in their power, that they had persuaded him that there was something wrong with him. He had tried to bring her to one of the sessions but she refused. The coroner announced that such treatment struck him as dangerous and he felt it was his duty and responsibility to bring the matter to the attention of the minister.

29 September 1942

Petrol restrictions

By the autumn of 1942 petrol in Dublin was scarcer than tea and on Tuesday 29 September there was a threat of even more cuts in supply. The owners of private cars had none and some tried with only moderate success to use wood or gas, the latter carried in blimps on roof racks. The bicycle was ubiquitous and the horse came into its own again as the main source of transport power. Some privileged people could still command fuel, including ministers of religion, doctors and veterinary surgeons. The latter two groups had already faced reductions during the previous two or three months and clergymen too were warned that their position was 'being reviewed'.

It was reckoned that there had been over-consumption of between 25,000 and 30,000 gallons per month during the summer and it was announced that the medics who owned cars of up to 10hp would continue to have eight gallons per month but those with engines between 10hp and 16hp would be cut by two gallons, leaving them with ten, while those with over 16hp would now receive twelve gallons. Those permitted private cars had a number of stringent conditions attached to their dole. They were not be used on holidays, for travelling to horse or dog races, to theatres, cinemas, dances or carnivals; for regular transport between home and work; for the conveyance of owner and family to school or church (unless as an officiating clergyman).

All repairs on permitted cars were to be carried out locally, owners not allowed to 'waste' petrol travelling long distances to the cities for the purpose. More ominous was the threat that with a continuance of the Emergency private commercial vehicles might go the way of private cars. Hearses, too, were not allowed to make long journeys when, grotesquely, 'alternative transport was available!'

30 September 1953

An Tóstal

An Tóstal (parade, display or pageant) was a Fianna Fáil-government approved sampler of Irish heritage and culture rolled out first in April 1953 and continued each spring until 1958 by Fógra Fáilte, the national tourism agency. On Wednesday 30 September 1953, aglow with the enterprise's success, Fógra Fáilte published its poster for the 1954 Tóstal. It main feature showed the Tóstal harp against a background of a map of Ireland. The arts of painting, drama, literature, music were represented symbolically, interspersed with others showing the national sports of hurling, football, shooting, horse racing and motorcycling. The legend was 'Ireland at Home' and the dates were 18 April-9 May. It was 'Ireland of the Welcomes' one year on.

The emphasis was on a balance between Ireland's quasi-glorious past and her future as a modern nation and as such was generally welcomed. In one respect the country still lagged behind – the most significant medium of the 20th century. BBC television had rushed to set up transmitters to enable the citizens of Belfast to watch the coronation of Elizabeth II that summer. Independent Television would not arrive in Britain until 1956. Only those viewers (and they were few) who lived on the east coast were capable of picking up the signal from Alexandra Palace (the 'Ally Pally' of the snowy black-and-white telly). On the day of the Tóstal poster's release Erskine Childers, the Minister for Posts and Telegraphs, happened to be speaking about the inexorable coming of television at the annual dinner of the Wireless Dealers' Association. He could never recommend a television service that was not first-class and directed towards the preservation of the national culture as well as for entertainment purposes. It seemed that the aspirations of both enterprises were in tune.

1 October 1937

An excursion that ended in tragedy

For the first half of the 20th century the bicycle was the usual means of personal transportation in Dublin, much outnumbering the far from ubiquitous car. The relative flatness of most of the city made it ideal for cycling, but not too far to the south where the Dublin-Wicklow mountain range began, the roads got steeper, narrower and more twisted. Cyclists were usually right in their assumption that as a general rule the only other road-users would be pedestrians so they treated the area as a kind of national park, a treasured amenity for city dwellers.

On 5 August 1937 Leo Deakon of McCaffrey's estate, Mount Brown, cycled to Ticknock to visit his brother in a camp there. He left at 9.50pm in the company of Mary Fox from Shaw Street, off Pearse Street, and two other women, Maura Clarke and Lily Murphy. All had bicycles but because the hill was so steep they walked down to the foot of Ticknock before mounting. As they rode off they saw a car approach about ten yards away. It was travelling at about thirty or thirty-five miles an hour, swerving from side to side. Deakon had not seen any headlights but did see small sidelights. He shouted to Mary Fox and accelerated to the front, aware that she was braking hard.

The car caught Deakon on the ankle, throwing him on to the bank, and he saw Mary being dragged for about five yards. His version was given under oath at the trial on Friday 1 October 1937 of Stanley Carlisle, 'Eden', Rathfarnham, on a charge of manslaughter. After the impact Mary Fox had been taken to the Meath Hospital, arriving there early on 6 August, but died the next day. The hearing was adjourned.

2 October 1949

An end to mosquitoes

For many years the suburbs of Howth, Sutton, Baldoyle and Raheny were plagued by mosquitoes. On Monday 2 October 1949 G. Bowles, the local health inspector, was able to announce that a campaign begun in May 1948 had been successful in eliminating the pest. Then Dr J.A. Harbison, Dublin City Medical Officer of Health, promised that the problem would be wiped out 'for once and for all'. The low-lying ground around Howth with its proliferation of stagnant pools had provided an ideal breeding ground for the two indigenous strains of the insect, coast-slobland and pool-sourced. The deadly anopheles mosquito that causes malaria is unknown in Ireland but a sting from the local variety caused a sharp pain and a resulting rash.

The first stage in the campaign was the spraying of larvaecidal solution composed of dichlorodiphenyltrichloroethane (DDT) and kerosene on all the stagnant pools and slow-moving streams in the locality. This treatment would not prevent recurrence so all the pools were drained by linking them with culverts to streams, which washed the larvae out into the bay. The swamp grounds were filled with rubble so that there was no moisture for the larvae to hatch out.

Research revealed that mosquitoes were capable of journeys of up to seven miles done in short bursts. By using a radial system of spraying the area of their first stopping place with 1300 gallons of the mixture a large proportion was eliminated. The sloblands were treated differently, with forty tons of impregnated sawdust. Finally drip-cans were fixed above known breeding streams from which a small quantity of the mixture was released every few minutes. The effect of these measures was an almost total clearance in a matter of months and Harbison's optimistic promise was manifestly kept.

3 October 1944

Charlie Kerins

The threat from the original IRA continued for years after Fianna Fáil had become the government party and crimes involving the dissidents were often tried in military courts. When Charles Kerins (26) of Caherina, Tralee, County Kerry was tried for the murder of Detective-Sergeant Denis O'Brien of Ballyboden, Rathfarnham, on 9 September 1942 the hearing was held at a sitting of the Special Criminal Court in Collins Barracks. The proceedings began on Monday 2 October 1944 and the following day Kerins refused to recognise the court and declined legal assistance. He refused to plead and made no attempt to refute the evidence for the prosecution.

This stated that the sergeant had been murdered near his home by assassins armed with Thomson guns and other weapons. A right ring-finger print of Charles Kerins had been found on a bicycle abandoned near the scene. He was an associate of Liam Quinn, a known member of the IRA, whose prints were also found on the bike. Hearing this, the president of the court announced:

> …the Court considers it right to inform you that at this stage that a prima facie case has been established against you. In order to give you an opportunity to consider your position and, if you so desire, to obtain legal advice and assistance to enable you to answer the case made against you…the Court has decided to adjourn until Monday morning, October 9th at 11 o'clock.

Then there was more detailed evidence of many weapons, including machine-guns, revolvers, bomb-making equipment, hand grenades and hundreds of rounds of ammunition that were found in Kerins's home. Garda witnesses gave evidence of finding maps and IRA documents there as well. Kerins still refused any recognition and after some discussion the court adjourned. Kerins was later condemned to death.

4 October 1949

Lift accident

Michael Gibbs, a 20-year-old repairman, from Iveagh Gardens, Crumlin, died in a lift accident in the premises of Nicholson Brothers, Drury Street, on 28 September 1949. The inquest was held in Mercer's Hospital on Tuesday 4 October and the jury returned a verdict in accordance with the medical evidence that death was due to shock and haemorrhage. They added that due to insufficient evidence they were unable to decide whether he had been killed when the lift was ascending or descending; neither could they determine whether there was negligence on the part of the lift attendant.

The victim had been working in the well of the lift shaft and it was arranged with the operator that he should warn Gibbs when the lift was being used. This was emphasised by Edward Hackett, who as dispatch manager of the firm had given the lift operator these instructions. James Paisley, a lorry helper, testified that he had rung the bell to have the lift brought down and that Thomas Maguire, the operator, of Chaworth Terrace, Phibsborough, had shouted a warning. Paisley had noticed some tools in the corner of the wall but did not see Gibbs. When the lift began to ascend again he could see his body at the bottom of the shaft, about six feet below street level.

The not very secure warning system had clearly failed on that occasion. Dr D.A. MacErlean, the city coroner, came to the conclusion that Gibbs had been in the well of the shaft when the lift had been sent down by Maguire, who had shouted his usual warning. Maguire had not, however, had a reply from Gibbs and assumed that he was out of the well and clear of danger. MacErlean thought it possible that the fatal injuries had been caused by the counterweights of the lift.

5 October 1959

Handel celebration

On Monday 5 October 1959, two hundred and seventeen years after the event it commemorated, a plaque was set in the wall of a building in Fishamble Street, the last remnant of what once was the Old Musick Hall. The plaque's inscription read:

> This bronze commemorates the first performance of George Frederic Handel's oratorio *Messiah*, given in the Old Musick Hall, Fishamble Street, on Tuesday, April 13th, 1742.

The site was part of a factory and the workers were given leave to watch the ceremony that was unveiled by Dr James S. Hall, chairman of the Deal and Walmer Handelian Society. Also in the party were representatives of the British Embassy and the German Legation, Councillor Daniel Morris, the Deputy Lord Mayor and members of the Music Association of Ireland.

In his short speech Dr Hall noted how the event they commemorated had brought happiness to millions of people and affected the social life of every country in the civilised world. 'In the British isles alone there are probably over a thousand choral societies, who totally subsist on their annual performances of this work.' He opined that although from a musical standpoint it was a bad thing, from a social point of view it was wholly admirable when it gave young people the opportunity to do something constructive and give pleasure to themselves and others.

He pleased his listeners by reminding them that the oratorio's reception in London was in sad contrast to 'the generous one you gave him here in Dublin'. This became the cue for Councillor Morris publicly to lament the lack of a concert hall dedicated to Handel, which was long overdue. That day Dr Hall also declared open an exhibition of Handel relics and manuscripts in the Civic Museum in South William Street.

6 October 1942

Objections to Roualt

George Roualt was seventy-one and recognised as (among other genres) the finest painter of religious paintings in his native France when his *Christ and the Soldier* was offered by the Friends of the National Collections as a gift to the Dublin Municipal Gallery. On Tuesday 6 October 1942 it was rejected by the advisory committee. The chief spokesperson for the committee was Kathleen Clarke, former Lord Mayor and widow of the oldest signatory of the proclamation of the Irish Republic at Easter 1916. She complained that it gave us Christ in an unusual way and it might be taken as a travesty and as this was a Christian country it would be offensive to put it on exhibition in a public gallery.

Dermod O'Brien, President of the Royal Hibernian Academy, took an entirely opposite view, saying that he had voted for acceptance and could not understand how anyone could regard such a reverent work of art as blasphemous. Some might find it grotesque but he wondered what they might have made of early Christian art. The characteristic black figure outlines made Roualt's work like a stained-glass window. He evoked the iconic name of Sir Hugh Lane, insisting that it was for the work of such artists that the Municipal Gallery had been intended.

Ireland at the time was in a state of almost Genevan public morality. Religious art was in general anodyne and unthreatening, and Roualt's bright colours may have put off people used to the art sold in many Catholic repositories throughout the country. A tribute from the editor of the *Catholic Herald* was dismissed by Mrs Clarke: even if she were assured that it was the greatest work in the world she still would maintain her attitude. The island of plaster saints remained secure.

7 October 1843

Monster meeting

At the beginning of 1843 the sixty-seven-year-old Daniel O'Connell announced that it would be 'The Year of Repeal'. The Tories under Sir Robert Peel were in power, leaving him free of any commitment to the Whigs, and he began a series of what Thomas Barnes, the hostile editor of *The Times*, pejoratively called 'monster' meetings. He spoke in Trim in March; Mullingar in March; Charleville, Cork, Cashel, Nenagh and Longford in May; Kilkenny, Mallow, Ennis and Skibbereen in June; Donnybrook, Waterford, Enniscorthy, Tuam and Castlebar in July; Tara on 15 August; Loughrea and Lismore in September and Mullaghmore on 1 October. The numbers attending ranged from 100,000 in Trim to 900,000 in Tara, with 500,000 the modal score.

The last meeting was due to be held in Clontarf on Sunday 8 October, the venue chosen because of its association with a glorious Irish past. That meeting was, according to publicity in organs such as *The Nation,* going to make the Tara host look like a caucus but on the Saturday evening, when many protestors would have left for the capital, Peel proscribed the meeting. Already warships rode at anchor in Dublin Bay and Clontarf was ringed with cavalry. O'Connell did not hesitate; he immediately cancelled the meeting with the agreement of the more radical Young Irelanders, although they afterwards denied it.

The decision was entirely consistent with his lifelong policy of non-violence; the prospect of a million people converging on the fields of north Dublin and the strands of the bay to be met with armed and trained soldiers was to him unthinkable. He organised stewards to turn back the crowds that were already reaching the city and went himself to the scene to stand in front of the riflemen and dragoons and shoo away any of his supporters who thought to defy the proclamation.

8 October 1984

The price of the pint

The twenty-fourth Dáil took office on 14 December 1982 and lasted 1546 days, until 10 March 1987. It was a coalition formed from Fine Gael that provided Garret Fitzgerald as Taoiseach and Labour, whose leader, Dick Spring, was Tánaiste. It coincided with a period of economic stringency, with a return to joblessness and high emigration. It was ever conscious of Charles Haughey, the leader of the opposition, whose tactics seemed opportunistic and cavalier, to put it no more strongly. One critic remarked that if you gave your purse to Garret he might mislay it, while Charlie would put it on a horse – and the horse might win!

In an attempt to alleviate the tax burden on serious drinkers Spring had reduced the excise duty on spirits in the 1984 budget, allowing the price of a small whiskey to drop from £1.06 to 98p. To the dismay of the denizens of many a snug, the price of a pint of Guinness remained at £1.18, leaving it 20p dearer than a ball of malt. Since the dark stuff was for centuries one of the defining features of the fair city, far more Irish, if much younger, than uisce beatha, voices were raised in protest, loudest among them from St James's Gate.

The story broke on Tuesday 8 October 1984 and, appropriately, it was Michael O'Halloran, Dublin's Lord Mayor, who announced that he would write to Dick Spring, Barry Desmond, the Minister for Health, and the Health Education Bureau to complain – on grounds of health, of course. 'This is a direct encouragement to people to consume a lot of spirits which are more harmful to health than beer.' He stated further with greater conviction that the pint in Dublin has long been a traditional drink and that this was an attack on it.

9 October 1662

Smock Alley

One of the more agreeable aspects of the restoration of Charles II in 1660 was the reopening of the theatres that had been closed during Cromwell's Commonwealth. In May 1661 John Ogilby, nominated Master of the Revels for Ireland by the king, applied for a licence to build Dublin's second theatre, the first, in Werburgh Street, having been closed by the Puritans in 1641. He built what became the first Theatre Royal in Smock Alley, which was almost on the banks of the Liffey until Essex Quay was developed in the 1720s. His office allowed him to licence the building of theatres anywhere 'in the Kingdom of Ireland' so his application for a patent was a mere formality.

Soon known as Smock Alley Theatre, from its unsavoury location where 'persons were met to make savoury bargains' it was the first purpose-built 'Restoration' theatre in these islands and became a stepping-stone for many Irish actors, writers and director on their way to the London royal theatres, Drury Lane and the Haymarket. It opened on Monday 9 October 1662 and saw the first dramatic works of the Derry-born dramatist, George Farquhar (1677-1707), and Dublin's own Richard Brinsley Sheridan (1751-1816). Peg Woffington (1720-60) appeared there before she became 'Sweet Peg of Old Drury', as did her lover, Charles Macklin (1690-1797), the great actor and playwright who was born MacLaughlin in Donegal. David Garrick (1717-79), Macklin's only rival, gave his first ever *Hamlet* there and, perhaps appropriately, later shared the amorous favours of Peg.

The theatre survived the collapse of the upper galleries in 1671 and did not finally close until 1787, when it had the ironic indignity of becoming a whiskey store. In 1815 it was transformed into the Catholic church of St Michael and St John when Fr Michael Blake, in the face of official opposition prior to Catholic Emancipation, oversaw the conversion. It survived as a place of worship until 1989-90. The building reverted to its original theatrical function in 2012.

10 October 1940

The Bell

Life in Ireland in 1940 was in the words of Seán O'Faolain (1900-91) himself 'pretty deadly dull', so he was immediately attracted to the proposition of Peadar O'Donnell (1893-1986) that they found a new magazine that would reflect the heart and mind of the real Ireland – the one hidden under the conformism and narrow-minded self-esteem of what O'Faolain had already called the 'grocers' republic'. O'Donnell took care of the business side while O'Faolain had the laborious and, as it proved, maieutic role of editor.

The former found the money and the paper, released by a civil servant who had been under his command during the Troubles. The print run was 3000 copies a month and they chose the name *The Bell*. As O'Faolain wrote in his first editorial: 'Any other equally spare and hard and simple word would have done; any word with a minimum of associations.' It was clear from that first item that it was a kind of manifesto and that, as O'Donnell had expected, O'Faolain would 'give it stature'. By Thursday 10 October 1940 *The Bell* had hit the newsagents for the first time and its distant tinklings may still be heard.

The editorial was entitled 'This Is Your Magazine' and O'Faolain called, indeed challenged, people to write for it. So he published early work by Patrick Kavanagh, Sam Hanna Bell, Brendan Behan, Flann O'Brien, Patrick Campbell, James Plunkett, Michael McLaverty and many other 'names' now familiar. He also sought work from non-writers, some who preferred to remain anonymous: 'An Old Nun', 'Lowbrow', 'Fisherman', 'Taken Down'. No rejection slips were ever used; each hopeful received a personal note from the editor. One entry, 'I Did Penal Servitude', was later a bestseller with the same title. The pseudonym, D83222, was in fact O'Faolain's telephone number.

11 October 1951

The Theatre Royal

The designation 'royal' applied to a theatre did not indicate any special recommendation by the current monarch but that the house had been granted a royal patent, without which theatrical performances were illegal. The practice dated from the restoration of the monarchy in 1660 and the use of the title persisted long after the licensing system was changed. Dublin had four Theatre Royals, the first in Smock Alley (1662-1787), the second in Hawkins Street (1821-80) until it burned down, the third (1897-1934) on the same site and finally, from 1935 the 4000-seater that supplied home-grown entertainment during the Emergency and afterwards. It became the Dublin equivalent of the London Palladium with its plethora of international stars, until it ceased to be profitable and closed in 1962.

Seven years before that sad occasion the management, conscious of its stellar thespian history, mounted an exhibition of playbills, programmes and photographs in the foyer of the dress circle, which opened on Thursday 11 October 1951. The show gave a sketch of the theatre's story and that of its predecessors. The site had at different times been a meat market, the headquarters of the Royal Dublin Society, a Mendicity Institute and a concert hall. It was during rehearsals for *Ali Baba and the Forty Thieves* that the second theatre was destroyed by fire on 9 February 1880; the manager perished in the conflagration.

During the years of the third Theatre Royal such Olympian names as Henry Irving, Forbes Robertson, Herbert Beerbohm Tree, Sir C. Aubrey Smith, Ellen Terry, F.R. Benson, Lily Langtry and Cyril Maude, Charles Chaplin and Mrs Patrick Campbell played there, all of whom figured among the memorabilia. Later stars like Danny Kaye, Fred Astaire, Bob Hope and Judy Garland were also remembered.

In its place now stand the modern building that houses the Screen Cinema and the twelve-storey Hawkins House, an office block.

12 October 1953

Lost in the Wicklow Mountains

Anthony Moore (17) an adventurous junior porter from 88 Derry Road, Crumlin, set out one morning with rucksack and rations for the Wicklow mountains but by noon next day, Monday 12 October 1953, he had not returned. In spite of his age he was an experienced member of An Óige but knowing how challenging the terrain around Glencree and Enniskerry could be, his parents informed the police. Gardaí from Rathfarnham, Enniskerry and Tallaght began a search immediately but had to abandon the attempt because of afternoon fog, endemic to the area.

They checked with the An Óige hostel in Lackendarragh but the warden reported that Moore, whom he knew well, had not called there during the weekend – nor had he been seen in the other hostels in Glencree and Slieve Cuilin. Motorists and local farmers could give no information. At An Óige headquarters in Mountjoy Square a party of thirty members with ropes, boots and emergency kit prepared to leave at dawn to try to find him.

His father told the press that Anthony had been a member of An Óige since the age of thirteen and 'knows every inch of the Wicklow hills'; although concerned, he still had good hopes of finding him safe. The boy had boarded the Enniskerry bus at 11am on Sunday, intending to go to a dance in the Scalp with other hikers and cyclists. In his rucksack he had enough food for one day, a primus stove and a torch. So it was a considerable relief to all the parties when he appeared fit and well and very hungry in Baltinglass on the Tuesday afternoon. He had lost his bearings and covered a total of fifty miles, sleeping out on the Sunday night and in a disused barn on the Monday.

13 October 1937

Full of sound and fury

The Gate Theatre was founded by Micheál MacLiammóir and Hilton Edwards in 1928 as a formal alternative to the Abbey Theatre, presenting, often on a shoestring, both the finest plays by international dramatists and the classical corpus. On Wednesday 12 October 1937 *The Irish Times* theatre critic, known only initially as A.E.M. in those reticent days, reviewed the Scottish play, that off-stage may not speak its name without dire consequences. The initials stood for Andrew E. Malone, the pen name of Laurence Patrick Byrne (1888-1939), the author of *The Irish Drama* (1929) and a trenchant critic. That old theatrical tradition is based upon the play's reputation for serious accidental injuries and even deaths afflicting its dramatis personae, and the belief that the witches' brew prepared in Act 4, Scene 1 contains elements of the satanic Mass.

Undaunted, the 'Boys', as they were affectionately known, delivered a *Macbeth* with Hilton as director and the eponymous Scot, and Micheál as his nemesis, Macduff. The 'fiend-like queen' was played by Coralie Carmichael, the Gate's leading lady of the time. The astute critic drew authoritative notice to the little girl playing Macduff's son. This was Peggy Cummins, then twelve, who afterwards made more that a dozen films in England and Hollywood. The production did not please Malone but he did allow that Hilton played the part 'with all the gusto of his Richard, giving the unhappy king a vigour, to which only desperation could have driven him.' The truth was that he had little regard for the play, dismissing it as 'a tale told by an idiot, full of sound and fury, signifying nothing'. (I wonder where he found that quotation.) He also suggested that the production 'in modern dress' could be 'an interpretation of the Ireland of fifteen or twenty years ago'.

14 October 1928

'The Boys'

The actor, stage designer and linguistically talented Alfred Willmore (1899-1978) began his stage career as a boy actor and after study in the Slade School fell in love with an idealised Gaelic Ireland and became proficient in its language. To complete the picture he changed his ultra-British name to Micheál MacLiammóir and came to Ireland to act with the repertory company of his brother-in-law, Anew McMaster. In the company was Hilton Edwards (1903-1982), who had joined the troupe in 1927, and they became lifelong partners.

Hilton was a fine character actor, stage electrician and adventurous director, Micheál a remarkably handsome lead, set designer, bi-lingual playwright and poet. (Forenames were de rigueur.) They decided to form a company that would present plays that were not generally available in other Dublin theatre: modern international plays, experimental theatre, Shakespeare and other classics. Lacking a theatre, they continued to work in the Taibhdhearc, the Gaelic theatre in Galway, opening it with Micheál's own play, *Diarmaid agus Gráinne*, in which he played the lead.

The first production of the entrancingly named Gate Theatre opened on Sunday 14 October 1928 in the Peacock, the Abbey's other place. Hilton played a remarkably buoyant Peer Gynt, the rackety eponymous hero of Ibsen best-known play. 'The Boys', as the pair was called, stayed in the Peacock, presenting dramas by Tolstoy, Elmer Rice and Eugene O'Neill, among others, until they found a home in the old Assembly building in Parnell Square in February 1930 where the hit of the season was the satirical dream play *The Old Lady says 'No!'*, by Denis Johnston. The contrast between the increasingly local offerings in the Abbey and the known – and, considering the mores of the time, generously tolerated – relationship between the Gate's founders led the Dublin wits to describe the art-theatre scene as 'Sodom and Begorrah'.

15 October 1842

The Nation

The Repeal Association of Daniel O'Connell was founded after the Liberator's achievement in 1829 of Catholic Emancipation. Its purpose was the removal of the infamous Act of Union (1800) that deprived Ireland of her own parliament but gave her no economic advantage to compensate. Three young men with more radical ambitions, intent upon using more radical means to achieve them, were the founders of an ancillary movement called Young Ireland. They were Thomas Davis (1814-45), a Protestant from Mallow, County Cork, Charles Gavan Duffy (1816-1903) from Monaghan and John Blake Dillon (1814-66) from Ballaghaderreen, County Roscommon, and they realised that what Young Ireland and the Repeal Movement needed was a popular newspaper that would inform, educate and inspire.

At Davis's insistence they called it *The Nation* and its first number was printed in 12 Trinity Street on 15 October 1842, with Duffy as editor. The text was written mainly by Davis and he turned the paper into an inexpensive and intensive weekly course in adult education, with a special reference to things Irish, including the language, and an inevitable touch of Anglophobia. It was an effective and fitting complement to the work of the reading rooms that O'Connell had established in his urge to make the grievously mistreated country, in the words of Davis's best known poem (published in *The Nation*), 'a nation once again'. It encouraged the writing of patriotic verse, some little more than doggerel but popular enough to allow the booklet *The Spirit of The Nation* to remain in print for more than a century.

The first sentence of its first editorial set the tone for its pungent style:

> With all the nicknames that serve to delude and divide us...there are
> in truth but two parties in Ireland: those who suffer from her national
> degradation and those who profit by it.

16 October 1949

Floods in Dublin

Sunday 16 October 1949 was a day of prodigious bad weather in Dublin, meriting many column inches in the next day's papers. 2.53 inches of rain fell that day, the highest for any October day since records were kept and the wettest day most people could remember. The city bore the brunt, although the country as a whole suffered as well. Pedestrians who braved the weather had to wade through six inches of ominously coloured brown water, and most cellars and basements needed the services of the over-worked firemen from Tara Street who had to answer more than three hundred and fifty emergency calls.

The four-storey tenements in the Coombe were saturated because of leaks in the roofs. In one house the ceiling of the top-floor flat gave way, raining down debris on the Curtis family: Patrick, Eileen, and three children aged three, two and a baby, five months old. Other families afflicted by the ruin of their furniture were the Suttles, the McCarthys, the O'Learys, the O'Higginses, the Corishes, the Whelans and the Smiths and all stated that their rooms were regularly flooded every time there was heavy rain.

The East Wall Road district was severely flooded, with Hawthorn Terrace, Seville Place, Oriel Street, Seaview Avenue and Church Road underneath a foot of water, larks for the barefoot children or those equipped with wellies but distinctly unpleasant for their parents. The local Garda officer found it necessary to patrol his beat in a horse and cart. Ringsend, Sandymount, Morehampton Road, Malahide Road, Fairview and other areas close to the Liffey and Dublin Bay had to bear not only the brunt of the torrential rain but the rising tide. Because of the storm damage to lines telephone services between the city and Belfast, Dundalk and Monaghan were dislocated, calls having to be routed through Liverpool.

17 October 1949

The smell of alcohol

John F. Morris, a sales manager from Nutley Park, was returning from Dún Laoghaire along the Stillorgan Road about 10pm on 17 June 1949 with his wife, son and daughter. As he neared Nutley Lane he noticed a car being driven erratically from the opposite direction about two or three hundred yards away. He slowed down and swerved but the other vehicle, a Baby Fiat, hit the right side of his car, wrecking it beyond repair. He managed to get out and, although his first concern was for his wife, he observed the woman driver, later identified as Mrs Adrienne Bethell (45) of Bray Head Hotel, Bray, lying on her back on the road with her feet and legs still in her car.

Soon a crowd gathered, including Gardaí and a priest, but the woman's immediate reaction was to cry, 'Take me away from these [expletive deleted] priests.' Garda W. Fortune, who had brought the priest, testified that he had 'got the smell of alcohol from her'. Later in the hospital she described it as 'like a concentration camp' and the couch was 'like the beach in Bray'. She also claimed that she was being threatened by 'black devils and priests'. The ambulance driver testified that she had made nasty remarks about him, the police and the Catholic Church.

The trial was held in the Dublin District Court on Monday 17 October 1949. Through her solicitor, Mrs Bethell expressed her most sincere regret for any unpleasant remarks she may have made on the occasion, when she was considerably upset. The charge of driving while drunk was dismissed but that of 'driving a motor-car in a dangerous manner' was upheld. She was fined £40 (£1250 today) and had her driving licence suspended until 31 March 1951.

18 October 1984

National Day of Remembrance

Although every effort was made since the founding of the Free State in 1922 to accommodate the residual elements of what might be called the ascendancy, imperial echoes continue to cause difficulties. Extremists of both sides could not help but exacerbate the situation when such matters as the Royal British Legion's National Day of Remembrance held in St Patrick's Cathedral to coincide with the ceremonies at the Cenotaph on 11 November each year was being planned. It was a diplomatic minefield, especially at the height of the Northern Troubles. Many Dubliners had fought in both World Wars and many members of their families felt that they should be remembered and indeed it seemed that the country would never be whole until it faced the question and agreed on the answer.

Even as late as the 1980s the matter required delicate handling, especially during the era of the coalition government of Garret FitzGerald. There was much parliamentary discussion and informal conversation between interested parties and the Legion but no satisfactory solution was found. On Thursday 18 October 1984 Lieutenant-Colonel Brian Clarke announced that no formal invitation would be issued to the Defence Forces. He refused to say whether he had been advised that the Defence Forces would not be in a position to take up the informal verbal invitation issued by him to the Adjutant-General, Major-General Brendan Cassidy.

Much had been expected by way of resolution from an all-party Oireachtas committee that would be set up to discuss a National Day of Remembrance but the Taoiseach rejected an allegation of bad faith on the government's party, suggested by Charles Haughey, leader of Fianna Fáil. Garret FitzGerald stated that an invitation had not even been received, let alone considered. It seemed that Clarke's lack of action was truly conceived 'to prevent further embarrassment and controversy'.

19 October 1745

Dr Swift DSPD

In his poem, 'Verses on the Death of Dr Swift, DSPD' which has 488 lines, W.B Years ironically anticipates the reaction to his demise, fourteen years before the actual event. Lines 483-6 are well known:

> *He gave what little wealth he had*
> *To build a house for fools and mad:*
> *And showed by one satiric touch*
> *No nation wanted it so much.*

The letters after his name in the title stand for (in Latin) 'Dean of St Patrick's, Dublin' but for Swift it was a life sentence after the disappointment of all his ambitions. He was never reconciled to 'dirty Dublin and miserable Ireland'.

Jonathan Swift (1667-1745), was famous for the satires *A Tale of a Tub* (1704) and *Gulliver's Travels* (1726). His exile in the land of his birth gave his work an even sharper edge. *The Drapier's Letters* (1724) ended an attempt at coinage devaluation and *A Modest Proposal,* suggesting Ireland's plethora of babies as a meat source, is unmatched for laconic savagery.

Swift's later years were clouded by Ménière's disease and dementia and his epitaph, composed by himself and inscribed over his tomb in St Patrick's, notes that the *saeva indignatio* which lacerated his life could no longer tear apart his heart. He died on 19 October 1745, aged seventy-eight.

> *Hic depositum est corpus/JONATHAN SWIFT STD/*
> *Ecclesiae Cathedralis Decani*
> *Ubi saeva indignatio/ulterius cor lacerare nequit. Abi viator/et*
> *imitare, si poteris, /strenuum pro virili libertatis vindicatorem.*

Yeats made a rhymed version of the epitaph:

> *Swift has sailed into his rest;/Savage indignation there*
> *Cannot lacerate his breast./Imitate him if you dare,*
> *World-besotted traveller; he/ Served human liberty.*

20 October 1971

NCAD

The National College of Art and Design (NCAD) was first so named in 1971 when its governing board was appointed by the Minister for Education. It had a long history and several avatars, including the Dublin Metropolitan School of Art (1877) and the National College of Art (1936). Attempts to move the NCAD from its Thomas Street site to Belfield after it became a constituent college of UCD were strongly resisted by students and graduates, keeping alive a reputation for protest against unreasonable authoritarian decisions, especially those of the Department of Education.

On Wednesday 20 October 1971 that department dismissed two part-time teachers, Paul Funge and Alice Hanratty, from the NCAD. They were staff members who taught first-year Foundation Course students. The reason for the termination of their contracts was their alleged failure to carry out their duties. When the news broke, forty NCAD students protested in front of the offices of the Department of Education in Marlborough Street and at a meeting in the college that evening fifty-six students pledged not to attend any classes until both teachers were reinstated.

The two teachers based their complaints on the refusal of the board to clarify the nature of their duties, the unusually high number of first years who had failed their June assessments and the charge that the exams had been improperly conducted. Both the dismissed were artists of reputation in the own right and it was clear that there was a serious clash in NCAD between established and innovative attitudes. The dispute led to the college being closed on Tuesday 26 October and by the time it was reopened on Monday 6 December, Pádraig Faulkner, the minister, had been asked many questions about the matter in the Dáil. A kind of normality was restored when Funge and Hanratty were reinstated on Tuesday 14 December 1971.

21 October 1901

Casadh an tSúgáin

The first formal production of a play in Irish was *Casadh an tSúgáin* (The Twisting of the Rope). The theatre was the Gaiety in King Street and it was staged for the first time on Monday 21 October 1901 as a postlude to *Diarmuid and Grania*, the product of an uneasy collaboration by W.B. Yeats and George Moore. It was not in fact the first acted dramatic piece in Irish. A scena involving St Patrick and Laoghaire, the pagan ard-rí, was produced as part of Aonach Thír Chonaill in Letterkenny, County Donegal, in 1898 and *Eilís agus an Bhean Déirce* (Eilis and the Beggar Woman) by P.T. Mac Fhionnlaoich had been acted by Inghinidhe na hÉireann in the Antient Concert Rooms the previous August.

However the Abbey Theatre 'record of work', published in *Samhain* (the Irish Literary Theatre's autumn journal) in 1909, is at pains to make clear that *Casadh an tSúgáin* was the 'First Gaelic play produced in a theatre'. The author was Douglas Hyde, the co-founder of the Gaelic League, and he played the part of the boastful Connacht poet Hanrahan, a character devised by Yeats, who tries to wreak havoc in a Munster household by his arrogance, jeering, boasting and attempts to seduce Oona, the daughter of the house, from her fiancé Sheamus. They dare not attack him because of his poetic status but they trick him into showing how much better súgán ropes are made from straw in Connacht. As the rope lengthens he is forced backwards to the open door and finally shut outside.

The play remains popular in both languages and features frequently in such folk entertainments as Tralee's Siamsa Tíre. Brendan Behan's original title for *The Quare Fellow*, his play about capital punishment, was *The Twisting of Another Rope*.

22 October 1953

Tempestuous hearing

The voyage of the MV *Munster* from Liverpool to Dublin on the night of 24-5 August 1953 was stormy in several senses. She rolled quite a bit in the choppy sea but the real tempest was human. The details emerged in the first hearing of a murder case in the Dublin District Court on Thursday 22 October 1953.

Joseph Riggs testified that as he was returning from holiday on the ship he saw three men struggling on the poop deck at 12.30am. The tallest of the three had his hand over the mouth of a smaller man, as he forced him on to one of the buoy-seats. The latter, the accused, Robert James Thomas (19) kept shouting and demanding to see the captain, and soon was rolling with the tall man about the deck. When next Riggs looked, Thomas was holding Ernest Humphries (20) against the rail and suddenly tossed him by the legs over the side.

Hayden Griffiths, who was third officer, said he was on watch duty on the bridge when a seaman reported: 'Man overboard!' He ordered the ship to be turned round with full floodlights and threw a lifebelt over starboard. They searched for an hour and a half before resuming the course for Dublin. The hearing was adjourned until 29 October.

That same day in the Children's Metropolitan Court a sixteen-year-old boy, who could not be named, tried to defenestrate himself while District Justice McCarthy was pronouncing sentence. His case had been remanded twice already because he had collapsed in the dock and when he heard that he was to spend two years in a reformatory he rushed to a side window, crashing his head against the pane, but was prevented from falling by storage heaters. He was carried screaming, kicking and biting, from the court.

23 October 1940

'Put them up'

For many years after the founding of the modern Irish state the level of serious crime was quite low. Killings, apart from occasional 'domestics', were usually connected either directly or remotely to the residual effects of the Civil War. The increase in shootings spawned largely by the drug problem and the spill-over of the Northern Troubles was a later phenomenon. When, on the night of Wednesday 23 October 1940 a young man was shot in the stomach and severely wounded it became an important news story.

The shooting occurred while he, along with two companions, was fixing posters of an unspecified nature on a dead wall at the junction of Langrishe Place that runs off Summerhill, beyond the Gardiner Street junction. It was then described as 'a poorly lighted alley' and somehow an altercation arose when the trio was approached by a detective officer. One of the men was arrested, the other, uninjured, party ran away. The injured man, whose name was not revealed by the police, had emergency surgery performed on him in Jervis Street Hospital.

The affair was so sudden and short-lived that most people in the vicinity would have been unaware of anything untoward, apart from the sound of the shot. One witness, Mr Cloone, a local shopkeeper, explained that he was standing at the door of his shop when he saw the flash of the gun and instinctively ducked down. He had heard some noises that he thought were children running but realised that it was the sound of a struggle. He saw that one of the men had stains of poster paste on his clothes. He also heard the detective saying, 'Put them up' and one of the men had done so. The other, taller and older, had not spoken but was holding his hands over his stomach.

24 October 1949

Noël Browne

With all the modern advances in the treatment of cancer it is difficult to realise what a killer it was sixty-five years ago, when the arrival of a now standard deep x-ray therapy system and diagnostic unit in Hume Street Skin and Cancer Hospital made newspaper headlines. The newsworthiness was a deliberate stroke on the part of Dr Noël Browne, the dynamic and controversial Minister for Health in the coalition government of 1948-51. Appointed on 18 February 1948, he began a crusade against tuberculosis that had a remarkably rapid initial success and now he turned his attention to the other great killer. He was present in the hospital at the inauguration of the equipment on Monday 24 October 1949.

He was welcomed by T.R. Gibson, the chairman of the hospital board, who said it was a happy coincidence that the installation had come at the same time as the formation by the minister of a nationwide agency for the early diagnosis of the disease. He was also pleased to announce that by the time of the next annual report they would have doubled bed accommodation. In reply Browne advised that cancer was the second highest killing disease in Ireland, striking at middle-aged and older people. In taking steps to deal with it he acknowledged he had the cooperation, assistance and advice of medical men associated with cancer work for many years.

C. Campbell SC proposed a vote of thanks to the minister, during which he noted that the annual number of cancer deaths had risen from three thousand in 1925 to four thousand in 1947 and that of the minimum requirement of two hundred beds in Hume Street they still had only sixty. Seconded by Professor C.J. O'Reilly, who said that Browne had the gratitude of thousands, the vote was unanimously adopted.

25 October 1949

Miraculous deliverance

The night of Tuesday 25 October 1949 saw one of the worst storms ever to afflict the volatile Irish Sea. One vessel that bore the brunt of its wildness was the 260-ton auxiliary schooner, *Windermere*, that limped into Dublin port on the Wednesday morning with her engine almost lifeless. Her crew of four – Michael O'Brien, John Coffey, Paddy Craine and T. Carroll, and her master, Captain William Tyrrell, from Wicklow, were all exhausted but otherwise unhurt. She had left Whitehaven, Cumberland, with a cargo of coal for Wicklow and had battled her way for twenty-five hours, twelve of them after all her distress rockets apparently went unheeded. In fact her signals were picked up by the Howth lifeboat, manned by its coxswain E. Harford. It searched the mountainous seas for seven hours, trying to find the *Windermere*, until it too had to head for home.

Tyrrell told the newspapers that he had never experienced such waves during his thirty years at sea. When he realised at 4am that they were near Rockabill (the two islands 'Rock' and 'Bill', six kilometres east-north-east of Skerries, that had a lighthouse) he decided to heave to. The seas, wind and haze were so bad that it was the only option. Everything on deck had to be lashed, while the crewmen worked tirelessly at the pumps and sealing the hatches.

They rode the storm for another eight hours and then headed for Dublin Bay. The wind had gone around from north-east to south-west and forced Tyrrell to heave to again. They had lost all the sails except the foresail and it was being shredded. The wind eventually turned east and drove them into Dublin Bay, where the water seemed almost smooth by comparison. Tyrrell praised his crew as 'splendid' and called his deliverance a 'miracle'.

26 October 1989

Family tragedy

On 15 February 1989 Éamon Daly, a thirty-seven-year-old from Ballyduff, County Waterford, took Aileen, his four-year-old daughter, to Lismore bridge over the River Blackwater and threw her into the water, where she drowned. Details of the ghastly story were revealed at the trial for murder of the father in the Central Criminal Court in Dublin on Thursday 26 October 1989. He was found guilty but insane after the testimonies of two psychiatrists. One of these, Dr Charles Smith, medical director of the Central Mental Hospital, described the event as 'a classical tragedy attached to a classical mental illness'. He said that Daly was in his opinion legally and medically insane at the time. He was suffering from a psychotic depression, with the delusion that he was destined for poverty and that his children would be better off not living.

On the day Daly's intention was to bring both Aileen and her three-year-old sister Linda but Eileen, his wife, managed in the struggle to wrest her from his arms. She was not able to save Aileen nor to prevent her father from taking the child off in his car. (Her body was found weeks after the killing eight miles downstream from Lismore bridge.) Kevin Haugh SC, the prosecuting counsel, said that the facts of the case were not in dispute, nor was the mental condition of the accused at the time. The jury had little difficulty in reaching their verdict in this undefended and horribly uncomplicated case. The trial judge ordered that Daly should be detained in the Central Mental Hospital pending a future court order and further psychiatric reports. The newspapers could do little more than report without commentary the known, harrowing facts as revealed, speculation about turmoil in the family being regarded as gratuitous.

27 October 1942

Lip service

A special session of the Oireachtas in the Mansion House in Dawson Street was called to discuss 'remedies for the ailments with which the Irish language was afflicted'. This particular one was covered in the Dublin press the following day, Tuesday 27 October 1942. The session was chaired by 'An Seabhac', the pseudonym (meaning 'the hawk') of the Irish-language writer Pádraig Ó Síochfhradha (1883-1964) (his surname usually rendered in English as Sugrue). He was from Dingle and had written two bestsellers: *Jimín*, a comic book for children, enjoyed (unusually) as a school textbook, and *An Baile Seo 'Gainne* (Our Town) a series of gently humorous sketches of his birthplace.

He could speak with some authority and charged the universities and the government with obstructing the language. He had written to a government department a letter in Irish and had been addressed in reply as 'Mr Sugrue'. As well as that revelation he quoted a letter sent to the president of the National University in which the writer stated that her son, having been educated through Irish at primary and secondary level, now found that in University College Dublin not one word was taught through Irish.

Pádraig Mac Con Midhe, the delegate from Belfast and president of the GAA, contrasted the situation in the north, claiming that one would hear more Irish spoken in Belfast in five minutes than in Dublin in a day. A paper read by Éamon de Bhaldran suggested that if the TDs and senators were real Gaels and Irish speakers there might be some hope of the population taking a greater interest in the language.

The debate was a refrain that had been heard often before and would be reprised often again. The term 'lip service' might have been invented to describe the attitude of the vast majority of members of the Oireachtas and the civil service to Irish, then as now.

28 October 1940

O'Dea's Bottom

The encircling gloom of the Emergency years could be temporarily dispelled by cinema and theatre. A typical example was a Gate Theatre production on Monday 28 November 1940 of *A Midsummer Night's Dream*, with the Edwards-MacLiammóir company playing a mile away from home in the Gaiety. *The Dream*, with its combination of farce, fantasy and frivolity, tends to drive directors to heights of all three 'f's: Herbert Beerbohm Tree had live rabbits running about the stage in 1900 and in the 1970 production by Peter Brook the actors played on stilts and trapezes before a plain white cyclorama.

The Gate company's stalwarts – Coralie Carmichael, Shelagh Richards and Meriel Moore – played Helena, Hermia and Titania, the last of these matched in an unequal struggle with MacLiammóir as Oberon. The latent animus between the two so obviously replicates the unease of Theseus and his conquered bride Hippolyta that many modern directors have doubled the roles. Puck, played by Dennis Barry, was kinder if no less mischievous than usual but the casting of Dublin's all-time favourite comedian as Bottom the weaver was a stroke of genius by Hilton Edwards in a generally elegant production, greatly enhanced by almost compulsory Mendelssohn music.

Jimmy O'Dea was then forty-one and almost at the height of his fame. He was the star of Christmas pantomime and revue. He had made five comedies for Ealing Studios and had a sideline of novelty discs. Few realised that he was a superb actor, having appeared in plays by Ibsen, Chekov and Shaw. But when, with a faraway look of wonder, he said: 'I have had a dream, past the wit of man to say what dream it was: man is but an ass if he goes about to expound this dream…' there were tears as well as laughter in the auditorium.

29 October 1946

Teachers' strike

For most of their public careers Éamon de Valera and Archbishop John Charles McQuaid seemed hand in glove, with a shared vision of an ideal Ireland. On one matter they were strongly at variance – the Dublin Irish National Teachers' Organisation (INTO) strike that lasted from 20 March until 31 October 1946. On Tuesday 29 October Dr T.J. O'Connell, INTO general secretary, directed his striking members to return to work on the Thursday. It was the public support for the teachers by McQuaid in direct opposition to the Fianna Fáil government's policy, as exemplified by Thomas Derrig (1897-1956), the Minister of Education, that caused the rift.

Derrig published new salary scales to take effect from 1 September 1945, which the teachers rejected by 4749 votes to 3773. The strike, which involved more than 1200 teachers and affected about 40,000 children, was financed by a levy of 12.5 per cent on teachers from outside the capital which gave the strikers about nine tenths of their salaries. All the ingredients were there for a long siege and neither side was prepared to yield. On 8 April McQuaid wrote to O'Connell, urging him to seek some means, without prejudice, of ending the impasse. O'Connell asked the archbishop to act as mediator between the INTO and the government but Derrig countered that 'no good purpose would be served by further discussion'.

Protests by the Corporation and street action by parents seemed to have no effect. At the Fianna Fáil ard-fheis on 8 October both de Valera and Derrig still refused to budge. It was an appeal by McQuaid to O'Connell in another letter on 28 October, using all the authority of a Church leader, that the good of the children 'who are my pastoral care' should be the teachers' prime consideration, that caused them to return. Great bitterness against Fianna Fáil remained, exemplified by their defeat in the general election of February 1948.

30 October 1986

Criminal incompetence

The increase in crime in Dublin has been a matter of grave concern, mostly drug-fuelled and aggravated by the rise of gangsterism. So it is something of a relief to find an example of gross ineptitude among thieves. John Walsh, aged thirty, of Joseph Plunkett Tower, Ballymun, had for some years been a not very successful criminal. His flat was raided on the suspicion of possession of cannabis with intent to supply on 30 October 1986 and as he threw four packets of the weed (worth £40 by current prices) out the window they were caught by Detective Garda Waters, conveniently placed to receive them. Equipment for the processing of the drug, with apparatus for weighing, cutting and packaging, was also found in his flat. When he was finally brought before Dublin District Court on 21 January 1988 on another charge, earlier misdemeanours were 'taken into account'.

Typical was his attempted robbery on 13 April 1986 of the Red Rooster shop in Ballymun in which he used a toy gun, a successful theft from the Towers pub of £85 and an unsuccessful raid on the Penthouse off-licence the same day using the same gun. At this latest court appearance he pleaded guilty to stealing £240, this time from his old target, the Penthouse, on 20 June 1987.

His solicitor, Michael Hanahoe, did what he could to mitigate the offences by diminishing his criminal status, claiming that his robberies were drunken escapades and his use of an imitation firearm was a measure of his client's innate fecklessness and criminal incompetence. He was well known about Ballymun and easily recognised at each of the scenes, being so foolish as to try them again. Walsh pleaded guilty to all the charges and was sentenced to eighteen months in Mountjoy jail.

31 October 1942

Rag day

Rivalry between Dublin's senior universities has varied in intensity throughout the 20th century, the animus propounded in the early days by differences in heritage, religion, class and politics. Nowadays most of the distinctions have become blurred and they are in general good-mannered. Apart from claims that 'Trinners are winners' and even more chauvinistic replies from UCD, the student bodies are complementary rather than at odds. Now and then, as during the UCD 'rag day' on Saturday 31 October 1942, things got heated.

A group of students thought it a jolly wheeze to make a foray in 'rag' costume into the Trinity campus and a group of equally jolly students of the older college decided to repel them. The result was a free fright that grew steadily more serious, spilling out on to College Green and causing traffic holds-up in that part of the city. Traffic then was considerably lighter than it is today, with practically no private cars and much horse transport, but at such a complicated intersection at the front gate of Trinity College the 'riot' – or Hallowe'en high-spirits, depending on your stance – was extremely disruptive. The Gardaí arrived in force and, ignoring the hail of turf sods, sticks, stones and tins, soon restored order. Another sortie of greater intensity was reported in Trinity's Lincoln Place gate and there the Gardaí were forced to draw batons and drove the assailants back along Nassau Street, from which they were taunted with cries of 'Flatfeet'.

The respectable part of Rag Day, the procession, showed signs of the bleak austerity of the time. All the floats, fewer than usual, were horse-drawn but they still showed elements of appropriate anti-government satire and caustic comment on the so-called 'Emergency'. *Gone with the Wind*, the blockbuster film of the time, was also effectively parodied.

WINTER

1 November 1920

'Mountjoy jail one Monday morning'

Kevin Barry joined the Irish Volunteers in October 1917 and was intermittently active while a medical student in UCD. On 20 September 1920 he took part in an IRA attack on an army lorry parked outside Monk's Bakery, Upper Church Street, near King's Inns. Three British soldiers were killed in the engagement and Barry was discovered under a van holding a pistol. He was arrested and charged with the killing of Private Marshall Whiteside, like him eighteen years of age. He was court-martialled and sentenced to death by hanging in Mountjoy jail.

Because of his age and the fact that he was the first Volunteer so to be sentenced there was an almost universal plea for clemency. The recent death by hunger strike of Terence MacSwiney (b. 1879) had greatly increased tension and both the Lord Lieutenant and the Irish Chief Justice came out strongly in favour of a reprieve. The authorities, advised (it is said) by Winston Churchill, refused. The unnecessary event, darkened by undoubted proof of torture of Barry while in prison, generated a score of ballads and one written anonymously by an expatriate Irishman in Glasgow is still sung and potentially rousing. It begins:

> *In Mountjoy jail one Monday morning high upon the gallows tree*
> *Kevin Barry gave his young life for the cause of liberty.*

It was the lines:

> *Just before he faced the hangman in his lonely prison cell*
> *British soldiers tortured Barry just because he wouldn't tell...*

that gave the ballad its particular punch and a sworn affidavit of the details of the ill-treatment caused widespread rage and dismay.

The 'Monday morning' was 1 November 1920 and as 8 o'clock approached two thousand people gathered to pray at the gates of Mountjoy. There was no inquest but at a military court of enquiry 'medical evidence was given...that death was instantaneous.'

2 November 1800

Buck Whaley

One of the more colourful characters of rakish 18th century-Dublin was Thomas Whaley (1766-1800), known variously as 'Buck' Whaley or 'Jerusalem' Whaley. He was born on 15 December 1766, the son of a magistrate known as 'Burn-Chapel' Whaley because of his liberal attitude to Catholicism. He was not of the same mind, being more interested in the high life and gambling than in priest-hunting. He inherited at the age of sixteen but had to leave Paris in a hurry because of a gambling debt of £14,000, lost in one night, which his bankers refused to cover. By the age of eighteen he was an MP in the Irish Parliament, in which role he later accepted bribes to vote both for and against the Act of Union.

Dining with the Duke of Leinster, he accepted a bet of £15,000 (£2m today) that he could travel to Jerusalem and back within two years. This he did triumphantly, with many tales of the Middle East, including parades of concubines and playing handball against the Wailing Wall in Jerusalem. He left Dublin in October 1788, sent off by a cheering crowd, and he was back to even greater acclaim in the summer of 1789 to collect the £15,000. With his expenses of £8000 his net profit was £7000.

A contemporary ballad recalls how:

> Buck Whaley lacking much in cash,
> And being used to cut a dash,
> He wagered full ten thousand pound
> He'd visit soon the Holy Ground.

He moved to the Isle of Man to avoid his debtors but made sure that his house was built on Irish soil by the neat device of importing enough to have a six-foot foundation throughout. This was part of yet another bet. He died on Sunday 2 November 1800 in Knutsford in Cheshire while travelling to London.

3 November 1937

Con man

At Dublin District Court on Wednesday 3 November 1937 Thomas P. Ryan (37) of Oakley Place, South Circular Road, was charged with attempting to obtain money under false pretences. His alleged victim was Canon Parkinson Hill of Zion Rectory, Rathgar, but at the hearing further charges of the same offence were entered involving three Dublin solicitors, S. Grant, M.C. Beatty and S.G. Rutherford. The case involved a farm that Ryan owned in Ballinafagh, Prosperous, County Kildare, and which he had made several attempts to sell.

The farm was only five acres in size, with a thatched cottage, but in his description he tended to exaggerate, saying that he owned a large slated house with up-to-date outhouses and farm effects, eight acres, two roods and twenty-eight perches and thirty acres of turbary. He told the solicitors and auctioneers that his absolute reserve price was £600 (£34,000 today). He was unable to produce the title deeds, claiming that he had never seen them.

He told his story to Beatty, whose office was in Eustace Street (off Dame Street) and received £20 from him, to Mr Walshe of D'Olier Street, from whom he obtained £10, to Mr O'Neill (of Abbey Street) from whom he netted £5 and an introduction to the manager of the Northern Bank, who gave him £25. Other sums obtained included £30 from the manager of the Royal Bank, £10 from the Ulster Bank, Kilcock, £11 from Reverend Mr Northridge 'by telling him a good story', and £10 from the National Finance Company, Abbey Street. He also got groceries from Findlaters in Rathmines, Geddings in Clontarf, the Duignan Meath Market and McCarthys, Parkgate Street.

In light of these charges and others revealed to the court a rather startled, near incredulous Mr Justice Conroy remanded the defendant for a week.

4 November 1949

Manslaughter charge

Early in the morning of Friday 4 March 1949 a car travelling on the Merrion Road in the direction of Blackrock overtook a taxi in Serpentine Avenue, mounted the pavement at the junction with Sandymount Avenue and crashed into a lamp standard. The car had been full of young people – eight in all – on their way from a dance in the Metropole but four of the backseat passengers had got out before the car had reached Ballsbridge. John Smart (20) and Monica Mary Barry (21), the two who stayed, died, the former that morning, the other several days later. Kevin Anthony Wilkinson (21), the driver, and Theodosia Antoinette Graham, the front-seat passenger, were injured but she was able to attend the Dublin District Court as a witness on Thursday 4 November 1949, when Wilkinson was charged with the manslaughter of Smart and Barry.

The case depended upon the quality of Wilkinson's driving and whether he had been imbibing alcohol. Dr Peter Storah, who had been at the dance, reached the scene soon after the crash and did what he could for the victims. He found no trace of liquor from Wilkinson, who was lying on the road when he arrived, and concluded that he was perfectly sober. Graham, propped up against railings, was diagnosed with scalp wounds and a broken leg. When she appeared at the hearing she needed the support of a stick and had a steel support on her right leg.

The case was adjourned until the following Monday for the hearing of evidence of speed of travel and driver's capacity. It was postponed again until Monday 14 November, when the judge dismissed the charges of manslaughter and dangerous driving but found Wilkinson guilty of careless driving. He fined him £5 and ordered him to pay costs of £11/9s.

5 November 1928

Na hAisteoirí Gaelacha in the Abbey

The Abbey, as Ireland's national subsidised theatre, had an implicit duty to stage work in Irish. This was especially true during the career as managing director of Ernest Blythe (1941-67), who insisted that his actors have proficiency in Irish and had their names printed in Irish in theatre programmes. Many thought that this cost the Abbey a number of excellent players and it was felt by detractors that national drama was being sacrificed to the language movement, especially when the most common productions in Irish were mediocre pantomimes. The result was a sharp division between supporters and execrators.

In the early years there were few Irish plays but those staged were actively encouraged and supported by all. Monday 5 November 1928 saw the opening of a playbill, not untypical, of early efforts that resulted in House Full notices appearing in the Abbey. A company known as the Gaelic Players presented two dramatic offerings: a one-act play called *The Quenching of the Light* by Seamus Wilmot (1902-77) and a translation of a scene from *The Rivals* (1775) by Richard Brinsley Sheridan (1751-1816), written when he was just twenty-three. (In later years the titles would not have been translated but boldly given as Na hAisteoirí Gaelacha, *Múchadh an tSolais* and *An Comhrac Aonair*.)

The first was in the tradition of Synge's *Riders to the Sea*, with poor peasants awaiting news of a missing vessel and the railing of one of little faith against God as the tragedy develops. The Sheridan piece was much more light-hearted, done in 18th-century costumes with lots of Anglo-Irish wit and wisdom, retained in translation, as Captain Absolute and Mrs Malaprop try to outwit each other and Bob Acres feels his courage ooze out of his palms in his aborted duel with the hot-headed Irishman, Sir Lucius O'Trigger.

6 November 1949

F.J. McCormick

On Sunday 6 November 1949 a painting called *The Vacant Throne* was unveiled by Seán T. O'Kelly, then President of Ireland, in what could without offence be called 'The Ould sh'Abbey'. Whatever about the condition of the theatre's décor there was no disputing the sterling qualities of the missing monarch, F.J. McCormick (1889-1947). The painting by Cecil Salkeld showed the face of the subject in eleven roles in which he was all but unmatchable. He was an early interpreter of O'Casey: the original Seamus Shields in *The Shadow of a Gunman*, Joxer Daley in *Juno and the Paycock* and Commandant Jack Clitheroe in *The Plough and the Stars*. No other Abbey actor came close to his excellence or versatility, although Barry Fitzgerald was a worthy colleague. He appeared in four hundred productions interpreting Shaw and Shakespeare, with a memorable Lear.

The significance of the painting's title was that its subject had died of a brain tumour on 24 April 1947 just as a new career as a cinema actor was waiting.

F.J. McCormick was born Peter Judge in Skerries, County Dublin, in 1889 and worked as a civil servant in Dublin and London until joining the Abbey in 1918. He was the half-antithesis of Oliver Goldsmith's description of David Garrick: 'On the stage he was natural, simple affecting;/'Twas only that when he was off, he was acting.' Off stage Judge was the least histrionic of personalities, having all the quiet reticence of the ideal civil servant. His appearance as Shell in the film *Odd Man Out* (1947), chock-full of Irish actors, made him an overnight star but he survived only to take part in *Hungry Hill* (1947).

Lennox Robinson, who was the master of ceremonies, advised his audience that the portrait would hang in the foyer. It may still be seen in the theatre today.

7 November 1980

The Legion of Mary

Although officially approving the active involvement of the laity in the religious life, often called Catholic Action, the Irish church establishment allowed as little autonomy as it could to those who were anxious to help. One such case was that of Frank Duff (1889-1980), an indefatigable worker for the poor of Dublin. He was born in 1889 and joined the civil service in 1908. In 1921, with Fr Michael Toher, he founded the Legion of Mary. In spite of the manifestly good work he was doing it was viewed with grave suspicion by the Dublin archbishops. It was many years before his work was given total assent.

He had become agonisingly aware of the condition of the underclass, who lived in squalor in some of the worst slums in Europe, as a member of the Society of St Vincent de Paul, which he joined in 1913. The local clergy seemed unwilling or unable to do much to help. Part of their approach was affected by the fact that in an attempt to survive, some of the women had become prostitutes, many working in Monto, Dublin's red-light district that had been an 'allowed' area for many years.

The legion had from the beginning a militaristic air with a vocabulary borrowed from Ancient Rome; other terms in use included *praesidium, acies* and *curia comitium*, chosen to emphasise that there was an endless battle against evil. Duff established the Sancta Maria hostel in 1922 for the rehabilitation of former prostitutes and five years later the Morning Star hostel for homeless men. The battle against Monto and its attendant streets was fought and won by 1925 but some have seen its dissolution as one of the generators of the notorious Magdalen laundries. Duff died on Friday 7 November 1980, having seen his *Legio Mariae* become an international organisation.

8 November 1956

Three experienced sailors lost

Dublin Bay is usually a quiet stretch of water but facing east it sometimes has to take the full force of an Irish Sea storm. At 7pm on Wednesday 7 November 1957 three experienced sailors, Captain Reginald Kearon OBE, the Dún Laoghaire Harbour Master, Cormac P. Maloney AMCEI, 41 Nutgrove Park, Clonskeagh, the engineer in charge of harbour services, and D.S. Cadogan of 40 Seapoint Avenue, Monkstown, a retired boat-builder, put to sea in a motor launch for a trial run. Some time later the engine failed just as the wind rose to gale force. After midnight on the Thursday Poolbeg Lighthouse radioed that there was a launch in distress at the Poolbeg rocks.

The Dún Laoghaire lifeboat was launched and in spite of deplorable weather conditions located the launch at around 1.30am. It was not able to get close because of the wind and the strength of the waves but the crew decided to try to float a line on a lifebuoy. John Jenkins, the coxswain, brought the vessel dangerously close to the rocks, shouting to the men on the launch to hold on and wait for a line to be shot across. Just as he stood up ready to fire a huge wave lifted the launch and smashed it against the rocks. The wreck took only a few seconds but, after an hour's search using its power light, the lifeboat gave up hope of finding the survivors.

Next morning at daybreak the lifeboat went out again but it was not until the afternoon that Maloney's body, wearing a life jacket, was washed up near the Pigeon House power station. The bodies of Kearon and Cadogan were recovered on the shingle near the Bull Wall. It was ironical that Kearon's special concern had been the provision of a rescue service for the bay.

9 November 1961

Filming The Quare Fellow

Brendan Behan's finest play, *The Quare Fellow*, had its first British production by the Theatre Workshop in the Theatre Royal, Stratford East, on 24 May 1956. It was directed and probably shaped by Joan Littlewood and its authenticity, based on an actual case and Behan's own prison experiences, made it a potent oblique case against capital punishment and the public piety of Ireland at the time. It had first been offered to the Abbey and had predictably been rejected by Ernest Blythe but was gladly welcomed by Alan Simpson for his Pike Theatre. Its British and American success made it an inevitable choice for some director for filming and an inevitable insertion of a love interest since all-male movies don't do well at the box-office.

A British company known as Liger (an unsubtle crunch of 'lion' and 'tiger' – an associate company was called Tigon) in cooperation with Braynstone Films and US Pathé began shooting on Thursday 8 November 1961 in the cellars of the International Hotel in Bray. The main location would be Kilmainham jail and Arthur Driefuss, the director, announced that the company would be making 'a substantial contribution' to the prison's restoration fund. Driefuss also wrote the scenario and grafted on the love interest, personified by Sylvia Syms and the idealistic young warder played by Patrick McGoohan. Behan himself had been signed up to sing the film's theme song, 'The Ould Triangle', and was intended to have a small role in the film.

Driefuss managed to preserve the integrity of the theme, using outside locations such as the Brazen Head, Dublin's oldest pub, merely as 'the counterpoint of the outside world'. The film provided parts, rather as *Odd Man Out* had done fourteen years earlier, for the great Irish repertory company of actors. Filmed in black and white, it still grips.

10 November 1861

The funeral of Terence Bellew MacManus

Terence Bellew MacManus (1811-61) was in many ways a typical 19th-century Irish nationalist: born in Tempo, County Fermanagh, in 1811, he became a successful shipping agent in Liverpool, where he joined the Repeal Movement. On his return to Ireland in 1843 he became an enthusiastic member of Young Ireland. With William Smith O'Brien and John Blake Dillon, he took part in the abortive engagement in Ballingarry, County Tipperary, in 1848 and, avoiding the death sentence, was transported to Van Diemen's Land in 1849. In 1852 he escaped and made his way to San Francisco, where he tried but failed to resume his career in shipping and died in poverty on 15 January 1861.

Both at home in Ireland and in the United States a new 'physical-force' movement known as the Irish Revolutionary Brotherhood (IRB) had come into existence. They soon began to call themselves Fenians after the Fianna of Fionn Mac Cumhaill in the great saga. One of the founders, Thomas Luby (1822-1901), hearing of MacManus's death, realised that the funeral in Dublin of the old Ballingarry warrior could be a significant piece of publicity for the movement. But Paul Cullen (1803-78), Archbishop of Dublin, who had dire experience in Rome of Garibaldi's revolutionaries, would not give permission for a lying-in-state of MacManus's body in the Pro-Cathedral, nor allow any priest of his diocese to officiate at his graveside.

The body was brought by slow stages from San Francisco to New York, each station being marked by a show of Fenian strength. When it reached Ireland it was laid out in the Mechanics Institute in Abbey Street (afterwards the site of the Abbey Theatre) and on Sunday 10 November 1861 MacManus was buried after a huge funeral, the attendance at which startled even the organisers. Fifty thousand men marched to Glasnevin Cemetery through streets crowded with at least twice that number.

11 November 1938

Embezzlement charge

The tenth day of the trial of Christopher Noonan on a charge of embezzlement was Friday 11 November 1938. Noonan worked for the Corporation's housing department and allegedly kept money received by him from Corporation tenants. Prompted by his counsel P. McGilligan, the Fine Gael TD and law professor, he gave evidence on his own behalf.

It appeared that some tenants preferred not to accept an office receipt because it would not show how much in arrears they were. In such cases it was his practice to put such moneys into a sealed envelope with the full details written on the outside. This would be left for the collector who would then post out receipts to the clients concerned. At this point Judge Davitt broke in to ask if there was anything in any book to show the passing of money from him to the collector and was told, 'No.'

Another complicated piece of procedure was the story of Mr Peppard and the cheques. Noonan explained that he had given rent money to Peppard and received cheques made out to the city treasurer and lodged with his account. On the night of 9-10 September the safe in Noonan's office was broken into. He had left the office at 5pm on the 9th, having locked the safe with his key, the only one he had. Next morning a clerk took out a key and said, 'There is your key.' Noonan produced his key and disclaimed all knowledge of the second. Both keys were tried and fitted, and it was clear that a robbery had taken place. Noonan added that when he was suspended the city manager told him that it had nothing to do with the robbery but was to do with two delayed cheques.

The hearing was adjourned until the following morning.

12 November 1872

The Fay Brothers

The Abbey Theatre owes its existence primarily to the aesthetic vision of three people whose talk one wet afternoon led to the setting up of the Irish Literary Theatre. They were the poet W.B. Yeats and the playwrights Lady Gregory and Edward Martyn, and their manifesto (published in 1897) began:

> We propose to have performed in Dublin in the spring of every year certain Celtic and Irish plays, which will be written with a high ambition and so build up a Celtic and Irish school of dramatic literature.

It was an ambitious project, especially for people who had then little experience of practical stagecraft.

The real dramaturgy and the renowned Abbey style of clarity of speech and economy of gesture and movement came when Yeats was introduced to William George (W.G.) Fay (1872-1947) and his brother Frank (1870-1931) by his friend Æ (George Russell) (1867-1935). Fay, who was born in Dublin, had trained as an electrician but soon toured Ireland with a number of 'fit-up' companies. Both W.G. and Frank had experience of Théâtre Libre in Paris, giving W.G. a thorough knowledge of experimental theatre and making him a superb comic actor and Frank a renowned speaker of verse.

It was their Dublin Dramatic School that found such Abbey stalwarts as Sarah Allgood (1879-1950) and in the first production of *The Playboy of the Western World*, W.G., also the director, played Christy Mahon, while Frank was Shawn Keogh. It was he who brought the Abbey patroness Annie Horniman to Dublin where, fascinated equally by Yeats and the idea of repertory theatre, she provided the money to buy the building in Lower Abbey Street that became the theatre's first permanent home. After some policy differences with Horniman the brothers left the company, W.G. having an impressive career in films.

13 November 1951

No word of the missing passengers

November is notoriously the month for fogs, although because of fuel changes and clean-air legislation the days of real 'pea-soupers' is largely gone. However in the 1950s coal was a contributory factor, especially on calm days of high meteorological pressure. Just after midnight on Tuesday 13 November 1951 a taxi with two women passengers was making its careful way in dense fog along City Quay on the south bank of the Liffey in the direction of Butt Bridge. The driver, Patrick Rogers, of 5 Leix Road, Cabra, found himself completely disoriented and drove into the river at a spot where there was no protecting parapet.

Finding the car lipping the edge he jammed on the brakes but was soon struggling to push open the door underwater. Two men, Patrick Donnelly of 3 Stella Gardens, Sandymount, and William Moran of 10 Newtown, Tallaght, told the newspapers that while on Butt Bridge they had heard a squeal of brakes followed by a splash and, seeing a man struggling in the water, threw him a lifebuoy. He failed to reach it at the first attempt but caught it when they threw it again and they were able to land him at the step at the foot of the bridge.

The police were quickly on the scene and when he was pulled from the water he told them about his missing passengers, two women, English, he thought. He had picked them up in Harcourt Street and intended to take them to a Fairview address. He was rushed to Sir Patrick Dun's Hospital and treated for shock. Meanwhile a diver had been sent for and attempts were being made to raise the car with a mobile crane. By the time the morning papers were on sale there had been no word of the missing women.

14 November 1825

The Pro-Cathedral

Dublin has two cathedrals, Holy Trinity, now generally known as Christ Church, and St Patrick's, sited less than a mile to the south. Both were in existence long before Henry VIII's break from Rome and in ecclesiastical law are still Catholic edifices, Christ Church's precedence having been established in 1300. The Catholic authorities still regard it as their cathedral and so when the Popery laws began to be relaxed and then repealed, at the turn of the 19th century, and the majority population was allowed to worship in any church of quasi-cathedral status that they might build, it could not usurp the primacy of Christ Church. The new edifice built in Marlborough Street was therefore called a pro-cathedral, *acting* until, in some imagined ecumenical future, the former possession might be restored.

By 1803, in spite of great disappointment at the non-delivery of the promised full emancipation, the diocese of Dublin under its conforming archbishop, John Thomas Troy (1786-1823), made the first faltering move towards building St Mary's Pro-Cathedral, with the purchase of Lord Annesley's townhouse in Marlborough Street, close to the city's main thoroughfare, Sackville Street. Funds were low (when Troy died in 1823 there was scarcely enough money enough to bury him) and it was not until 1814 that the house was demolished, enabling Troy to lay the foundation stone in May 1815. The building, designed by George Papworth, was the first Catholic episcopal seat built in these islands since the Reformation. It was Daniel Murray (1768-1852), Troy's successor, who officiated at its opening on Monday 14 November 1825.

The effect on Catholic morale was incalculable; Catholicism was no longer a hole-in-corner sect and the impressive building, so close to the city centre, was a matter of pride and focus, not only for the citizens of Dublin but for the country as a whole.

15 November 1937

The R&R&G&S

It may seem something of a message in code to say that the R&R loves G&S but most Dubliners can decipher the message. The Rathmines and Rathgar, the quintessential Dublin music society, was founded in 1913 at a meeting held in 48 Summerville Park, Rathmines. C.P. Fitzgerald, the young organist in Rathgar's Church of the Three Patrons, wanted to establish a musical society whose membership would be formed from residents of the townships of Rathmines and Rathgar. The principle still adhered to more than a hundred years later is that, although professional technical help is sought and used, the performers, chorus and leads, are amateurs.

From the start the operettas of Gilbert and Sullivan played a large part in the R&R repertoire. The first production, *The Mikado*, was staged in the Queen's Theatre, Pearse Street, in December 1913. The following year, also in December, the society performed for the first time in the Gaiety Theatre, with another G&S operetta, *The Yeomen of the Guard*. As the society developed and membership expanded it was decided to complement the society's G&S performances by including other musical comedy productions in its repertoire. But the coded message still holds.

For its silver jubilee year the society presented two of the most popular G&S operettas on alternate evenings in the week beginning Monday 10 November 1937. They followed the chronology of composition by staging *HMS Pinafore* that evening and *The Pirates of Penzance* on the Tuesday. The venue was the Olympia Theatre in Dame Street and the audience enjoyed again Captain Corcoran who 'never – well hardly ever – said a big big D', the 'somewhat triangular' Deadeye Dick and Sir Joseph Porter, who became the 'ruler of the Queen's navee by polishing the handle of the big front door'.

16 November 1928

The Valkyrie *in Dublin*

The cultural needs of Dublin in the late 19th and early 20th centuries were fairly well catered for with home products but the city always had a welcome for the big stuff: the touring companies of Charles Doran and Anew McMaster for classical drama and the Carl Rosa Opera Company for the really big stuff. When that company hit town you could be sure of full houses and audiences who could if necessary prompt Puccini, *Cav* and *Pag* and the great Irish trio *Maritana, The Bohemian Girl* and *The Lily of Killarney.*

The Carl Rosa Opera Company was founded in 1873 by Carl August Nicholas Rosa, a German-born musical impresario, to present opera in English, employing a mix of established opera stars and young singers, reaching new opera audiences with popularly priced tickets. He started the company along with his wife, Euphrosyne Parepa-Rosa, and popularised opera in Britain and America, performing standard repertory in English, as well as operas by English composers. It survived Rosa's death in 1889 and with frequent revivals never quite disappeared from the 20th-century popular operatic scene.

On Friday 16 November 1928 the company had a sell-out in the Gaiety Theatre, when it presented *The Valkyrie*, the second and most accessible of the four sections of Wagner's Ring cycle. If it was not *Die Walküre* as played in Bayreuth it was, by local standards, epic enough. It had been an ambitious offering on the company's last visit and now it confidently repeated its success with fine performances by Leslie Jones as Wotan, King of the Valkyries, Ethel Austin as Brunnhilde, his daughter, William Boland as Siegmund and Pauline Maunder as Sieglinde. The orchestral highlight was of course was the famous 'Ride' and special applause was reserved for Arthur Hammond, the conductor.

17 November 1960

Learning French

From the 1960s Ireland's thoughts were focused on Europe. It was with some disappointment that at the annual distribution of prizes in Mountjoy School, Malahide Road, on Thursday 17 November 1960 William Tate, the headmaster, expressed his concern about the numbers of pupils who had dropped French in their Leaving Certificate years. He also deplored the reaction of many parents to compulsory religious instruction as taking up the time that should have been devoted to secular subjects. He had resisted the pleas of some parents that their children be excused attendance because even apart from the religious aspect he believed that dropping a subject merely encouraged laziness and the wastage of time.

He revealed that out of seventy-five senior boys only thirty-four were studying French. He insisted that it was essential that every boy and girl should have even a smattering of a continental language since 'the world is growing increasingly smaller.' Commenting on the increase in the take-up of science, he acknowledged the support of the Schools Scientific Education Trust established by Guinness but was less that enthusiastic about it as a general subject, suggesting it was essentially a subject for those with a distinct flair.

The platform party included the Most Rev Dr R.B. Pike, Bishop of Meath, who took up the question of religious instruction and its necessity for a full education: 'The world is full of very clever people who are foolish in the things that matter.' He appealed for recruits for the ministry as the Church was desperately short of vocations and asked teachers to be on the look out for possible future clergymen. As usual in these matters F. La Touche Godfrey, the guest who presented the prizes, admitted that he had never won a prize in the past fifty years.

18 November 1937

Driving with physical disability

In the years before compulsory testing was introduced all a Dublin citizen had to do to obtain a driving licence was to pay a fee and drive off. In 1937 the fee was 10s and although bans of various durations were imposed by magistrates for various offences there was rarely a question of disqualification. Peter McBride of 28 Upper Pembroke Street had had his left arm amputated at the shoulder in 1918 but by 1928 had devised means of driving by putting his hand through the gaps in the steering wheel when he needed to change gear. The police got to hear about this practice and McBride became the subject of a disqualification appeal by Superintendent Hurley, under the Transport Act of 1933. He argued that McBride's lack of left arm constituted 'physical disability' and required his appearance in the Dublin District Court before Mr Justice Lennon on Thursday 18 November 1937.

McBride's solicitor stated that he had been driving for nine years without accident and now the gear stick had been lengthened so that it was easily reached from the steering wheel. He described how his client had subjected himself to a police test and that one of the Gardaí from the Carriage Department had found him entirely capable, with a performance that he described as 'remarkable'. The judge was not impressed by the arguments, saying that sooner or later 'any man who drives with frequency will…be involved in an accident.' He was, however, reluctant to make the order but did so when the counsel for the State Solicitor suggested he might otherwise allow anyone with a physical disability to make the declaration and secure a licence. He remained sympathetic to McBride's special ability and suspended the operation of the order in case of an appeal.

19 November 1798

'So bad an anatomist'

By September 1798 all the attempts at insurrection by the United Irishmen had been frustrated but Wolfe Tone, the most charismatic of all the movement's leaders, had one final card to play. Two significant invasion attempts had come to nothing, the French fleet unable to land in Cork because of bad weather in Bantry Bay in 1796 and a Dutch fleet annihilated in Camperdown in 1797. A last attempt had a small French fleet leave Brest on 16 September 1798, with Tone travelling in the flagship *Hoche* and 3000 troops under Admiral Bompard.

On 10 October the invasion fleet was met by a British squadron off the north coast of Donegal. Tone refused to transfer to the schooner, which could outrun the fastest enemy ship, but chose to act as gunnery officer until, on 31 October, he was brought ashore in leg-irons in Buncrana in Lough Swilly. He was taken to Dublin Castle via Derry jail and there his request to be 'shot by a platoon of grenadiers' was refused. The sentence of hanging was to be carried out on 12 November on the insistence of Lord Cornwallis, the Lord Lieutenant.

John Philpot Curran and other Irish friends tried to obtain a stay of execution on the grounds that he was a French officer over whom the British military had no authority. By the time the approval came Tone was already very ill, having tried to cut his throat on the day fixed for his execution. In fact he severed his windpipe but missed the jugular vein. He was attended by an émigré French surgeon to whom he croaked in French. 'I am sorry I have been so bad an anatomist.' He lingered in great pain for a week, until 19 November, dying most probably of septicaemia from the infected wound.

20 November 1960

Killed in the Congo

On 8 November 1960 an eleven-man platoon from the Irish 33rd Battalion, on peace-keeping duties in the Congo, was ambushed in Niemba by a hundred Baluba tribesman while attempting to mend a bridge over the Luweyeye River. Nine of them, including the platoon commander, Lieutenant Kevin Gleeson, were killed, by guns, by poisoned spears and arrows and some by being beaten to death. On Sunday 20 November, the bodies lay in state in Casement Aerodrome, Baldonnel in a temporary mortuary in one of the hangars and were visited by hundreds of people who made the journey to pay their respects. The coffins were placed on four trucks while that of Gleeson was carried on a jeep-towed trailer.

An escort party, led by Captain Donal Crowley, had travelled with the bodies and stayed for the funeral, which took place on the following Tuesday in Glasnevin cemetery. The bodies were received by the Rev T.J. Flanagan, chaplain to the Air Corps, and more than a thousand people knelt for prayers in the hangar. After the prayers four Air Corps servicemen took up guard duty around the coffins, the personnel changing every half-hour. The caskets were draped with Tricolours and the United Nations flag.

That Sunday, Masses were celebrated at a specially erected altar and all that day a steady stream of people moved round the hangar, many weeping, stopping to read the names at each catafalque and saying individual prayers. It was clear that when the funeral made its way back into the city, led by a motorcycle escort, the crowds in the centre would be huge. On the day of the funeral, O'Connell Street, North Frederick Street, Berkeley Road, Doyle's Corner, Phibsborough Road and Finglas Road were crowded with mourners, slowly coming to accept the reality that Irish soldiers had been killed in action.

21 November 1938

'Always something new'

Largely because of the artistic pre-eminence of his opus, Shakespeare, the glover's son of Stratford, has been the subject of continual attack as to the authorship of the plays. There is in fact more documentary evidence about his life than any of his literary contemporaries and the final death to the naysayers came when Ronald Knox mockingly proved beyond doubt that Queen Victoria was the true author of Tennyson's *In Memoriam.*

In the 20th century few non-cranks bothered to challenge the Warwickshire origin of all that grandeur but odd lateral attacks on his dramaturgy continued. On the afternoon of 21 November 1938 Professor Wilhelm Keller of the University of Münster proposed to an audience in the Graduates Memorial Building, Trinity College, that Shakespeare wrote his dramatic works not primarily as plays for the very dismissive theatre of the Tudor and Jacobean age but as intended books. Surprisingly he suggested that some plays that were 'much too long for the purposes of the theatre'.

He especially mentioned *Hamlet* and *Richard III* and his comments reflected not the history of the Globe or the Rose of Shakespeare's time but the cumbersome heavily décor-rich late Victorian and Edwardian productions, with elaborate changes of set for every scene and real rabbits for the forest of Arden. Shakespeare himself talked in *Romeo and Juliet* of the 'two hours' traffick of our stage' and as an actor-writer-shareholder he knew exactly what he was talking about. The only works he seemed anxious to have published were the sonnets and that for political and well as personal reasons. The afternoon was tactfully brought to a close by the vice-provost of Trinity who concluded that although people had been writing about Shakespeare for hundreds of years there was always something new to be said about him.

22 November 1955

Archival treasure

Nowadays when news comes continuously throughout every minute of the year to a variety of electronic receivers it is difficult to imagine (or remember) a time when the only pictorial source was the weekly newsreel in the cinema. In 1955 television was an east-coast phenomenon and the Irish newsreels supplied visually what was heard only on the radio. The material was mostly home-grown, filmed in black and white and with a preponderance of sporting coverage. Those without television but with access to the external giants like Movietone, Gaumont British and Pathé Gazette, with their world coverage, tended to sneer at the 'parochialism' of the items and assumed that they were not shown outside the four green fields.

A survey published on Tuesday 22 November 1955 told a rather different story. Twenty-five items from the Irish newsreel company Universal News had been screened in many other countries, including Britain, USA, Canada, South Africa, Singapore, Norway, Spain, Holland, Turkey, New Zealand, India, Hong Kong, Japan, Jamaica, Ceylon and the Arab countries. The distributor was the British movie mogul J. Arthur Rank, who had literally worldwide outlets. The clips gave a rich and rare portrait of the peaceful country at the time: a quarry blast in Kildare, an Ireland-England rugby match, the famous Tulyar's new colt, the wedding of the son of the champion jockey, Sir Gordon Richards, a fashion show of Irish-designed blouses and many shots of all kinds of sports.

The event that achieved the widest distribution was that year's Dublin Horse Show, which was shown in cinemas in most of the countries listed above. The Soapbox Derby was very big in Japan and Norway and the Ireland-Scotland soccer international was included in Arabic newsreels. These reels still exist and have become a rich archival treasure of all our yesterdays.

23 November 1942

'The Chief'

Of the great personalities of Irish history, none had a career more amenable to drama than Charles Stewart Parnell (1846-91). Robert Emmet is a much more romantic hero, bewitching the young, but the 'dead king', as Mr Casey calls him in Joyce's *A Portrait of the Artist as a Young Man,* is the character for the older and sadder. 'Parnell,' as many including Yeats have rhymed, 'loved his lass,' and she was English and married. His absolute temperament precluded the necessary compromise. Cecil Rhodes, who admired the man greatly urged, 'Divorce, marry and return,' but all miscalculated the wary tolerance of the Church and even the moralistic Liberal party and the Titan fell. His death at the age of forty-five may well have set back the cause of Ireland by a hundred years but his life and death were the very stuff of drama.

On Monday 23 November 1942 a new play about the lost leader was presented in the Gaiety Theatre by the Edwards-MacLiammóir company in their half-yearly vacation from their home in the Gate. The play, by Anne Schaeffler, had Hilton Edwards as Gladstone, Meriel Moore as 'O Shea who must be obeyed', to use the crack of Tim Healy, Parnell's closest enemy, and the meteoric MacLiammóir as the 'Chief'. A wider cast included such characters as Healy, Michael Davitt, the O'Gorman Mahon and the egregious Captain O'Shea, the blackmailing 'wronged' husband, played with appropriate unction by Michael Hennessy.

The play, enjoyable as it was, gave no new light as to how a classical tragedy with loads of hubris and inevitable nemesis came to happen but it created a splendid evening of theatre and a part for its star as definitive as his earlier Emmet in *The Old Lady Says 'No!',* Denis Johnston's brilliant fantasy-satire of 1929.

24 November 1949

'Very savage and cruel' assault

Una Melody from Castle Avenue, Clontarf, was twenty-one when she was subject to a 'very savage and cruel' assault, as District Justice Fitzpatrick described it in court on Thursday 24 November 1949 when he sentenced her assailant, John Moriarty (39), of Swilly Road, Cabra, to three months' imprisonment. He was employed as an effects operator with Radio Éireann and although married with four children was separated from his wife. Melody and he had, as they say, history.

Moriarty was working as a conjuror at an amusement arcade in Eden Quay when he saw Melody spending money in slot machines. They seemed to 'click' and soon she was working as an assistant in his act, although she was then not much more than fifteen. Their relationship for the next six years was complex, with frequent changes of mood. She was his partner when he did his act at various gigs about the country and later kept turning up at his workplace.

On 24 September 1949 she ran into him in Lower O'Connell Street and, although her account is vague and contradictory, it seems she agreed to accompany him to the Phoenix Park, near where he lived. When they reached the Polo Ground he knocked her down and kicked her, accusing her of having a relationship with the manager of one of the Mooney pubs in the city. He sent her home but inexplicably she met him in town again and returned with him to the park, where he beat her again. The doctor who examined her the following night confirmed that she had black eyes and other superficial injuries on back, body and thighs, enough to confine her to bed until 1 October. The judge decided that in spite of the unreliability of some of her evidence there was sufficient to convict, fixing bail at £10.

25 November 1913

The Irish Volunteers

In January 1913 Northern unionists in their opposition to the Home Rule Bill that was certain to be passed in Westminster, because the Irish Parliamentary Party led by John Redmond held the balance of power, formed a militia known as the Ulster Volunteer Force (UVF). An article by Eoin MacNeill in *An Claidheamh Soluis*, the Gaelic League newspaper, entitled 'The North Began' suggested that nationalists in the south should organise a similar force. Little more than three weeks later, on Monday 25 November 1913, he and Bulmer Hobson, a member of the Irish Republican Brotherhood (IRB) from Holywood, County Down, formed the Irish Volunteers in the Rotunda Rooms in Parnell Square.

The manifesto, already prepared and read by MacNeill, indicated that its object was 'to secure and maintain the rights and liberties common to all the people of Ireland'. The document ended with a non-specific call and a reference to an 18th-century precedent:

> In the name of national unity, of national dignity, of national and individual liberty and manly citizenship, we appeal to our countrymen to recognise and accept without hesitation the opportunity that has been granted them to join the ranks of the Irish Volunteers and to make the movement now begun, not unworthy of the historic title which it had adopted.

The IRB, already considering the possibility of an armed rising in keeping with their Fenian traditions, joined in considerable numbers. They remained quiescent until the outbreak of the First World War, when they broke with the majority who followed Redmond and his call for them to join the British war effort. When, in 1916, it seemed that the time was ripe the radical breakaway group, now numbering 15,000, prepared for the Easter Rising. Both O'Neill and Hobson disapproved and took no part.

26 November 1972

The Dublin bombings

Dublin, like many other cities, was touched by the overspill of the euphem-istically named Northern Troubles. On four occasions – 26 November 1972, 1 December 1972, 20 January 1973 and the most catastrophic, 17 May 1974, when twenty-six Dubliners lost their lives – the city was afflicted by explosions, mostly as a result of car bombs. Most were later shown as likely to have been of UVF origin, the force admitting to its involvement in the 1974 outrage (on this occasion five people were also killed in Monaghan) in 1993.

The first event occurred at 1.25am on Sunday 26 November 1972 outside the back door of an art-house movie centre in O'Connell Bridge House during a late-night film show. The bomb exploded in a laneway that led from Burgh Quay to the Leinster Market, injuring forty people, inflicting serious facial, leg and bowel wounds. The cinema audience numbered a hundred and fifty-six, with three attendants; many were blown out of their seats and those who could do so ran to the exits for fear of another device. Shops and houses in the immediate vicinity were badly damaged.

No organisation admitted responsibility for the attack but the Garda Síochána felt it was probably the work of the Provisional IRA. Seán Mac Stíofáin, then chief-of-staff, had been taken to the Mater Hospital for treatment for the ill-effects of his hunger and thirst strike, and tensions were high as he was kept under heavy guard. The next night an armed IRA unit tried unsuccessfully to rescue him. It is now regarded as 'more likely than not' that the bomb was an IRA reaction to the passage of punitive anti-subversive legislation in amendments to the Offences against the State Act, although an official enquiry by the Irish Supreme Court Justice, Henry Barron, in its report in November 2004 found no absolute proof of that organisation's involvement.

27 November 1928

'Hands Up!'

From a country that emerged out of violence Ireland soon settled down to one of minimum crime. In the 1920s, however, there were still a number of weapons in circulation and one was used on the night of 14 November 1928. James Timble from Ward's Hill (now disappeared) entered a spirit grocery on St Alban's Road, off the South Circular Road, pointed a gun at the owner Denis P. Mordant and in time-honoured fashion said, 'Hands up!' The full story was related by witnesses a fortnight later, Tuesday 27 November, when the case came to court.

Mordant described how at five minutes to eleven o'clock that night he was in the adjoining dairy when the man standing in the dock and whom he had identified the previous evening in Newmarket police station had entered and threatened him. At the same time another man came in and tried to shut the door behind him. Mordant then picked up a four-gallon milk can and offered to strike Timble with it. At this both men bolted from the shop and ran off in the direction of Blackpitts. He phoned for the Gardaí and within ten minutes the flying squad had arrived. Hearing that Timble's mother had said that he had been ill and had not left the house for three weeks, the judge adjourned the case for a week.

In another case Robert McEvoy, a deserter from the Free State Army, was charged with loitering with criminal intent in Rathmines. Captain T.P. O'Gallacher from Portobello Barracks said that McEvoy had been absent from his regiment since 13 November and before that he had been on compassionate leave, claiming that his father had died. The judge handed him over to the military authorities.

28 November 1871

She Stoops to Conquer *in the Gaiety*

The Gaiety Theatre in King Street, near St Stephen's Green, opened on Tuesday 28 November 1872 and is the oldest surviving theatre in the city. Designed by architect C.J. Phipps and finished in under seven months, it was extended by the great Frank Matcham in 1883. It has been mainly a musical theatre, although it has also presented straight plays. The Gaiety pantomime has long been a feature of Dublin's entertainment scene and this was especially the case in the golden years of Jimmy O'Dea.

The theatre played its part in the growth of the Irish Literary Theatre of Yeats, Lady Gregory and Edward Martyn, who in their 1897 manifesto 'proposed to have performed in the spring of every year certain Celtic and Irish plays...' *The Last Feast of the Fianna* by Alice Milligan and *Maeve* by Edward Martyn (19 February 1900) and the following night *The Bending of the Bough* by George Moore, provided that year's spring offering. The group was pleased to have seen their work in a 'real' theatre. On 21 October 1901 they were back in the Gaiety with Yeats's *Diarmuid and Grania* and *Casadh an tSúgáin* by Douglas Hyde.

At the time of the theatre's opening the Irish Renaissance was a distant dream. There were few native plays and as the Lord Lieutenant, Earl Spencer, was the guest of honour the management achieved a diplomatic stroke; they chose Oliver Goldsmith's *She Stoops to Conquer*. It was unquestionably Irish – Goldsmith had been born in Longford and reared in Lissoy, and the shenanigans around the Three Jolly Pigeons is pure Westmeath. The gallants, on the other hand, are clearly English so the choice was apposite. It was preceded by a burlesque, *La Belle Sauvage*, based upon the story of Pocahontas, the native Virginian princess.

29 November 1956

Christmas illuminations

These days, when Easter eggs appear in January and Hallowee'n witches are replaced overnight by Santa Clauses on 1 November, it is something of a relief to realise that the dread spirit of Yuletide was once held off almost until December. On Thursday 29 November 1957 Robert Briscoe, the Lord Mayor, switched on the Christmas illuminations in the George's Street and Exchequer Street areas. The much-looked-forward-to event had its source in the George's Street Association, then twenty-nine years old. On that occasion the eleven-year-old Ethel Minogue, the daughter of Michael Minogue, the association's chairman, presented a bouquet of flowers to the Lady Mayor's wife.

The ubiquitous Father Christmas was there, in a strange reversal of role receiving presents rather than dispensing them, as the switch-on coincided with the opening of the children's toy fund. The previous year his doppelganger had acquired 80,000 gifts for the cause and it was expected that the number should be greater this year. The centrepiece of the display was a candle, that most elegant of symbols, and at six feet it looked well to last for the whole of the festive season.

Meanwhile in Capel Street crowds had gathered to await the arrival of a young man carrying a simulated 'Olympic torch' that would be the signal for the lights to be switched on in that part of the city, which was densely supplied with a remarkable variety of shops. Just before the actual enlightenment a crowd of Irish dancers from the Comerford School enacted an inner-city version of the age-old dancing at the crossroads where Capel Street and Bolton Street meet. The only uneasy note was unwittingly struck by collectors for the Hungarian Relief Fund, a reminder that the workers' uprising there had been brutally crushed by Soviet tanks twenty-five days earlier.

30 November 1938

External affairs and the king

The amendment to the Irish constitution that rescinded the title Saorstát Éireann (the Irish Free State) and changed it to Éire (in Irish) and Ireland (in English) was passed by plebiscite by 685, 105 votes to 526, 945 on 1 July 1937 and became law on 29 December. It was the kind of 'freedom to achieve freedom' step that Michael Collins has envisaged on signing the Anglo-Irish Treaty of 1921. The comparative closeness of the result, the difference being 14 per cent of the total, reflected not objection on the part of the Nos to the principle but to the fact that it was sponsored by Éamon de Valera's ruling Dáil party Fianna Fáil. They would continue to be the party in power until the 13th Dáil, 1948-51 and in 1948 the coalition government removed the country from the British Commonwealth and created the Republic of Ireland.

The Éire amendment, although generally approved, gave rise to a number of complicated and even embarrassing legal difficulties. On Wednesday 30 November 1938 General Seán Mac Eoin TD, later to be Minister for Justice and Minister for Defence, asked the Taoiseach, Éamon de Valera, about the procedure for the appointment of ministers plenipotentiary from Éire to foreign states. With a commendably straight face de Valera replied that letters of credence had to be signed by King George VI and countersigned by the Minister for External Affairs.

Mac Eoin, with equal sober mien, asked how the signature was to be obtained. 'Does the king come across to External Affairs or does someone from External Affairs go over to the king?' Here Brendan Corish, the Labour TD from Wexford, broke in with, 'I didn't see him here lately,' a remark causing general laughter in the chamber. The Taoiseach, with some relief, replied that the matter was one for the High Commissioner's office, to which they had a confidential post.

1 December 1969

Godot

Waiting for Godot, Beckett's most popular and accessible play, opened in the Abbey Theatre on Monday 1 December 1969. It was not the first Dublin production of the Irish-born dramatist's work; that honour goes to the brief but stellar career of the bijou Pike (1953-8) run by Alan Simpson and Carolyn Swift, which introduced Beckett to his home nation on 28 October 1955, a few months after its first English-language production in London. Certainly the board of the Abbey at the time would not have considered it, nor London West End theatres. But with the urgings of shame and time Dublin and the Irish National Theatre finally decided to cash in on the guru's reputation.

The lyrical, logical, lissom and ultimately static tramps, Vladimir and Estragon, were played by two of the leading theatrical stars of the time, Peter O'Toole and Donal McCann, the former making his first appearance on the Abbey stage. The play demands techniques more properly suited to, if not the actual circus ring, then old variety stages. The business with the bowler hats is straight from Laurel and Hardy and there are traces of Buster Keaton in Vladimir's travails.

McCann's louche acceptance of their situation makes it clear that it is an Irish play, in spite of its French birth, and he provides a harmless Mr Hyde to Vladimir's Dr Jekyll optimistic pessimism. O'Toole had all the grace of a ballet dancer when it was needed and it was he who most clearly demonstrated their mutual interdependence. They were the ideal leads in play in which, notoriously, 'nothing happens twice'. The casting of Éamon Kelly as Pozzo now seems unwise. The genial Kerry seanchaí, renowned for his usual shtick of tall stories, was unconvincing as the ranting slave-driving bully. His innate kindness kept breaking through.

2 December 1811

The Kildare Place Society

In the early years of the 19th century the living conditions of the poor both rurally and in Dublin and their lack of hope of amelioration because of the poverty trap roused some philanthropic businesspeople and lawyers, mainly Quakers, to attempt to supply some relief through education. Some Church of Ireland parishes in Dublin had reported success in their Sunday and day schools and with this model in mind a group of concerned individuals set up the Society for the Promoting the Education of the Poor in Ireland on Monday 2 December 1811. The rather unwieldy title was soon shortened to the Kildare Place Society (KPS), taking its name from the society's headquarters.

Its aim was to provide popular, non-sectarian education and as such it was in line with current government policy. It was on that account given considerable amounts of state money. Imbued with 'an anxious desire to diffuse the blessings of education throughout the country, without suffering its progress to be impeded by those sectarian distinctions which have so frequently opposed an insurmountable barrier to the amelioration of the peasantry of Ireland', the KPS won the support of some prominent Catholics, including Daniel O'Connell, who saw in it an ally in his work of recreating an Irish nation. By 1830 it was providing instruction for 137, 639 pupils in 1621 schools.

One important aspect of the curriculum was the daily reading of the Bible by all the children together 'without note or comment'. This proved to be its undoing as a non-sectarian agency. Some of the more vigorously evangelistic Protestant sects, aflame with the prospect of a 'second reformation', could not resist the opportunity for proselytism and the KPS's perceived financial support to openly proselytising schools rang alarm bells not only among Catholics but also with the government authorities, who withdrew support and finance in 1831.

3 December 1928

A cultural desert?

Histories of the modern Irish state can sometimes paint a picture of a bland not to say Philistine cultural desert, whose practitioners grew steadily less courageous as the Church and the Fianna Fáil government became more controlling. The capital was compared to Calvin's Geneva and one letter writer to the papers in the 1950s suggested that the only totally acceptable theatrical performance would be a production of Gilbert and Sullivan's *The Gondoliers* staged by a girls' convent school. The seeds of this control were set in the first decade with the passing of a film censorship act in 1924 and a much more swingeing Censorship of Publications Act in 1929 which banned books with little discrimination.

In this respect Dublin was less at the mercy of crosier and the PP's blackthorn stick. There was never any formal censorship of plays and music was regarded (incorrectly) as morally null. So that on Monday 3 December 1928 Dubliners had the choice of a glorious piano recital by Myra Hess, then thirty-eight, the leading virtuoso of the time, who later organised 1700 lunchtime concerts and played in a hundred and fifty of them in the National Gallery in London during the six years of the war in spite of the Luftwaffe air raids. The alternative was a very fine Abbey production of *Hamlet* by Anew McMaster (1894-1962), Ireland's own (Monaghan-born) actor manager. It was hardly a cultural desert.

Tall and strikingly handsome, McMaster had formed his own touring company in 1925 and brought the classical dramas of Sophocles, Shakespeare, Ibsen, Chekov and the rest to every small town in Ireland. His appearance as Hamlet in Stratford in 1933, when he was thirty-nine, was memorable and he had in his company such notables as T.P. McKenna, Harold Pinter and his own brother-in-law, Micheál MacLiammóir.

4 December 1966

The Censorship Reform Society

On Sunday 4 December 1966 a packed audience in the Gate Theatre heard of plans to enrol members in a Censorship Reform Society. It was typical of a number of events that finally persuaded the government that while some kind of bulwark against pornography might be thought essential, the current definition of 'indecency' was hopelessly flawed. The items included a reading by actors Maureen Toal and T.P. McKenna of passages from Edna O'Brien's novel, *Casualties of Peace,* held at the time by the Irish customs. Bruce Arnold gave a short history of the legislation and showed how an excess of chauvinist moral isolationism had made the censors so resolute in their interpretation of their duties.

The Censorship of Publications Act (1929) permitted the banning of 'indecent' books by a Censorship Board that for nearly seventy years seemed to many deliberately to target the work of Irish writers, in spite of their artistic excellence, as somehow constituting a disgrace to the country. Among many writers banned for 'indecency' were Seán O'Faolain, Frank O'Connor, Austin Clarke, Kate O'Brien. Edna O'Brien, John McGahern. Brian Moore and Benedict Kiely. Most serious modern writers from other countries were also banned, lumped with the purveyors of the most extreme pornography.

In the 1940s O'Faolain and O'Connor did what they could to expose the essential injustice of the system but it would require a radical change in public opinion before the board's authority would be challenged and finally rendered obsolete. The introduction of an appeal system by the Minister for Justice, Brian Lenihan, in 1967 weakened it effectively and the surge in paperback publication made its implementation almost impossible. The Gate Theatre event was one of many that finally dislodged the Mrs Grundys from their perches by the most successful of all weapons, mockery.

5 December 1994

Garda improvements

In 1991 someone in Garda headquarters in the Phoenix Park had the bright idea of initiating a staff suggestion scheme for improvements within the force. They correctly surmised that it was those on the job who best could suggest greater efficiencies in procedure that would save time and money, these being effectively the same goal. Sergeant Bernard Finnegan, based in Garda headquarters, won the top award out of a hundred and twenty proposals and on Monday 5 December 1994 was presented with the prize of £1000. It was formally handed over by the Garda Commissioner, Patrick Gilligan, in the workplace, while the sergeant's mother looked approvingly on. The prize amount, according to the rules, was worked out as a percentage of the estimated savings that the improvement would realise.

Finnegan's idea had to do with typewriter maintenance in the Phoenix Park and elsewhere. Although the Garda was as high-tech an organisation as any other similar institution, electric typewriters were still used for filling out such important forms as summonses and details of reported crime and since these played a large part of the day-to-day business of police stations, deterioration in the machines was considerable. Finnegan recommended that a fixed-cost contract be made with outside commercial firms for maintenance, replacement of parts and repair of breakdowns. It was reckoned by the number crunchers that the scheme would save £58,000 a year.

Other prizewinners included Inspector Michael Colman, also in headquarters, who got £250 for a new rostering system; T.J. Cormican, a retired sergeant from Thurles won £100 for inventing a means of endorsing summons served by post; Detective Sergeant Michael Reilly, also stationed in the 'Park', suggested standardising the certificates that Gardaí give for character references for visa applications and Garda Richard Conway from Wexford received two awards, including one for a standardised intruder alarm form.

6 December 1949

Houses of sale

When the crowds attacked the first staging of *The Plough and the Stars* in 1926, shouting, 'There are no women like that in Ireland!' in response to the character of Rosie Redmond, there may have been some who actually believed it. Twenty-three years later they had printed proof, not only that there were such people in Ireland, but that there were 'houses of sale' as Polonius described them in *Hamlet*.

On Tuesday 6 December 1949 the judge-president of the Dublin Circuit Civil Court affirmed sentences of three months' imprisonment and a £100 fine on Mrs Elizabeth Brown of 119 and 120 Capel Street for permitting the premises of which she was the lessee to be used as a brothel. Another woman, Mrs Elizabeth McCann, the manageress of the house, had a three-month sentence confirmed for aiding and abetting the management of a brothel. The judge was particularly severe on Alexander Ryan, an ex-policeman, whom he described as 'the most despicable character I've ever seen' and increased his sentence to one of six months' imprisonment: 'I regret very much I cannot give him more.'

The account of the Garda investigation of the affair must have amused the hardened newspapermen of the city, who may not have regarded the case as one if burning national importance. Garda Michael Collins said he had the house under observation on different occasions during the month of August. One night he had seen eight men and nine women enter between 11.05 and 2.15. One of these he had seen many times in the early hours of the morning, usually with different men. Detective-Sergeant Corry had visited the house in October and found Mrs McCann asleep on the couch and the house full of known prostitutes. Nevertheless Mrs Brown insisted that she was running a private house where you could get bed and breakfast.

7 December 1967

Foot and mouth

Neil Blaney (1922-95) became Minister for Agriculture and Fisheries in 1966 and was faced early on with the challenge of a virulent strain of *Aphthae Epizooticae,* or foot-and-mouth disease (FMD) as it is generally known, occurring in Northumberland. The effect of contagion on a cattle-exporting country like Ireland could be disastrous, so there were few lengths to which he would not be prepared to go to keep the country FMD-free. Already travellers from Northern Ireland had to go through rigorous hygiene procedures, forbidden to bring food in quantity across the border and having vigorously to wipe their footwear on mats heavily impregnated with disinfectant.

On Thursday 7 December 1967 Blaney called a press conference to announce a number of measures to lessen the risk of 'carrying'. The number of people entering Ireland by air and sea would be restricted to between 1500 and 2000 people a day and all would be fully disinfected. He said, however, that only in the face of the gravest emergency would he contemplate the total closure of the ports. That would have had to last at least two months and cause a loss to the economy of between £35m to £40m, as well as causing long-term damage to Irish trade.

Even more absolute was his three-pronged appeal to the Irish in Britain not to come home for Christmas: a letter from him to the employees of the firms who dug the mass graves for the slaughtered cattle to be included in pay-packets, reminding them that because of the nature of their employment they could be carriers; letters from the Irish Embassy in London to 4000 parish priests asking them to appeal to their Irish parishioners to stay away; another appeal from the ambassador with the same message to three hundred Irish organisations in Britain.

These extreme methods worked: Ireland stayed FMD-free.

8 December 1922

'Orders of frightfulness'

The first executions of 'Irregulars' in the ghastly Civil War of 1922-3 were carried out in Kilmainham jail on Friday 17 November 1922. The men were James Fisher, Peter Cassidy, John F. Gaffney and Richard Twohig and they had been found guilty of 'taking part in or aiding or abetting any attacks upon the national forces'. On Monday 27 November, Liam Lynch, the self-styled commander of the IRA, wrote in a letter to the Ceann Comhairle, Michael Hayes: '… as the illegal body over which you preside has declared war on the soldiers of the Republic…we shall adopt very drastic measures to protect our forces.' Three days later, in 'orders of frightfulness' sent to all company commanders with immediate effect, he announced that all TDs who had voted for the legislation should be shot on sight.

It was a time of great bitterness and emotional exaltation and it did not take long for a response to happen in Dublin. On Thursday 7 December 1922 Seán Hales TD, while travelling to the Dáil in an open car with Pádraic Ó Máille, Leas-Ceann Comhairle, was shot dead and his companion seriously wounded. The cabinet met in emergency session and, risking a cycle of even more violent retaliation, ordered the execution of four leading anti-Treatyites: Rory O'Connor (who had been Kevin O'Higgins's best man), Liam Mellows, Joe McKelvey and Richard Barrett – all significant figures, allegedly one from each province. The sentences were carried out the following morning in Mountjoy jail. The action was ruthless but effective, as from them on no further attacks were made on TDs. But the wound inflicted by the decision festered for years and led to the killing of O'Higgins's father in his home in County Laois the following year and of O'Higgins himself, believed to be the main architect of the policy, four and a half years later.

9 December 1994

Sexual assault

It is probably an illusion based upon reticence in reportage but the sexual assault in Dublin of one male by another seems to be a new and unpleasant fact of urban life. On Friday 9 December 1994 it was revealed that a fifteen-year-old youth had admitted to having sexually assaulted a thirteen-year-old boy in the Temple Bar area of the city two weeks earlier. A file was to be sent to the Director of Public Prosecutions in respect of the charges.

Details of the investigation were revealed by the detective branch, which had identified a pattern of robberies, usually of teenagers, in the city centre north of the Liffey over the previous months. As many as twenty teenagers had complained of being held up by a young man armed with a knife. In at least one case there was an attempted sexual assault.

The assault took place south of the river in Temple Bar on Monday 28 November, when two thirteen-year-old boys on a day out in the city were confronted by a youth who said he was armed with a knife. He forced one of the boys into a shrubbery behind the Civic Offices in Fishamble Street. The lad's companion was able to make his escape and ran to Nassau Street, where he got help. The boy who had been attacked was not seriously injured and, although greatly shocked, insisted on travelling home on the DART. He was confused about what exactly had occurred but later the Gardaí announced that they had evidence that he had been the victim of a serious sexual assault.

The fifteen-year-old who could not be named because of his age was arrested and, accompanied by a parent, interviewed by the Gardaí. It was later announced that security cameras were to be installed in the Temple Bar area.

10 December 1952

Inter-union dispute

In the 1950s the members of the orchestra in the Theatre Royal were not all in the same union, fourteen being members of the Irish Federation of Musicians (IFM) and five in the Irish Transport and General Workers' Union (ITGWU). On Wednesday 10 December 1952 a dispute that had been smouldering for six months flamed into strike action when the theatre organist and the thirteen Federation members of the orchestra downed instruments, so to speak, and the show, that in age-old theatrical tradition *must* go on, had only nine instrumentalists and a substitute organist.

The germ of the dispute was the employment of a trumpeter during one of the highlights of the Royal's history, the appearance in Dublin of the manic, tongue-twisting American comedian, Danny Kaye. The musician, although a Federation member, had not the three-year residence qualification that was part of an agreement between the Irish Theatre and Cinema Association and the ITGWU that made it obligatory for the Federation's members to be members of the latter to obtain employment in the Dublin theatres. This agreement was about to expire and after a meeting on 12 November the Federation announced that they would no longer be members of the ITGWU.

Inter-union disputes can also be the most bitter and houses began to suffer, since only the hardy would pass the Federation's pickets. Harry Roy, a leading British band leader, who was booked as the top-of-the-bill act for the following night, said he could not risk involving his band members in such a dispute. The stagehands and other theatre employees who were ITGWU members said they would not work with Federation members after 20 December. The lines were drawn for a damaging and ultimately pointless dispute, in which the IFM was very much the weaker party against the giant ITGWU.

11 December 1956

Forgery charge

Forgery is usually a middle-class crime perpetrated by the 'respectable'; it rarely involves violence and remains in the area of 'what a pity!' rather than 'how heinous!' When Joseph Griffin (40) was returned for trial on Tuesday 11 December 1956 on the charge of having forged a letter 'purporting to be signed by Gilbert S. Reeves, intending to use it in evidence in the High Court with intent to deceive' he was allowed bail – his own of £10, with independent surety of £600 or two of £300 each. Griffin who lived in 'Mentone', Military Road, Killiney, was also charged under the Debtors' Act with falsely representing that the letter was true and signed by the aforesaid with the purpose of obtaining the consent of his creditors to an agreement.

Noel Harnett, for Griffin, began by asking for a dismissal on the grounds that the prosecution had not produced adequate evidence to sustain the charges. As argument proceeded it became clear that Griffin was bankrupt and in Hartnett's words 'was going around with almost pathological optimism trying to get his former business associates to help him'. He also had difficulty in keeping his solicitor interested in the case. Harnett pointed out that there was indisputable evidence that the letter had been written in London, not in Dublin, as the charge alleged. He reminded the court that Griffin had, under oath, stated that he did not write the letter.

In rebuttal, William Ellis for the prosecution said that all the evidence pointed to the fact that the letter was sent to Griffin's solicitors for the purpose of providing them with material sufficiently persuasive to secure agreement by his creditors to allow the terms of the bankruptcy. District Justice Lennon returned Griffin for trial after he had refused the offer of calling any witness.

12 December 1967

No priests in the theatre

The Second Vatican Council lasted from 11 October 1962 until 8 December 1965 and in some countries the senior clergy seemed reluctant to implement the reforms. In this matter Ireland was not the slowest to conform but still made the mills of God seem quite nippy by comparison. One frivolous prohibition was still on the canonical books in 1967 but by 12 December of that year it looked as if the lumbering, ponderous machinery of Church law was about to lift the ban on Irish priests attending the theatre.

With typical aplomb the banned theatre fans had long found ways of circumventing the letter of the law by sitting in the wings or taking up room in the lighting-box – a Irish Catholic solution to an Irish Catholic problem. It is difficult to discern the reason for the ban in the first place. It couldn't logically have been the reason given by Dr Johnson to Garrick: 'I'll come no more behind your scenes, David; for the silk stockings and white bosoms of your actresses excite my amorous propensities.' The priest in the wings would be exposed to all kinds of déshabillé and picturesque language as quick costume changes and entrances were made – far more, indeed, than if he had had a seat in the stalls.

The pointlessness of the legislation was underscored by the fact that the prohibition did not apply to the cinema, nor to the multiplicity of amateur productions about the country, most of them parish-sponsored. Often, too, one might find oneself sitting beside a priest not in 'civvies', who would explain with an airy wave of his hands that he wasn't on the Irish mission. Further the lawmakers did not seem to realise that the prohibition applied only to a minuscule minority. What happened to the sound maxim, *De minimis non curat lex?*

13 December 1994

Moveable Feasts

The calendar, even one as accommodating as the Gregorian, is full of awkwardnesses for the tidy-minded and the bureaucratic. The old or new date of Easter caused a lot of trouble at the 7th-century Synod of Whitby that also dealt with monks' haircuts. The world is still divided between those who love the rule for fixing Easter as 'the first Sunday after the first full moon after the vernal equinox' and those who would prefer the second Sunday in April. In a rational society the second option would make things handy for school-meals-caterers, bus time-tablers and travel agents. The perceived quixotry of the existing allows the rationalists from time to time to try to emend what has worked romantically for centuries, so far, I'm glad to say, without success.

On Tuesday 13 December 1994 Mary O'Rourke, acting Minister for Enterprise, produced a discussion paper on holiday legislation in which she recommended that the state, employers and trade unions should consider moving three public holidays, St Patrick's Day, and the June and October public holidays. The discussion mentioned the most controversial first. The presumed death date of our national saint (who was neither an Irish national nor a canonised saint) had for years been celebrated in the teeth of wind and weather, especially in America, and now the lady was for turning its celebration, not to a date in summer in the expectation of more clement conditions, but so that the holiday would happen at a weekend. She also wanted to postpone the June holiday to a Monday later in the month than the first and move the October holiday from the last Monday to the first. It is not clear who in the end discussed the document but the status is still quo.

14 December 1918

Swan song for the Irish Parliamentary Party

The general election of 1918 was for most of the United Kingdom a reassuring sign that things were getting back to normal after the extended horrors of the First World War. Polling began on Saturday 14 December – elections were more leisurely in those years – and soon it was clear that if Lloyd George (1863-1945) were to continue as prime minister he needed to placate his Conservative (and unionist) coalition partners, led by Andrew Bonar Law (1858-1923). This secured the position of the Ulster unionists in the demand for their version of Home Rule and stimulated the movement in the south for direct action, later canonised as the 'armed struggle'. Many of the leaders, already in prison after the Easter Rising, were candidates but even the most sanguine could not have been entirely prepared for the landslide victory of Sinn Féin. The movement had been formed and named by Arthur Griffith (1872-1922) in 1905 but had developed its own momentum in ways Griffith could never have anticipated.

When the results were finally known one stark fact emerged: the Irish Parliamentary Party, led by John Dillon since the death of John Redmond, had its majority representation reduced to six seats, while Éamon de Valera led a party with seventy-three MPs, none of whom, even those who were free to do so, were prepared to take their seats. Sinn Féin's formation of its own regime, the first Dáil, in January 1919, was essentially a declaration of secession from the United Kingdom.

Dublin had nine constituencies plus three university seats, two in Trinity returning a Unionist and an Independent Unionist and one in UCD returning a Sinn Féin MP. The city divisions went over almost entirely to Sinn Féin (including the victory in St Patrick's Division of Constance Markievicz, the first woman ever elected to Westminster). Only Rathmines, the most Protestant of boroughs, stayed loyal to unionism and re-elected the popular and liberal Sir Maurice Dockrell (1850-1929), greatly assisted by his support in the past for woman's suffrage.

15 December 2000

Fire in Trinity College

Since its foundation in 1592 Trinity College has had twenty-three chancellors, the current incumbent being Mary Thérèse Winifred Robinson (b. 1944), appointed in 1998 and the only woman so far to have filled the post. She was also first woman President of Ireland (1990-7) and United Nations High Commissioner for Human Rights (1997-2002). Well used to public events, which she invariably graced, on the afternoon of Friday 15 December 2000 she was almost upstaged by the Dublin Fire Service.

It was winter graduation day (commencements as they are known in TCD) and the ceremony had just begun when, at 3pm, the college security staff noticed smoke coming through the roof of the Graduate Memorial Building. The fire alarm sounded in the building and the students inside left in a hurry. The fire had begun in the attic where many records of some of the college's oldest student societies were stored. Old papers, antique books and other materials belonging to the Historical and Philosophical societies had been damaged but most were 'salvageable' according to a Trinity spokeswoman. Before the fire tenders arrived the college authorities had begun to remove to safety valuable portraits of past dignitaries.

The fire-fighters managed to confine the eight-foot bursts of flame that shot out of the chimney to the attic where the fire began but it took three hours finally to extinguish the blaze. Roof timbers and slates were damaged but the building was otherwise secure. There was general relief that there was little overall damage and no injuries. The ceremonial procession of graduands went ahead with its usual pomp and there was something almost symbolic about the evidence of the continuance of tradition and learning as the chancellor, who had been an undergraduate and professor of law in the university, led the way past the fire engines and the crowds of bystanders.

16 December 1964

Aer Lingus spreads its wings

The mid-1960s was a time of relative prosperity and low unemployment in Ireland, evidenced by a surge in consumer spending and an increase in leisure activities. It was a time, too, of the realisation of the country's tourist potential. Aer Lingus, the national carrier, decided to flutter its wings, so to speak, and set up a number of inclusive package tours with British travel agencies to destinations in Ireland. On Friday 16 December 1964 the company announced plans for 1965, consisting of a hundred different inclusive holidays.

There were five different categories on offer: centred holidays in fourteen selected resorts with a wide choice of hotels; coach holidays, incorporating the pick of Ireland's tourist sites and centres; drive-yourself hired cars 'for those who prefer to discover Ireland for themselves'; sporting holidays, for golf enthusiasts (high handicap or low, starting with Portmarnock) and fishermen (game, coarse or sea); specialised holidays, for those who require holidays 'tailor-made' by a travel agent (basic ingredients to include pony-trekking, sea and river cruising or caravan).

The announcement was accompanied by the publication of two million full-colour booklets giving the details of the offerings with which the company intended to saturate travel agents in Britain. The costs quoted seem in these inflationary days to be ridiculously low. Even the dearest: fourteen nights in a Grade 'A' hotel, flying at weekends between 13 July and 13 September, was to cost £72 from Liverpool and £81/3s from London. The British government's imposed spending limit of £50 for travellers worked to Ireland's advantage since the British pound was very acceptable, as holding parity with its Irish equivalent. In addition, the concept of the inclusive air tour, so general today, was considered quite daring fifty years ago.

17 December 1949

Convict at large

Cecil Robinson, a 25-year-old ex-British airman, was serving a seven-year sentence in Maryborough (Portlaoise), for the shooting of Marie Doran (20), of Churchtown Great, Rathgar, in a railway carriage on the embankment in Lower Beechwood Avenue, Ranelagh. He had been arrested in a Dublin hotel the day after the attack on Doran. At his trial he startled the court by saying he was not going to appeal his sentence. He had been diagnosed as suffering from psycho-neurosis, aggravated by war wounds, and the persistence of the symptoms while in the prison led to his transference to Dundrum Criminal Asylum for observation.

While in Dundrum Robinson had befriended a member of the travelling community, also called Doran, who had originally been sentenced to ten years' penal servitude for robbery with violence. They both managed to escape from the asylum by piling up a heap of boxes and debris against the 30-ft perimeter wall but had separated after the escape.

Robinson was a man of enterprise and somehow managed to make his way to Newhaven, a port on the south Sussex coast. As he boarded the Dieppe ferry on Saturday 17 December 1949 he was arrested by the Lewes police and held until three members of the Garda came to collect him. They travelled by train northwards to catch the Dublin boat and true to form they had to change in Crewe. Robinson asked permission to use the toilet on the platform, had his handcuffs removed for the convenience and suddenly jumped on to the line, oblivious of any danger, running up the track to escape. He was still at large the following Monday, although with warnings flashed to police stations in Cheshire, Staffordshire and Shropshire, the authorities were confident of an early arrest. He was captured a week later near his mother's house in Cheshire.

18 December 1969

The battle of Hume Street

Thursday 18 December 1969 was a not untypical day it what the papers called the 'Battle of Hume Street'. The short street that runs from Ely Place to St Stephen's Green was, at least in façade, a jewel of Georgian Dublin. An Taisce and other cultural agencies wanted it to be preserved as an essential part of the 18th-century city. In June 1969 a number of houses were bought by the Green Property company, which intended to redevelop them. Workmen moved in to demolish the interiors with an intention of total demolition. The Corporation had refused permission for the development but its decision was overruled by Kevin Boland (1917-2001), the Minister for Local Government.

A group of architecture students then occupied the houses and tried to stop the workmen who had already entered the buildings and begun the demolition. Later that afternoon about 1000 protesters gathered at the corner of Hume Street and Stephen's Green, among them Garret Fitzgerald (1926-2011), Justin Keating (1930-2009), Noël Browne (1915-97) and Senator Mary Bourke (later President Mary Robinson). For many months later the struggle between the developer and the squatters continued. The affair became a cause célèbre to which the newspapers and other media returned for copy.

That day the squatters received an ultimatum: they were to leave or face the consequences. They said through a spokesman, 'We will hold out at all costs,' and organised an all-night guard. They also attempted to repair some of the damage, calling for volunteers and building materials. They hung out large sheets with appropriate slogans and put out more flags.

The Hume Street campaign ended in an unsatisfactory compromise. The interiors of the houses were gutted but the London-based company that owned the properties were persuaded to build a neo-Georgian façade for their replacement buildings.

19 December 1924

The voice of constitutional nationalism

The history of the *Freeman's Journal*, the newspaper that appeared for the last time on Friday 19 December 1924, was a kind of schematic map of the history of the country as a whole. It was published without a break from 1763 and in its one hundred-and-sixty-one years it had gradually become greener politically. Its support of the Treaty led to the burning of its works and the destruction of its presses by the IRA in March 1922 and for the remaining years of its life it became a kind of Free State government agency. It was bought by the much more profitable *Irish Independent*, which for many years included in its masthead the legend: 'Incorporating the *Freeman's Journal*'.

In its early years, it was associated with the 'patriot' opposition in the Irish parliament in College Green and for a while was a creature of Dublin Castle. In 1831 the *Freeman* was purchased by its first Catholic editor, Patrick Lavelle, an advocate of the repeal of the Act of Union. He died in 1837 and in 1841 his widow sold the paper to Sir John Gray (1815-75). It stayed with the Gray family and for the next fifty years it was the voice of constitutional nationalism and as such a strong supporter of Parnell. This support continued briefly after the 'split' but it was finally persuaded to accept the reuniting of the Irish Parliamentary Party under John Redmond.

Its last years showed it incapable of the modernisation that so characterised the *Independent*, its complementary rival. However, its place in literary history is assured as its offices were visited by Leopold Bloom in the 'Aeolus' chapter of James Joyce's *Ulysses* and each paragraph is prefixed by a bold heading from the edition of 16 June 1904, such as **In the Heart of the Hibernian Metropolis** and **O, Harp Eolian**.

20 December 1820

'Nature did me that honour.'

Dion[ysius Lardner] Boucicault (1820-90) was one of the most prolific of playwrights ever, being responsible for more than one hundred and fifty plays, mostly melodramatic adaptations, some topographically changed to suit to the location of the theatre of presentation. Thus *The Poor of Chicago* could swiftly become *The Poor of New York*, *The Poor of Liverpool, London, Boston*, even *Dublin*, wherever a multi-storey tenement could be seen to catch fire on stage. His theatre blossomed in the golden age of 'sensation drama' with burning skyscrapers, instantly mobile scenery, round towers revolving to show actors seen clinging to ivy, trains, ships sailing across the diorama, horse races, transparent ghosts and for *The Colleen Bawn* (1860), his most famous play, one of the lakes of Killarney.

Boucicault was born in Dublin on 20 December 1820 to the sister of the Irish poet George Darley, a year after she had separated from her Huguenot husband, Samuel Boursiquot. His father was Dr Dionysius Lardner, a lodger in her Lower Gardiner Street house, and wished him to become an engineer. After a year in London University he became an actor called Lee Moreton and had his first dramatic success with *London Assurance* at the age of twenty-one. (It was revived with great success by the Royal Shakespeare Company in 1974.)

The plays that have secured Boucicault's place in theatrical history are *The Colleen Bawn, Arrah na Pogue* (1864) and *The Shaughraun* (1874), with star comic parts written for himself. Disparaged by later purists as the source of 'stage Irish' he rather dismissed the stereotype and in a good-humoured way endowed his Irish characters with dramatic dignity and Daedalian ingenuity. Both Shaw and O'Casey owed their skill in dramaturgy to his influence. Asked once if he were Irish he replied, 'Nature did me that honour.'

21 December 1938

Dead of gas poisoning

Rainsford Avenue runs parallel to Thomas Street in the oldest part of inner-city Dublin. There in two houses on opposite sides of the street on the morning of Wednesday 21 December 1938 two elderly people were found to have died of gas poisoning. They were Mrs Hughes, a widow, who worked as a cleaner, and Henry Ball, a seventy-year-old, who lived in No 7 across the street. There was a gas leak in the neighbourhood and several other residents, affected by the fumes, had to receive medical treatment.

Mrs Hughes's body was discovered by a friend, Mrs McGrath, who arrived at the house at 11am to find out why she had not turned up for work. Unable to open the door, she had help in forcing it open. The men who entered were almost overcome by the smell but they made their way to the bedroom where they found the body of Mrs Hughes, apparently lifeless. She was taken to the Meath Hospital but was declared dead on arrival. When Ball's room was entered he was found lying on the floor. It was assumed that, feeling the effects of the gas, he had tried to make his way out of the bedroom.

The Gardaí from Kevin Street and Newmarket began intensive enquiries to try to find the cause, having sent for Dublin Gas Company engineers. They began to dig up the road. Susan Oliver, who had a room next door to Mrs Hughes, was responsible for saving the lives of a family who lived in an adjacent room. Smelling gas, she entered and found Patrick Monaghan, his wife Kathleen and their two children, George and Frank, lying unconscious on the floor. She opened all the windows and doors and in a few moments the Monaghans were able to breathe normally.

22 December 1960

Brendan Behan the hostage

Wit and broader humour were over the decades not entirely unknown in Irish courts. It gave counsel the risky opportunity to score points over each other and for the judge to show that he too was capable of the occasional *jeu d'esprit*. One 19th-century justice dismissed a defendant with the words, 'You leave this court with no other stain on your character than that of being declared innocent by a Limerick jury.' A counsel harangued the judge that he had left his resourceless client 'between the devil and the deep blue sea'. To which his honour replied: 'I would spare him the second; so he can go to the first with costs.'

It was reassuring to realise, on the evidence of a court appearance on Thursday 2 December 1960 of the best-known Irishman of the 1960s, Brendan Behan, described as 'author and playwright' of Anglesea Road, Ballsbridge, that the old capacity for Attic wit was still extant. The rattling boy from Dublin town was there not as a miscreant but as bailsman. He was just back from America and although his play, *The Hostage*, as modified by Joan Littlewood, was a Broadway hit, aspects of the trip had had a negative effect on his health.

Anthony Maxwell Swift, a thirty-four-year-old car salesman, was accused of larceny by means of a trick, fraudulent conversion and false pretences. When Behan had been sworn in, District Justice Kenneth Reddin, himself a published novelist and playwright, observed, 'You have come here to offer yourself as hostage?'

Behan replied, 'That's about the height of it, your worship.' He said he would go bail for the whole £250, when the judge offered him the alternative of paying half then in cash.

The business finished, Reddin thanked him and welcomed him back to Dublin, and Behan replied: 'Happy Christmas.'

23 December 1946

Yuletide closedown

On Monday 23 December 1946 CIÉ (Córas Iompair Éireann) announced with regret that all its road passenger services would close down at 3pm on Christmas Day. The prospect had been flagged in the local papers for some days but the reality came as a blow to Dubliners who wished to or needed to escape from the dyspepsia, the paper hats and the debris of Christmas at home. In 1946 cars were the property of the rather well off, while ordinary punters were almost totally dependent on tram and bus. It was an effective immobilisation for the majority of citizens.

The members of the Irish Transport and General Workers' Union had never had a specific agreement about Christmas Day working and there was no negotiation mechanism to cover the particular case. Individual members of the ITGWU agreed that the cessation of service would cause inconvenience if not actual hardship to the public. The relief visits to grandparents of children already on edge with the excitement of Santa's toys would require a taxi and they were not plentiful and quite expensive during what was then the most shut-down holiday of the year. The washing-up would have barely started by 3pm and the sports, pantomimes and near normality of St Stephen's Day seemed aeons away.

In an attempt to gain some consensus the matter had been referred to the Labour Court but there seemed to be some discrepancy between the management's version and that of the ITGWU and there was no record of any discussion of a special wage for those who might agree to volunteer for Christmas Day work. With no agreement achieved it was clear that when the buses and trams were garaged on the day it was the first Yuletide closedown.

24 December 1823

Architect of Georgian Dublin

When George IV made his state visit to Ireland in 1821 he landed in Howth, much the worse for wear with drink. His visit to the Emerald Isle was marred by 'looseness', requiring a 'sanitary engine' to be made ready for any emergency in the Curragh, his main Irish interest. Dún Laoghaire (Dunleary as it was then spelled), the port from which he departed on 3 September, was renamed Kingstown in his honour and retained the name for a hundred years.

The royal visit was a time for the scattering of favours and one seventy-eight-year-old who lived in a self-designed house in Canonbrook in Lucan was expected to be knighted. He was wheeled down to the road that was the royal route to the Curragh in his bath chair, ready for the expected accolade from Beau Brummel's 'fat friend'. For some reason, perhaps the king's comfort, the route was changed. The meeting and expected dubbing did not take place and James Gandon, the great architect of Georgian Dublin, was wheeled home again. He died on Wednesday 24 December 1823, a few months after refusing gracefully to help found the Royal Hibernian Academy.

Gandon was born in London on Wednesday 20 February 1743 and without much parental help made himself into a brilliant architect. He rejected an offer of an official military post as an architect in St Petersburg in favour of a contract to come to Dublin in 1781 to build a new Custom House, against much local opposition. The city merchants had campaigned against the location of the replacement downriver from the old but were outsmarted by the wily John Beresford (1738-1805), the first commissioner of revenue. It remains one of the glories of Dublin, despite the fact that it was not all reinstated after being set on fire in an IRA attack during the War of Independence, and takes its honoured place with other Gandon piles, the Four Courts and King's Inns.

25 December 2000

God and Mammon on Christmas Day

In 2000 Christmas Day fell on a Monday, normally a working day, and it seemed an appropriate time for the leaders of the main religions in Dublin to speak about God – and Mammon. Dr Walton Empey, during his Christ Church service, spoke of the discrepancy between different perceptions of the meaning of the word 'glory' when applied to the nation:

> In Christian terms the glory of a nation lies not in its wealth or its power but in how it uses that wealth and how it cares for its minorities. How did our recent budget, for example, reflect our glory as a nation? The short answer is that it did not.

He drew attention to the fact that under the proposed changes in the taxation system a person in long-term unemployment would gain £8 a week while a person with an annual income of £40,000 would be £64 a week better off. 'It could hardly be thought that this was a brave attempt to bring the poor out of the poverty trap. It is not a reflection of the nation's glory.'

Dr Desmond Connell, speaking in the Pro-Cathedral, attacked the 'widening gap between the rich and the poor': The worship of riches takes its toll in apathy…in theft from employers and sharp practice, in devious forms of corruption, in neglect of families.' He also found it imperative to attack the permissiveness that was eroding social respect for marriage and preparing a new generation ill-adapted to life in society.

The Rev Richard MacCarthy, Dean of St Patrick's, also attacked the budget in his peroration:

> Although there are huge numbers of people still animated by Christian concern for their less fortunate fellows, they need mobilising. In view of recent provisions to enable the rich to get richer, they certainly need mobilising at the next general election.

26 December 1949

Seasonal cheer in Dublin

If Christmas Day in the age before television was mainly concerned with over-indulgence, paper hats and torn crackers, St Stephen's Day usually meant going to the theatre or the 'pictures'. Dublin had plenty of seasonal cheer to offer: the Irish-born George Farquhar's *The Recruiting Officer* in the Gate; *Niall agus Carmelita*, the Irish pantomime, in the Abbey, an O'Dea/O'Donovan offering, *Alive, Alive, O!* in the Gaiety and *Jack and the Beanstalk* in the Cine-Variety House Capitol, which also had an Oirish film called *Top o' the Morning*, with Bing Crosby and Ann Blyth. It dealt with the dire results of the theft of the Blarney Stone. The *New Yorker* magazine responded with four words: 'The Irish should sue!' but in the city there were no complaints, especially as Crosby was regarded as virtually Irish.

If 'Der Bingle' was popular, Jimmy O'Dea was loved and there was no better interpreter of O'Donovan's witty scripts. He was splendid in drag in the character of 'Biddy Mulligan, the Pride of the Coombe', whose theme song, modernised from an old pantomime ditty by W.S. North, was sung throughout Ireland. Also in the cast was Maureen Potter, O'Dea's theatrical heiress, who almost filled the comedic gap left by her mentor's death in 1965.

In spite of the language barrier the Abbey pantomime was very popular, as much for the excellence of the production values as the all-round ability of young performers such as 'Raymond' McAnally, Ronnie Masterson and the great interpreter of Beckett, Jack McGowran. For film goers there was a rich choice of stars: Cary Grant, Margaret Lockwood, Gene Kelly, David Tomlinson, Van Heflin and many others. But houses for the only respectable Restoration dramatist in the Gate were also good and the critics welcomed the skill of players such as Godfrey Quigley and Aidan Grennell.

27 December 1938

Cinderella

For nearly forty years one artiste bestrode the narrow world of Dublin entertainment like a Colossus, although physically he was no giant. This was Jimmy O'Dea, pantomime dame, songwriter, actor in films, radio, television and gramophone. In the Gaiety in King Street and the Olympia in Dame Street, whether in revue or pantomime, his reputation went beyond popularity, reaching adulation. Seeing the O'Dea pantomime was a necessary part of Yuletide celebration, known by the shorthand phrase 'going to see Jimmy'. His great creation, although not original, was 'Biddy Mulligan, the Pride of the Coombe' but he was equally at home in 'straight' roles. With a pair of sparkling eyes, a fine tenor voice and the graceful movements of a ballet dancer, he was applauded equally on entry and exit.

On Tuesday 27 December 1928, the Dublin papers were full of praise for the Gaiety panto, this year the perennial *Cinderella* with her 'glass' slipper, a mishearing of Charles Perrault's 'vair' (fur) as 'verre'. By far the most popular of all Christmas shows, it gave plenty of opportunities for the highly appreciated 'transformation' scenes, mice and pumpkin magically rendered as footmen and a coach and four and the gradually stripping of Cinders's grand robes as she flees the ball on the stroke of midnight and is reduced once again to rags.

O'Dea played Buttons, Cinderella's only friend in Baron de Shook's castle, with lots of business including repartee and physical comedy, such as walking bow-legged about the stage for too long after riding in on a huge draught horse. Also in the cast as Myrtle, the more abrasive of the two ugly sisters, was a coming star in the Dublin showbiz firmament, the extremely tall Noel Purcell. As one paper said: 'Everyone must go and see *Cinderella*.'

28 December 1928

An Irish Grand Prix

Motor racing first took place in the Phoenix Park in 1903 when the Irish Gordon Bennett Race speed trials were held on the main straight. (The horse racing course had been opened a year earlier.) One interested party was the Society of Irish Motor Traders who hoped to sponsor the first Irish Grand Prix in the summer of 1929. A lot depended on the response of the Society of Motor Manufacturers and Traders and on Friday 28 December 1928 the Irish body was able to announce that the British arm of the trade would participate in the races. They informed as a matter or priority the Royal Irish Automobile Club (RIAC), the participation of whose members was essential for the success of the venture. That done, all systems were put in motion to publicise the races due to be held the following July.

The cost was estimated at £12,000 (in excess of £630,000 today) and it was optimistically stated by the committee that the receipts from entrance fees, admission charges etc. should make it unnecessary actually 'to make any claim on foot of the guarantee now about to be sought from the public'. Nevertheless the committee needed to have the guarantee; otherwise it would be reluctantly compelled to withdraw from the project. They pointed out the great benefit that would accrue to the country as a whole, by reason of the publicity and the influx of visitors.

The guarantee list would open on the 31 December, the following Monday, and the list of guarantors would be published each Saturday morning in *The Irish Times*, the *Irish Independent* and the *Cork Examiner*. The committee further asked that people willing to assist in the organisation of the races should communicate with the secretary of the RIAC, stating in which capacity their services could best be utilised.

29 December 1956

Mamie Cadden: angel of mercy

Mary Anne ('Mamie') Cadden set up a private nursing home in Rathmines in 1931 in her fortieth year. It fulfilled its formal role adequately, as she had trained as a midwife in Holles Street maternity hospital, but she had several predictable sidelines. One was what used to be called in Victorian times 'baby-farming' – the disposal of unwanted babies – the other illegal abortion. She served several sentences for abandoning a baby in County Meath and for procuring abortions by medical and surgical means. In 1951 she set up a one-room clinic in Hume Street and resumed her career as a backstreet abortionist. When the body of Mrs Helen O'Reilly, one of her patients, was found on the pavement outside her home, she was arrested and sentenced to death by hanging. She had managed to avoid conviction for a similar offence five years earlier.

The appeal was held in December 1956 and after a hearing lasting five days it was dismissed on Monday 29. The sentence was reaffirmed by Conor Maguire, the Chief Justice, and Messrs Justice Teevan and Murnaghan. One argument for appeal was that the advice by the trial judge on the nature and effect of circumstantial evidence was not sound. This was dismissed, as was the question of whether the judge should have advised that the jury could bring in a verdict of manslaughter. The date of 10 January 1957 was fixed for the execution but after widespread appeals for clemency and the assertion that this 'angel of mercy' (as she was called) to so many Irish women had not had any murderous intention she was reprieved. Her sentence was commuted to life imprisonment in Mountjoy jail but she was soon declared insane and moved to Dundrum Criminal Lunatic Asylum. She died there of a heart attack in 1959.

30 December 1965

'No Through Road'

The clash between the freedom of the individual and authority is an unpleasant fact of modern life, caused partly by the rise of the compensation culture. Charges that we live in a 'nanny state', ruled by an unpleasant deity called 'Elthan Safetee', are heard everywhere. A moment's thought might convince that rules are essentially the defenders of freedom but when in individual cases rights seemed to be transgressed such a thoughtful moment has no force.

On Thursday 30 December 1965 motorists, some of them sea-anglers, hardy swimmers and sightseers anxious to view the bay, drove past the famous Pigeon House electricity station in Ringsend in south Dublin on their way to the South Wall, to find their passage blocked by a number of warning signs and a barrier. The first sign read: 'Danger, Barrier Ahead', the second some feet away had: 'Notice. Entry Prohibited. ESB.' On the left of the barrier was a board reading: 'No Through Road' while on the right was a much older message from Dublin Port and Docks Board advising pedestrians, cyclists and drivers that 'all persons entering and travelling on the Great South Wall' did so at their own risk.

The barrier was constructed of ten iron stakes with enough space in the middle to permit single vehicle access but designed so that it too could be blocked off. There were two separate clashes with the Electricity Supply Board, one involving those who felt their 'rights' had been diminished and a more official one involving the Port and Docks Board, which discouraged cars but said that the ESB had no right to prohibit entry. The ESB countered that their notices were not to prevent access to the wall but to the sand dunes, where they intended to build a new station.

31 December 1961

The birth of Teilifís Éireann

On the evening of Sunday 31 December 1961 an unwonted crowd gathered outside the Gresham Hotel in O'Connell Street in spite of the snow. Inside an unusual degree of excitement was being generated. There were many arrivals of VIPs from politics, media and especially showbiz. That night Ireland's first native home-grown television station went on air from Donnybrook and the gala opening was being relayed from the hotel. To be honest, television was not exactly unknown in Ireland; there had been patchy east-coast reception from BBC transmitters in Sutton Coldfield and Holme Moss from 1949. To coincide with the coronation of Elizabeth II loyal east Ulster came on stream in 1953 and by the end of the 1950s 60 per cent of the country could receive BBC1 and ITV.

It was clearly time for a national service, as there was already some inkling of the medium's popularity and its power. The early jerky, snowy pictures gave no indication of this power and most politicians were able to dismiss it as 'an expensive luxury' but it was clear by the end of the 1950s that the hour of Teilifís Éireann had come.

The service was launched on New Year's Eve by President Éamon de Valera, who thundered: 'Never before was there in the hands of men an instrument so powerful to influence the thoughts and actions of the multitude' – hardly telespeak. The programmes for the evening included poetry readings by Siobhán McKenna and Micheál MacLiammóir and a variety show with Jimmy O'Dea and Maureen Potter, the other stars in the Irish firmament. The first OB, as people soon learned to call it, was from the Gresham ballroom and the compère was Ireland's leading sports commentator, Micheál O'Hehir. The couples dancing inside were filmed, as was the multitude outside.